Southern Literary Studies
Louis D. Rubin, Jr., Editor

Old Clemens

Old Clemens and W. D. H.

and W. D. H.

The Story of a Remarkable Friendship

Kenneth E. Eble

Louisiana State University Press
Baton Rouge and London

Library of Congress Cataloging in Publication Data

Eble, Kenneth Eugene.
    Old Clemens and W.D.H.

    (Southern literary studies)
    Bibliography: p.
    Includes index.
    1. Twain, Mark, 1835–1910—Friends and associates.
2. Howells, William Dean, 1837–1920—Friends and associ-
ates.   3. Authors, American—19th century—Biography.
I. Title.   II. series.
PS1333.E24   1985   818'.409 [B]   85-5236
ISBN 0-8071-1227-5

The author gratefully acknowledges permission to reprint from the following: Dixon Wecter,
ed., *Mark Twain to Mrs. Fairbanks* (The Huntington Library, New York), copyright © 1949
by the Mark Twain Company, reprinted by permission of the Huntington Library; Henry Nash
Smith and William Gibson, eds., *Mark Twain—Howells Letters: The Correspondence of
Samuel L. Clemens and William Dean Howells, 1872–1910*, copyright © 1960 by the
Mark Twain Company, © 1960 by Mildred Howells and John Mead Howells, © 1960 by
the President and Fellows of Harvard College, reprinted by permission of the Mark Twain
Foundation and William W. Howells; George Arms, Richard H. Bollinger, Christoph K.
Lohmann, and John K. Reeves, eds., *W. D. Howells: Selected Letters* (6 vols.), copyright ©
1979 by G. K. Hall and Company and the Howells Edition Editorial Board, reprinted by
permission of G. K. Hall and Company, the Howells Edition Editorial Board, and William W.
Howells; Mildred Howells, ed., *Life in Letters of William Dean Howells*, copyright © 1928 by
Doubleday, Doran and Co., Inc., © 1928 by the Bookman Publishing Co., Inc., reprinted
by permission of William W. Howells. The letters of William Dean Howells are quoted herein
by special permission of William W. Howells.

Portions of this work have been published previously, in slightly different form, as "Howells
and Twain: Being and Staying Friends," *Old Northwest*, X (Spring, 1984), 91–105.

To Ed Lueders and the late Robert Schaaf, longtime friends

Contents

Acknowledgments

I wish to acknowledge my debt to Henry Nash Smith and William M. Gibson, whose *Mark Twain–Howells Letters* first brought the friendship of Mark Twain and William Dean Howells to my attention. I am grateful for the courtesies extended me at the Library of the Mark Twain Memorial, Hartford, Connecticut; the Houghton Library, Harvard University; the Howells Edition Center, Indiana University; and the Mark Twain Papers, the Bancroft Library, University of California, Berkeley. Special thanks to the late John N. M. Howells and to W. W. Howells for their cooperation with this and my previous study of William Dean Howells. Thanks also to my colleagues Don D. Walker, Beth Burdett, and Jim Fife. Edward Lueders and Robert Schaaf deserve special mention not only as longtime friends but as the earliest readers of the manuscript. Thanks also to Lewis Leary and Louis D. Rubin, Jr., whose encouragement helped to get the manuscript into print. Finally, thanks to my daughter Melissa for once again being my typist and far more than that.

Old Clemens and W. D. H.

Mark Twain.
From William Dean Howells,
Literary Friends and Acquaintance
(Bloomington, Indiana, 1968).

William Dean Howells.
From his *Criticism and Fiction*
(New York, 1891).

One

Beginnings of a Friendship

The distance from Hartford, Connecticut, to Boston, Massachusetts, and on to Kittery Point, Maine, is less than two hundred miles. By car and in any weather except a winter blizzard, it is an easy and pleasant trip. Domestic and familiar might best describe it, for central Connecticut and Massachusetts are tamed and green. The spectacular, as New England has it, lies on the edges—the northern Maine coast, or the true mountain country of New Hampshire and Vermont, the Berkshires during the fall color season. Moving toward Boston is toward urbanization, but the terrain from the freeway hides its population and even its industry, and the prevailing woods may be even more abundant now than they were a century ago following the clearing that accompanied settlement.

Skirting Boston, one cannot escape all the facts: the mills that had already begun to claim the waterways in Thoreau's time, and industrial parks and housing developments that appear like rock outcroppings amid the vegetation. Still, those are no more reminders of modern reality than the freeways themselves. Soon enough, the traveler is north of Boston and north of Massachusetts shortly after. The sign for Kittery appears just after the freeway crosses Portsmouth Bay and enters Maine. The land runs out at Kittery Point itself, and only the Atlantic provides further passageway east.

Mark Twain's house, Hartford, Connecticut

W. D. Howells' house, Kittery Point, Maine

At one end of this three- to four-hour trip is the Mark Twain house in Hartford, at the other, William Dean Howells' summer place at Kittery Point. Both Howells' obscurity and Mark Twain's fame are reflected in the houses now preserved to honor them. Mark Twain is still known around the world; it was Howells who rightly called him "the Lincoln of our literature." As to Howells himself, though he wrote so many books that he said they must have been written by a trust named after him, he is a largely forgotten figure today. Paradoxically, it is the Mark Twain house that has been all but overcome by American success; Hartford's eminence as an insurance capital leaves little room for eminence of another kind. Nook Farm, the "suburban grove" in which Samuel Clemens built his house among kindred spirits after the Civil War, is now hemmed in by modern Hartford. Beyond the immediate small square that preserves the former homes of Mark Twain and Harriet Beecher Stowe and Katherine S. Day, the large and substantial houses set in spacious lawns that so attracted Clemens are not to be seen. Rather, one confronts urban blight—multiple, faceless, often abandoned dwellings, stores and shops boarded up, a poster speaking to the area's present condition: "War on Rats!"[1]

In these respects, Howells' house has fared better. The property at Kittery Point, except for changes made by Howells and his heirs, is much as it was when he purchased it in 1904. It is a solid, comfortable house with a mansard roof and three bay windows looking out on the bay and to Gerrish Island and the Isle of Shoals, which shelter the bay from the open sea. In the summer of 1902, Mark Twain was living at York Harbor, just a short trolley-car ride away.[2] Another hot summer, in 1905, Henry James, on a rare visit to the United States, stopped by.

1. William Dean Howells, "My Mark Twain," in Marilyn Austin Baldwin (ed.), *My Mark Twain: Reminiscences and Criticisms* (Baton Rouge, 1967), 84; William Dean Howells to Joseph A. Howells, December 9, 1906, in Mildred Howells (ed.), *Life in Letters of William Dean Howells* (2 vols.; Garden City, N.Y., 1928), II, 231.

2. Henry Nash Smith and William M. Gibson (eds.), *Mark Twain–Howells Letters: The Correspondence of Samuel L. Clemens and William Dean Howells, 1872–1910* (2 vols.; Cambridge, Mass., 1960), II, 742–44.

Few tourists are likely to follow the complete route from Hartford to Kittery Point, though many will go as far as Boston, not to seek out Howells' dwelling places but to establish a base for visiting the Revolutionary War shrines and the literary landmarks that lie all around. Although both Howells and Clemens grew up on the western frontier, the commonplace reality of New England lives on in the white frame house at Kittery Point, just as the materialistic aspirations of the Gilded Age display themselves in Mark Twain's flamboyant house in Hartford.

The birth and death dates of Samuel Clemens and William Dean Howells span almost a century of American life, from 1835 to 1920, embracing the full geographical expansion of the country, its rise to international power, and its suffering through two wars whose scars are still with us. Both were young men from the provinces, schooled as country printers, separated from their native ground by the necessity of seeking their fortunes as journalists and writers. In midlife they were constrained to stay in the East, in close touch with the editing and publishing upon which their incomes depended. Both married women whose places of birth and upbringing provided additional reasons for settling in New England. In the end, both were American nomads, having no settled place of existence for very long, visitors back to the mid-America from which they came as they were to the great cities of both Europe and America.

Samuel Clemens and William Dean Howells first met late in 1869 in the office of James T. Fields, then editor of the *Atlantic Monthly*. What each knew of the other must be guessed at; such guesses, however wide they may be of the precise truth, help place both men before the reader. Howells was thirty-two, married and the father of two children, three years back from serving as consul in Venice, author of *Venetian Life* and *Italian Journeys*, and both a contributor to national magazines and assistant editor of a recently established one. Clemens was thirty-four, to be married within a few months to Olivia Langdon of Elmira, New York, and despite a considerable reputation as a western humorist, more or less unemployed. Howells had come to his present situation by a combination of hard work, having an eye out for the main chance, and exploiting a talent for writing about his domestic and foreign experiences. Cambridge, where he had settled down, had more than an adventitious attractiveness to him; he was ambitious to be a writer among American writers, and the best place to begin was within the literary village that was the center of American letters. Clemens' route is both more interesting and less literary. It took him out of Mississippi River towns, where he had grown up and served as a journeyman printer, to New Orleans, Nevada, San Francisco, the Sandwich Islands, and then back east to New York via the Isthmus. Possessed of the same kind of journalistic talent as Howells, he promoted himself into a European trip in 1867 that provided the material for his first successful book, *Innocents Abroad*. His being unemployed in 1869 was a matter of having given up on Washington, D.C., as a base for a free-lance journalist, and of not having arrived at any other steady employment. True, his lecturing was going well, but in places of less than world renown: Titusville and Franklin, Pennsylvania, Geneseo and Auburn, New York, for example, on successive nights in 1869.[3]

The two men might have met earlier if their time in New York had coincided. Clemens arrived there in mid-January, 1867, and left the first of March, off on a visit and lecture to St. Louis and Hannibal, and in early June aboard the *Quaker City* bound for the Holy Land. Howells' time in New York the year before was as brief. He was there looking for a job in the fall of 1865, just after his return from Venice. "New York has waked me up," he wrote to his wife, Elinor, in September, giving her an accounting of three free-lance pieces he had sold for seventy dollars.[4] By October E. L. Godkin had taken him on as editorial assistant on the newly-established *Nation*, and he was able to have Elinor and his two children join him at a boardinghouse on Ninth Avenue before the end of the year. For the few months he was with the *Nation*, he did the column "Minor Topics" that found as much copy in the violent and coarse side of

3. Smith and Gibson (eds.), *Mark Twain–Howells Letters*, I, 6; Dixon Wecter (ed.), *Mark Twain to Mrs. Fairbanks* (San Marino, Calif, 1949), 72.

4. William Dean Howells to Elinor M. Howells, September 23, 1865, in William Dean Howells Papers, Houghton Library, Harvard University.

New York life as Mark Twain had found in San Francisco. In February James T. Fields of the *Atlantic* made him an offer that moved him to Boston and a literary editorship for which he had long been preparing. There he stayed until familiarity and conscience altered his views about the superiority of Boston as a place to live.

Although it is likely that Howells, had he stayed in New York as a young, ambitious journalist and free-lance writer, would have met Mark Twain the next year, they did not have the same circle of acquaintances. Howells' journalistic bent was literary; he was disinclined to be a reporter; his strength displayed itself best in editorial capacities. Mark Twain's besetting sins as a reporter, as he himself seemed to declare, were laziness and irresponsibility, both of which he compensated for by being able to invent what his disinclination kept him from covering. An Oakland, California, newspaper gives an account of Mark Twain in confusion in April, 1868. A citizen comes upon him near the Oakland and Alameda ferry landings searching for a dinner he is supposed to attend.

"Well," responded Mark, with a bewildered look, "that's the question. I agreed yesterday, or the day before, or the day before that, or some time or other, to go somewhere to a dinner that was to come off today, or maybe to-morrow, or perhaps to-morrow night, at some d----d place, across the bay. I don't know exactly where it is, or when it is, or who I agreed with. All I know is, I'm advertised in the newspaper to be somewhere, some time or other this week, to dine, or lecture, or something or other—and I want to find out where the d---l it is, and how to get there."[5]

His laziness and irresponsibility were true aspects of his nature, but in part were deliberately created aspects of his public character. His life-long work habits alternated between intense periods of concentrated effort and periods of deliberate idleness. In midcareer he described his habits to his friend, Mrs. Fairbanks. "One shouldn't have a single interest in the world outside of his work. He should work 3 months on a stretch, dead to everything *but* his work; then loaf diligently 3 months & go at it again. . . . Solitary impris-

5. Paul Fatout (ed.), *Mark Twain Speaks for Himself* (West Lafayette, Ind., 1978), xii.

onment, by compulsion, is the one perfect condition for perfect performance."[6]

What Mark Twain liked to do, early and late, was talk. He was fascinated by it, what he exchanged and overheard in the streets and what was delivered, often at a handsome price, from the lecture platform. From his beginnings as a writer, he was to draw on that pokebag full of talk and the experiences that lay behind it, from his boyhood in Hannibal to the mining camps of Nevada. With his sensitivity to the vernacular, he broke American writing away from the literary language of the nineteenth century and pointed the way for later writers to develop a literary idiom closer to the actuality of living speech.

Howells, despite his upbringing in near-frontier Ohio, was literary in a way that Mark Twain never was. He was to wait years before he turned back to making use of his Ohio past, and his style, graceful and lucid as it is, has in it some of the formal characteristics of nineteenth-century literary prose. His New York acquaintances inclined to literature more than Mark Twain's. Bayard Taylor and Richard Henry Stoddard were both in their early forties and established writers. Both were poets of the kind Howells was trying to be. Edmund Clarence Stedman was only a few years older than Howells, but already established in New York as a poet, journalist, and stockbroker when Howells met him. Thomas Bailey Aldrich, who was to become a close friend of both Howells and Mark Twain, was also established in New York in 1865. He left for Boston about the same time as Howells to become editor of *Every Saturday*, and later, in 1881, to succeed Howells as editor of the *Atlantic*. All of these men did the kind of miscellaneous journalism and correspondent work that supported more literary aspirations. All were poets, though all had the multiple talents Howells was to display. Taylor had enjoyed the greatest success, first from his travel letters describing a European walking tour in the 1840s, and in 1850 with a book about California and the forty-niners. He was the first eminent literary man that Howells had met, in his last year in Columbus in 1859. By

6. Wecter (ed.), *Mark Twain to Mrs. Fairbanks*, 206–207.

that time Taylor had established himself as a poet and translator, anticipating his widely accepted translation of *Faust* in 1870–1871. Taylor's time in the West preceded Mark Twain's by a decade. They were later to become friends; Taylor and family sailed on the *Holsatia* along with the Clemenses when Taylor was appointed minister to Germany in 1878, shortly before his death.

Justin Kaplan says, "Sam Clemens came to New York not as a pilgrim but as a miner staking out a claim and beginning to work at it."[7] Like Howells, but for the California newspapers with which he maintained connections, he was finding copy in the streets of New York and reacting somewhat as Howells had reacted to the slums, to the evidences of wealth and power, and to the variety of New York life. As Howells had sought out journalists and literary men he had met on his first trip to New York in 1860, so Clemens sought out old friends. One was Frank Fuller, war-time governor of the Utah territory, who urged him to give his western lectures in New York. Through Fuller, Clemens met Henry Ward Beecher, the most celebrated pulpit orator in the United United States, and soon to be even more celebrated through the *Tilton* v. *Beecher* adultery trial, which ended in a split decision in Beecher's favor in 1875.[8] Another western acquaintance was Charles Henry Webb, an easterner who migrated to California where he worked on the San Francisco *Bulletin* and established the *California* magazine, and through these publications, made his early acquaintance with Mark Twain. In 1866, the magazine having foundered, he had come back to New York to try to keep afloat on generally marginal schemes having something to do with publishing. Webb saw potential profit in exploiting Mark Twain's "Celebrated Jumping Frog" story, which had appeared in Henry Clapp's *Saturday Press* in 1865. (Although Howells knew of the *Saturday Press*, having published in it prior to going to Venice,

---

7. Justin Kaplan, *Mr. Clemens and Mark Twain* (New York, 1966), 20.

8. See Milton Rugoff, *The Beechers: An American Family in the Nineteenth Century* (New York, 1981). Mark Twain observed after Henry's death that it was a pity "that so insignificant a matter as the chastity or unchastity of an Elizabeth Tilton should clip the locks of this Samson and make him as other men, in the estimation of a nation of Lilliputians creeping and climbing about his shoe-soles," 514.

he may have missed the story, since it appeared during a busy period of leaving Venice and reestablishing himself.) Webb did succeed in compiling a collection of Mark Twain's pieces into a first and not very successful book. Frank Fuller became responsible for launching Mark Twain's lecturing career in New York. He rented Great Hall, the Peter Cooper auditorium in New York, which held over two thousand people, packed it by distributing free tickets to school teachers when no paying audience seemed likely to appear, and got Mark Twain off to an auspicious start on May 6, 1867. Another friend of Mark Twain's, Ned House, used his connection with the New York *Tribune* to write a laudatory review: "No other lecturer, of course excepting Artemus Ward, has so thoroughly succeeded in exciting the mirthful curiosity, and compelling the laughter of his hearers."[9]

It is likely that Howells and Clemens were at least vaguely aware of one another's writings, even though during the period of each writer's first publications they were at almost opposite points of the globe. In the years just before the Civil War and his removal to Venice, Howells was both a western journalist in Columbus, Ohio, and a free-lance writer looking for markets. In both capacities, he was exposed to American periodicals that might publish his work, though his gaze went to the East rather than the West, where only San Francisco was supporting literary enterprises. One of his earliest disappointments was not being able to get money in 1861 for a tour of western cities, which was to provide substance for a series of articles he had proposed to the *Atlantic*. Howells' early inclinations, however, were mostly toward poetry, and his aspirations to be a poet continued on through his Venetian years.

How much Mark Twain was inclined to explore the periodicals of either Boston or New York as literary marketplaces was limited by his much looser style of operation. He had published in Harper's *New Monthly Magazine*, in December of 1866, "Forty-three Days in an Open Boat," an account of the burning of a clipper ship *The Hornet*, whose survivors were taken to the Sandwich Islands. His fame was small enough and typesetters chronically careless enough

9. Kaplan, *Mr. Clemens and Mark Twain*, 34.

to cause his name to be printed as *Mark Swain*, both in one of the original newspaper reprintings and in the annual index of *Harper's*. Howells, beginning work on the *Nation* at the end of 1866 and moving to the *Atlantic* the next year, could hardly have avoided coming upon Mark Twain's work. Mark Twain's early lecturing, resumed after his trip to the Holy Land that summer, concluded in San Francisco in 1868 with the topic "Venice, Past and Present." There is no clear indication, however, that he had read Howells' *Venetian Life*, published in 1866, at this early date. In his tribute to Howells in 1906, he said that he had "read his Venetian Days about forty years ago." What we know is that neither man makes specific mention of the other in their notes or correspondence or writings before Clemens' mention, in a letter to Livy, of meeting a cousin of William D. Howells in Pittsburgh in October, 1869.[10]

There were, to be sure, personal differences at that point in their lives that might have kept an acquaintanceship from developing into a friendship. Howells was married and a father, conscious of his acquired learning in Italy as a point of entry into literary circles higher than journalistic ones. "Stoddard admires greatly my Italian translations of poetry," he wrote Elinor from New York in September, 1865. "Everybody regards me here as having *scholarship*."[11] Sam Clemens was a bachelor, with no pretenses to literary culture, a fondness for strong drink, and prey to the kind of moods and activities that landed him in jail overnight in both New York and San Francisco. Both were concerned with making money, and journalism seemed to be the best source of steady income. But Howells' route was via Boston and literary respectability along the way. Mark Twain's was by doing what he could do best and for which the public, if it could be reached by subscription book salesmen or from the lecture platform, would pay large sums. He was the public entertainer as Howells was the litarary editor, and both found their other selves sometimes at odds with their most serious aims as writers.

Senator William Stewart of Nevada offers a lively, if biased,

10. Kenneth E. Eble (ed.), *Howells: A Century of Criticism* (Dallas, 1962), 79; Dixon Wecter (ed.), *The Love Letters of Mark Twain* (New York, 1949), 115.
11. M. Howells (ed.), *Life in Letters*, I, 101.

glimpse of what Mark Twain was like as he gradually moved toward a career as writer and lecturer. He describes the beginning of Clemens' short career as his private secretary, which began in late November, 1867. "I was seated at my window one morning when a very disreputable-looking person slouched into the room. He was arrayed in a seedy suit, which hung upon his lean frame in bunches with no style worth mentioning. A sheaf of scraggy black hair leaked out of a battered old slouch hat, like stuffing from an ancient Colonial sofa, and an evil-smelling cigar butt, very much frazzled, protruded from the corner of his mouth. He had a very sinister appearance . . . I suppose he was the most lovable scamp and nuisance who ever blighted Nevada." The senator, who was described at eighty-three as being "straight as a juniper, as hard as a blacksmith, as keen of eye as an eagle," is not an entirely reliable witness. He had mixed feelings toward Mark Twain as toward his own mining days in Nevada, jealous of the notoriety Twain had gained as a teller of tales he himself had lived. Another oblique glance at Mark Twain's early days comes from his account of booking passage on the *Quaker City*. The voyage was designed and heavily advertised as of particular appeal to clergymen, and Clemens had a friend introduce him to the tour's promoter as a Baptist minister from San Francisco. Although Clemens revealed the hoax to the promoter the next day, the deception rankled in his mind ten years later when he described how Mark Twain had appeared, filling his office with "the fumes of bad whiskey." Mark Twain wrote: "For a ceaseless, tireless, forty-year advocate of total abstinence, the 'captain' is a mighty good judge of whiskey at second hand. I was poor—I couldn't afford good whiskey. How could I know the 'captain' was so particular about the quality of a man's whiskey?"[12]

Howells' recollections reveal something of the raffish side of Mark Twain as well as a side of Howells, probably more marked at seventy-three when he wrote the piece than at thirty-two when he experienced Mark Twain for the first time.

12. George Rothwell Brown (ed.), *Reminiscences of Senator William M. Stewart of Nevada* (New York, 1908), 219–20; Franklin Waller and G. Ezra Dane (eds.), *Mark Twain's Travels with Mr. Brown* (New York, 1940), 111–16; New York *World*, February 18, 1877, in Kaplan, *Mr. Clemens and Mark Twain*, 28.

He had the Southwestern, the Lincolnian, the Elizabethan breadth of parlance, which I suppose one ought not to call coarse without calling one's self prudish; and I was often hiding away in discreet holes and corners the letters in which he had loosed his bold fancy to stoop on rank suggestion; I could not bear to burn them, and I could not, after the first reading, quite bear to look at them. . . . At the time of our first meeting, which must have been well toward the winter, Clemens (as I must call him instead of Mark Twain, which seemed always somehow to mask him from my personal sense) was wearing a sealskin coat, with the fur out, in the satisfaction of a caprice, or the love of strong effect which he was apt to indulge through life. . . . With his crest of dense red hair, and the wide sweep of his flaming mustache, Clemens was not discordantly clothed in that sealskin coat, which afterward, in spite of his own warmth in it, sent the cold chills through me when I once accompanied it down Broadway, and shared the immense publicity it won him. [13]

We have no such description of Howells by Clemens, though we can create one of our own from photos of the period and references to Howells. His own poetic, if not Bohemian, urges were more restrained. Howells' moustache never flamed, though it took on a drooping luxuriance in midlife that it lacked both earlier and later. Mark Twain was almost a head taller, and his head emerged out of his shoulders like an eagle's, quite the opposite of the way Howells' head sat down upon a stocky frame. We have a pen sketch of Howells, done by Elinor in Italy—his hair dark and thick, his eyes deep-set enough to be poetic, a kind of cape over his shoulders, quill pen in hand—which comes as close to depicting the artist Howells as any sketch or photo. But it is still a proper artist, a literary artist, one even to be trusted as editor of a respectable Boston literary magazine.

Mark Twain's early writings support the impressions made by his physical appearance. The exaggeration, the propensity to tease and deceive and shock, the dozens of tricks and turns by which the coarse and vulgar as well as the revered could be made comic, were there in the sketches that Webb put together in 1866. Exposure to the mass of newspaper squibs, lecture materials, and the like adds

13. W. D. Howells, "My Mark Twain," 5–6.

to what we can guess about the nature of Mark Twain's maverick genius. For a St. Louis lecture audience, he offered to eat a child on stage for their entertainment if someone would but provide. A routine coverage of a baby's being left on a doorstep in San Francisco provided the last line of his story in the *Call*: "It appeared to be a good enough baby—nothing the matter with it—and it has been unaccountable to all who have heard of the circumstance, what the owner wanted to throw it away for." Or, a piece of throwaway invective, "Let his vices be forgotten, but his virtues remembered; it will not infringe much upon any man's time." Or a description of the chorus girls in a New York theatrical piece, *The Black Crook*: "a wilderness of girls . . . dressed with a meagerness that would make a parasol blush."[14]

By 1867 Howells had accomplished a tamer, more literary body of work. During all his time in Venice, he had nursed a hope of becoming a poet, modeled chiefly on Longfellow both with respect to the kind of poetry he wrote and to the substantial income and reputation Longfellow had gained by it. Although he had some poems accepted in the *Atlantic* and elsewhere, he had had more rejected, and his return to the United States marked a time of giving up poetry both as a main literary ambition and as a means of earning a living. He had already found a market for his travel letters in periodicals, and it was an obvious next step to put them into a book. *Venetian Life* in 1866 was followed by *Italian Journeys* in 1867, and both must have surprised Howells himself in the favorable reception they received. But besides that and an abundance of miscellaneous journalistic endeavors, Howells was writing heavier pieces: "Modern Italian Poets" and "Henry Wadsworth Longfellow" in the *North American Review*, and reviews of two different translations of Dante Alighieri's *Divine Comedy*. In joining the *Atlantic* Howells had found the journalistic basis he sought and one which enabled him to pursue literature all the same.

The early years of Howells and Clemens' friendship was a time

14. Edgar Branch (ed.), *Clemens of the Call: Mark Twain in San Francisco* (Berkeley, 1969), 49; Fatout (ed.), *Mark Twain Speaks for Himself*, 9; Waller and Dane (eds.), *Mark Twain's Travels with Mr. Brown*, 86.

of putting their western pasts behind them and establishing themselves in a more conventional eastern milieu. Howells was married during his years in Venice and returned to pursue a career with the responsibility of both wife and child. Clemens was about to give over a bachelor's life and enter into a courting that swept him off his feet fully as much as it did Olivia Langdon. The subsequent marriage moved him into respectability and affluence even more quickly than did the publication of *Innocents Abroad*, which preceded the marriage by less than a year. The house his father-in-law Jervis Langdon provided for him was a step toward the house in Hartford, the center for his domestic life and the base from which he established his professional reputation.

For both Howells and Mark Twain, journalism was an obvious vocation, and yet it was seemingly not respectable enough for the families into which both men married. Owning and publishing a paper afforded a more solid kind of business career, but neither Howells nor Mark Twain responded favorably to becoming businessmen early in their careers. Howells' father-in-law, Larkin G. Mead, Sr., saw an opportunity to buy a paper in Columbus, Ohio, and put Howells in charge of it, and though neither such an opportunity nor James Russell Lowell's urgings to practice journalism in the West were met with enthusiasm, Howells wrote to Elinor, "It is well to keep a lookout in all directions."[15] Jervis Langdon's loan of $12,500, enabling Clemens to buy a third interest in the Buffalo *Express*, did little more than prove that his son-in-law was not ready to become a businessman. Still, Mark Twain established himself in Hartford in as much affluent respectability as any eastern businessman might wish. Although Howells was to outgrow Cambridge, Boston, and the *Atlantic Monthly*, and even grow enough to have journalism on his own terms in Boston and New York, he settled into Cambridge at the time easily enough. The smugness of finding such a place as he and his wife and children found within the very cradle of civility and culture appears in *Suburban Sketches*, Howells' first attempt at domestic realism in which Cambridge and environs were treated as if they were Venice or Florence.

15. M. Howells (ed.), *Life in Letters*, I, 100–101.

Both men's careers, their remarkable friendship, too, are tied to their family situations. Both felt loyalties and financial responsibilities to the parental families they had left behind. Although *The Celebrated Jumping Frog* did not sell greatly in 1867, Clemens authorized his agent to collect the royalties and send them to Jane Clemens in Hannibal. Until his mother's death in 1890, he contributed to her support, frequently castigating himself for being late with money or for not sending enough. In 1870, largely at his advice, his mother and sister moved to Fredonia, New York, near the Clemenses in Elmira and Buffalo. Orion, somewhat like Howells' brother Sam, had a record of improvidence that stretched a merciful brother's patience but never severed the family tie.

Howells similarly looked to his Ohio family interest, sending clothes, Christmas gifts, and money, albeit with a thriftiness that was a part of Howells' character. He directly assisted his father in acquiring a transfer as consul from Quebec to Toronto in 1878, and later helped his brother Joe get a consular post in the West Indies. Earlier, when circumstances made it seem possible that Joseph would be drafted and thus deprive the family of a main source of income, Howells honestly expressed his disinclination to leave Venice for the printing office in Ohio, but concluded, "You have only to say come, and I come."[16] He wrote regularly, once a week, to his family in Ohio most of his life.

The inevitable movement away from the parental family was succeeded by the even stronger and insistent claims of their own wives and children. Literary critics, who are impatient with what gets in the way of their idea of an author's complete fulfillment, have a way of regarding both Livy Clemens and Elinor Howells as enemies to their husbands' gifts. Whatever emasculation either accomplished on her spouse's literary texts, they bore them children in a conventional way and with conventional results: the mixture of blessings and adversities that is the lot of most parents at any time. Neither plunged into marriage, and both were conventionally responsible husbands and fathers. Clemens' affection for Livy had in it that sentimentality, fierceness of attachment, playfulness, worship of his

16. *Ibid.*, 91.

own gods and damning of the rest, that is in his writing. Howells'
bond to Elinor was as conventional and cool as the ties between
married couples in his fiction. As seen through his fictional couple,
Basil and Isabel March, it was often dutiful on both sides, seldom if
ever passionate, condescendingly masculine at times, and a part of
a commonplace reality of life both to be suffered and treasured.
Mark Twain and Howells were, in some aspects of their personal
friendship, captives swapping tales of their captivity. Their children
were loved and cared for and worried over, additional hostages to
fortune from which neither man was free to move into the romantic
world his mind and spirit created. As for Livy and Elinor, both suffered ill health to the point of invalidism during much of their
middle and late lives. When Mark Twain first met her, Olivia Langdon
was suffering from a back injury sustained from falling on the ice at
age sixteen. Howells begins speaking of Elinor's ill health as early
as 1879, and she was a semi-invalid from 1889 till her death. Dixon
Wecter, literary editor of the Mark Twain estate, makes a wise comment about both husbands and wives. "By a legend of Mark's own
creation, Livy was supposed to play the heavy domestic tyrant—
vetoing his pet schemes, and upon the mildest remonstrance flying
into volcanic rages—as reflected particularly in the letters Mark
wrote the husband of another gentle and semi-invalid wife, William
Dean Howells, who enjoyed fabricating for himself a similar hen-
pecked role. It was their private little joke which a few other friends
shared, and it was good for a laugh precisely on the score of its
improbability."[17]

This, then, provides some background to the friendship that was
to begin sometime in late November or early December, 1869, in the
office of the *Atlantic Monthly*. A letter from Clemens in Pittsburgh to
Olivia Langdon, October 31, 1869, indicates that he was aware of
Howells, at least in the position he occupied on the *Atlantic*: "I
walked all around town this morning with a young Mr. Dean, a
cousin of Wm D. Howells, editor of the *Atlantic Monthly*. He kindly
offered to give me a letter of introduction to Mr. Howells, but I

17. Wecter (ed.), *Love Letters*, 11.

thanked him sincerely & declined, saying I had a sort of delicacy about using letters of introduction . . . I prefer to be casually introduced, or to call ceremoniously with a friend." Clemens may have been showing his polite side to Livy, for writing to his mother in 1866 he said: "I am taking letters of introduction to Henry Ward Beecher, Rev. Dr. Tyng, and other eminent parsons in the east. Whenever anybody offers me a letter to a preacher, now I snaffle it on the spot."[18] Whatever his deference to Howells as editor (in fact, assistant editor) of an important literary magazine, Clemens' interest in calling on him was stimulated by the favorable, unsigned review of *Innocents Abroad*, which appeared in the *Atlantic*'s December issue. In Boston for lecture engagements, he stopped at the *Atlantic* office, 124 Tremont Street, apparently meeting James T. Fields, and was introduced to Howells and apprised that Howells had written the favorable review. It was a long review in comparison with others Howells was writing and longer than reviews he was to write of Mark Twain's next few books. But, then, *Innocents Abroad* was a big book, as Howells pointed out in expressing the *Atlantic*'s disdain of subscription publishing. Most of the review follows; the chief deletions are illustrative passages Howells quoted from Mark Twain's text.

The character of American humor, and its want of resemblance to the humor of Kamtschatka and Patagonia—will the reader forgive us if we fail to set down here the thoughts suggested by these fresh and apposite topics? Will he credit us with a self-denial proportioned to the vastness of Mr. Clemens's very amusing book if we spare to state why he is so droll or— which is as much to the purpose—why we do not know? This reticence will leave us very little to say by way of analysis; and, indeed, there is very little to say of *The Innocents Abroad* which is not of the most obvious and easy description. The idea of a steamer-load of Americans going on a prolonged picnic to Europe and the Holy Land is itself almost sufficiently delightful, and it is perhaps praise enough for the author to add that it suffers nothing from his handling. . . . It is out of the bounty and abundance of his own nature that he is as amusing in the execution as in the conception of his work. And it is always good-humored humor, too, that he lavishes on

18. *Ibid.*, 115; Albert Bigelow Paine (ed.), *Mark Twain's Letters* (2 vols.; New York, 1917), I, 122.

his reader, and even in its impudence it is charming; we do not remember where it is indulged at the cost of the weak or helpless side, or where it is insolent, with all its sauciness and irreverence. The standard shams of travel which everybody sees through suffer possibly more than they ought, but not so much as they might; and one readily forgives the harsh treatment of them in consideration of the novel piece of justice done on such a traveller as suffers under the pseudonym of Grimes. It is impossible also that the quality of humor should not sometimes be strained in the course of so long a narrative; but the wonder is rather in the fact that it is strained so seldom. . . .

Of course, the instructive portions of Mr. Clemens's book are of general rather than particular character. . . . Yet the man who can be honest enough to let himself see the realities of human life everywhere, or who has only seen Americans as they are abroad, has not travelled in vain and is far from a useless guide. The very young American who told the English officers that a couple of our gunboats could come and knock Gibraltar into the Mediterranean Sea; the American who at a French restaurant "talked very loudly and coarsely; and laughed boisterously, where all others were so quiet and well behaved," and who ordered "wine, sir!" adding, to raise admiration in a country where wine is as much a matter of course as soup, "I never dine without wine, sir." . . .—these are all Americans who are painted to peculiar advantage by Mr. Clemens, and who will be easily recognized by such as have had the good-fortune to meet them abroad.

The didactic, however, is not Mr. Clemens's prevailing mood, nor his best, by any means. The greater part of his book is in the vein of irony, which, with a delicious impudence, he attributes to Saint Luke, declaring that Luke, in speaking of the winding "street, called Straight" in Damascus, "is careful not to commit himself; he does not say it is the street which *is* straight, but the 'street which is *called* Straight.' It is a fine piece of irony; it is the only facetious remark in the Bible, I believe." . . .

As Mr. Clemens writes of his experiences, we imagine he would talk of them, and very amusing talk it would be: often not at all fine in matter or manner, but full of touches of humor—which if not delicate are nearly always easy—and having a base of excellent sense and good feeling. There is an amount of pure human nature in the book that rarely gets into literature. . . .

Under his *nom de plume* of Mark Twain, Mr. Clemens is well known to the very large world of newspaper readers; and this book ought to secure him something better than the uncertain standing of a popular favorite. It is no business of ours to fix his rank among the humorists California has given us, but we think he is, in an entirely different way from all the others, quite worthy of the company of the best.[19]

Throughout the review as published, "Clemens" was spelled *Clements*, an error probably attributable to Howells, since he had sole charge of the book reviews as well as considerable responsibilities for proofreading. The fact is unimportant except as it suggests, as does the substance of the review, that Howells had little or no firsthand acquaintance with Mark Twain's other work. He knew his reputation, as is made clear in the last paragraph, but had "The Jumping Frog" or any other sketches really registered with him, he might have been expected to mention them.

What is most remarkable about the review and what Clemens must have most welcomed is the difference Howells finds between Mark Twain and the other California humorists. It was a difference he was to progressively define in reviews of works which followed; he summarizes Mark Twain's effects in a review of *Connecticut Yankee* in 1890: "The delicious satire, the marvellous wit, the wild, free, fantastic humor are the colors of the tapestry, while the texture is a humanity that lives in every fibre. . . . Mr. Clemens's humor seems the sunny break of his intense conviction." From the first, it is his humanity and his convictions that catch Howells' attention, even though at the outset he does some convincing of himself and the *Atlantic* readers that Clemens' humor is not vulgar or cynical or dispiriting. He will work no harm upon you, Howells seems to say, or, as he did say at the end of the review of *Roughing It*: "Its humor is always amiable, manly, and generous."[20]

In his recollection of the meeting in *My Mark Twain*, written in 1910 immediately after Mark Twain's death, Howells wrote: "In 1869 I had written rather a long notice of a book just winning its way into universal favor. In this review I had intimated my reservations concerning the *Innocents Abroad*, but I had the luck, if not the

19. W. D. Howells, "My Mark Twain," 89–94. In its original publication, the essay appeared anonymously among "Reviews and Literary Notices: *Innocents Abroad, or the New Pilgrim's Progress* . . . By Mark Twain (Samuel S. Clements[*sic*])."

20. *Harper's New Monthly Magazine*, LXXX (1890), 319–21, in W. D. Howells, *My Mark Twain*, 124, 128; *Atlantic Monthly*, XXIX (1872), 955, in W. D. Howells, *My Mark Twain*, 96.

sense, to recognize that it was such fun as we had not had before. I forget just what I said in praise of it, and it does not matter; it is enough that I praised it enough to satisfy the author. He now signified as much, and he stamped his gratitude into my memory with a story wonderfully allegorizing the situation, which the mock modesty of print forbids my repeating here. Throughout my long acquaintance with him his graphic touch was always allowing itself a freedom which I cannot bring my fainter pencil to illustrate."[21]

Mark Twain's biographer, Albert Bigelow Paine, said that the remark was: "When I read that review of yours, I felt like the woman who was so glad her baby had come white."[22] More careful recent scholars point out that Clemens specifically records this remark in a letter to Howells about his review of *Roughing It*. It seems highly likely that he did both. The connection between talk, his own and all that he listened to, and his writing is very close in Mark Twain's work. He probably did not invent the comparison on the spot in 1869, and if he did, it went into a vast reservoir of sayings to be drawn out whenever the occasion seemed appropriate.

Little more than these pleasantries seems to have taken place at the time of and shortly after their first meeting. Howells' account acknowledges "a gap in my recollections of Clemens, which is of a year or two," and the first document that establishes their acquaintance is a telegram in January, 1872, from Clemens to "W D Howells, Editor Atlantic Monthly," about an obscure poet, W. A. Kendall.

Please telegraph the following to Bret Harte immediately at my cost W A Kendall the poet writes that he is friendless & moneyless & is dying by inches as you know doctors say he must return to California & by sea wants to sail the fifteenth will you petition the steamship Company for a pass for him & sign my name & Howells & the other boys to it & forward said pass to Kendall at three twenty three Van Buren street Brooklyn I will send him fifty dollars get him some money if you can I do not know him but I know he is a good fellow and has hard luck.[23]

21. W. D. Howells, "My Mark Twain," 5.

22. Albert Bigelow Paine, *Mark Twain: A Biography: The Personal and Literary Life of Samuel Langhorne Clemens* (3 vols.; New York, 1912), I, 390.

23. Smith and Gibson (eds.), *Mark Twain–Howells Letters*, I, 9.

The tone of the telegram suggests that Clemens was confident enough of his acquaintance with Howells to single him out for this personal charitable purpose. The group signatures being requested confirms other evidence that Clemens and Howells and other literary friends had gotten together when Clemens was in Boston. A letter of November 12, 1871, to his publisher, E. P. Bliss, in Hartford, asks him to send copies of *Innocents Abroad* "(*marked with my compliments*)"[24] to Howells, Aldrich and Keeler, and notes they have been having a good many dinners together. Howells confirms such meetings, though not precisely as to date, by resuming his reminiscences of Clemens, after a gap of a year or two, with an account of a lunch in Boston given by Ralph Keeler and including Aldrich, Fields, Bret Harte, lately come from California, and Clemens.

Whatever the exact times or the missing details, we know that the two writers had become more than mere acquaintances between 1869 and 1872. Although Mark Twain's stature towers above Howells' today, that was not quite true at the beginning of their friendship. Howells was the one firmly established in the recognized literary line; Mark Twain was the outsider seeking and needing encouragement for his individual works, but also needing opportunities, acquaintances, and publications that might channel his energies into a literary career. For heretofore, and to a degree throughout his life, Clemens was linked with subscription publishing and the lecture circuit, both of which were dubiously related to literature. The *Atlantic*, for example, did not ordinarily review books from subscription publishers; *Innocents Abroad* was a notable exception. There was something crass about subscription publishing; any enterprising hawker of goods could set up shop and send salesmen on the road and door to door as easily for books as for brushes and potato peelers. The firms that put encyclopedias into the supermarkets or who sell "Fifty Golden Oldies" through television spots today occupy roughly the same position as subscription publishing firms did then. Lecturing was a mixture of uplift and entertainment; literary figures were among its performers, but the star was more likely to be a reformed

24. *Ibid.*, 7.

alcoholic like John Gough or an orating minister like Henry Ward
Beecher than an eminent writer like Emerson or Thoreau. Although
Clemens had intimations that he could become such a star and have
his books hawked in great numbers door to door besides, he was not
sure that was the course he wanted to take. With his marriage to
Livy, his need for respectability increased and so did his need to
support himself and her in the wealthy style that her family had established. His signing on with James Redpath's Boston Lyceum in
1869 lent some respectability to that part of his career, and Howells
and the *Atlantic*'s endorsement of *Innocents Abroad* lent support to
his literary aspirations.

The gap Howells speaks of between first meeting Mark Twain
and the renewal of their acquaintance is not surprising in light of the
personal events of Mark Twain's life. The fall and early winter of
1869 marked his debut as a lecturer in Boston. "During November
and December," Kaplan says, "he lectured nearly every night and
spent his days in Redpath's office on School Street smoking and talking shop with Nasby and Josh Billings."[25] But with the ending of the
circuit, which had begun in Pittsburgh and ended in Jamestown,
New York, Mark Twain was to see little of Boston for the next two
years. He cancelled his lecture appearances for 1870–1871, and
though he had *Roughing It* in mind as his next book, writing had to
give way to other demands. In August, 1870, Jervis Langdon died,
bringing Livy to a nervous collapse and adding to the responsibilities his marriage had already imposed. In October, Livy had a near
miscarriage and in November gave birth to a son, Langdon Clemens, whose frail condition intimated that he would not survive infancy. The writing of *Roughing It* was proceeding poorly that fall,
and Mark Twain's own pessimism was at times overpowering. It was
only with his moving to Hartford and the resumption of his lecturing
in the fall of 1871 that he had much opportunity to revisit Boston
and to pick up the acquaintance with Howells. It was from this time
that the close personal friendship of Howells and Mark Twain began.

25. Kaplan, *Mr. Clemens and Mark Twain*, 111.

Two

You Must Come to Hartford to Live

The Mark Twain house—now on a busy main street of Hartford, its grounds diminished, the stream and meadow gone—still conveys a monstrous lot of Mark Twain. It is not quite a gingerbread house, and "gaudy" does not adequately describe it. Neither does "mansion" or "castle" or "estate." A reporter in Hartford, seeing it not yet finished in 1874, called it "one of the oddest looking buildings in the State ever designed for a dwelling, if not in the whole country." A present-day biographer describes it as "part steamboat, part medieval stronghold, and part cuckoo clock."[1] Mark Twain himself recognized what it might be—"a gaudy and unrestful Palace of Sham"—but he made it a home fashioned by and to his own personality, but both intelligently and whimsically modified to embrace and indulge his wife and children and friends. He had carved into the library mantelpiece a quotation from Emerson: "The chief ornament of a house is the guests who frequent it." Howells later put the quotation in the mouth of Bartley Hubbard, the not-so-villainous villain of one of his novels, who bears a resemblance to both Howells and Mark Twain.

1. *Hartford Daily Times*, March 23, 1874, in the Mark Twain Library and Memorial Commission, *Mark Twain in Hartford* (Hartford, 1958), 8; Kaplan, *Mr. Clemens and Mark Twain*, 181.

The house at 351 Farmington Avenue was the most permanent home either Howells or Mark Twain was to have, and it had about it that same mixture of foolish peasant, knight errant, penitent, and prince that made up Mark Twain's personality. Few structures better display the struggle between order and disarray, symmetry and asymmetry, fecundity and control. Justin Kaplan counts three turrets, five balconies, nineteen large rooms, five baths, in addition to "innumerable embrasures" and "a forest of chimneys."[2] My own recent count of windows came to one hundred of various kinds, not counting those in the glass conservatory on the south side. The order in the structure comes from within, from a felt necessity to make the assemblage of bricks and stones and tile a comfortable dwelling place. Thus, a three-story dark oak spiral staircase occupies the central position. Open balconies and passageways at all levels open the house out to the surrounding grounds and bring within view the outlying terrain from a variety of perspectives.

"We had a particular pleasure," Howells wrote of one visit, "in looking off from the high windows on the pretty Hartford landscape, and down from them into the tops of the trees clothing the hillside by which the house stood. We agreed that there was a novel charm in trees seen from such a vantage, far surpassing that of the farther scenery. He had not been a country boy for nothing."[3] So sensitive was Mark Twain to the way a house embraces both inner and outer visions (and both able and willing to pay what that sensitivity may cost) that he had the flues of the dining room fireplace offset with a window cut directly above the mantel. Thus, he could watch the flames and falling snow at the same time. The same sensitivity prompted Mark Twain to have a tin roof put over one bedroom so he could hear the sound of the rain.

The house speaks eloquently of human vanity. But standing on the balcony off the third-story billiard room looking down at the parking lot, which now covers the stream that once ran there, one is not so much ashamed of human vanity as regretful that it is enjoyed so briefly. Moralizing is not the most easily aroused response from

2. Kaplan, *Mr. Clemens and Mark Twain*, 181.
3. W. D. Howells, "My Mark Twain," 14–15.

walking through the Mark Twain house today. Nor was it in Mark Twain's time. The house is there to be enjoyed, and the ghosts left behind are of those who enjoyed it greatly while alive—Clemens and Livy and their children and the Howellses and Warners and Twichells—and even Bret Harte, whose carping about the house and Clemens and, unforgivably, Livy rankled Clemens all his life.

In order to expand Mark Twain into the world he occupied in the 1870s, it must be pointed out that he was not singlehandedly responsible for the house. The architect was Edward Tuckerman Potter, whose hand can be seen in other houses which make use of differently colored brick laid in a variety of patterns.[4] He and his half-brother, William A. Potter, were sought-after architects of the period, engaged in designing church and public buildings as well as private dwellings of the well-to-do. The Church of the Good Shepherd in Hartford, commissioned in 1868 by the widow of Samuel Colt and erected directly behind the Colt Rifle Manufactory, is a good example of Potter's work, and it bears some of the same trademarks as are found in Mark Twain's house.

Potter was one of the earliest American architects to respond to the currents of medieval romanticism that affected English and American literature and the arts in general. While Clemens was contemplating what kind of house he would build, Howells was continuing his association with the Dante circle in Cambridge, contributing his command of present-day Italian to the assistance being rendered Longfellow in his translation of Dante's *Comedy*. John Ruskin, whose presence lies behind the High Victorian Gothic style that Potter followed most, had opted for "reading a building as we would Milton or Dante, and getting the same kind of delight out of the stones as out of the stanzas."[5] Potter is cited by architectural

4. See Sarah B. Lindau, *Edward T. and William A. Potter: American Victorian Architects* (New York, 1979), and Wilson H. Faude, *The Renaissance of Mark Twain's House: Handbook for Restoration* (Larchmont, N.Y., 1978). Illustrations of Ruskinian Gothic in New England, including views of Mark Twain's house, are in Wayne Andrews, *Architecture in New England: A Photographic History* (Brattleboro, Vt., 1973), 114–20.

5. George L. Hersey, *High Victorian Gothic: A Study in Associationism* (Baltimore, 1972), 29.

historians as an originator of the High Victorian Gothic in the United States found in the Mott Memorial Library at Union College in Schenectady. Hartford itself has the distinction of being the site of an even earlier appearance of the Gothic in Daniel Wadsworth's cottage built on its outskirts in 1818. And the state capitol at Hartford, erected in 1878, was listed among the ten best buildings in the United States by the *American Architect* in 1885; it is still often cited as an example of Venetian or Ruskinian Gothic.

The trend in architecture of the era makes Mark Twain's house much less idiosyncratic than it may seem, though having the servants' quarters closest to the street was Livy's idea, so her husband said, in order to keep them from running from back to front to see what was happening. Livy had much to do with choosing and furnishing the Hartford home. Returning to visit the house in 1895 after having left it as a permanent home four years earlier, Clemens wrote Livy, "You did it all, & it speaks of you & praises you eloquently & unceasingly."[6]

The polychromy of the building's exterior was a prominent aspect of Potter's style, following Ruskin's call for "every variety of hue, from pale yellow to purple, passing through orange, red and brown. . . . Penetrative ornaments of different sizes" should also abound, as well as "varied and visible masonry."[7] The Colt mansion, built in 1857–1858 in Hartford, is a more bizarre structure than Twain's house, combining medieval, Italian, and oriental modes, and attempting to harmonize a square Italianate tower with two trellised, bulbous domes. Twain might have pushed that far, though it is doubtful that he would have called the mansion, as Colt did, *Armsmere*.

The spot upon which Mark Twain chose to erect his castellated pleasure dome relates to his establishing a residence specifically in Hartford. Kenneth Andrews' *Nook Farm: Mark Twain's Hartford Circle* admirably recreates the immediate environment and the circle of individuals who gathered there. Curious as it may seem to have Mark Twain settle in Hartford—as curious as finding him buried in

6. Wecter (ed.), *Love Letters*, 312.
7. Hersey, *High Victorian Gothic*, 185.

Elmira, New York—the city was an excellent, almost inevitable choice.[8] Hartford in the 1860s was both a green and handsome New England village and a place of sufficient size and enterprise to be a base from which a writer might make a living. Hartford came to Clemens' attention in both professional and personal ways. The professional invitation came first, not precisely to move to Hartford, but to come see Elisha Bliss, the subscription publisher, and discuss making a book out of the *Quaker City* travel letters. Carrying out the responsibilities that had made his American Publishing Company a successful firm, Bliss wrote to Clemens right after he returned to New York from Europe. Along with Philadelphia, Cincinnati, and Chicago, Hartford was a leading subscription book center, and it was also a major center of cigar manufacture, as supportive of Mark Twain's vicious habit as the city's moral atmosphere was of Livy's quiet piety. In January, 1868, Clemens first visited Bliss, who lived across the street from Joe Twichell's church, to discuss a contract, and he returned a number of times to work on the book before it was published.

The place one signs the contract for a first book often becomes special for the author. Mark Twain's satisfaction was apparent in the letter he wrote to his old friend, Will Bowen: "I have made a tip-top contract for a 600-page book, & I feel perfectly jolly. It is with the heaviest publishing house in America, & I get the best terms they have ever offered any man save one."[9] The terms were 5 percent of the subscription price (he gambled on the royalties being larger than the $10,000 Bliss offered outright), and the promises of large sales were backed up by the army of disabled veterans, schoolteachers, clergymen, handicapped persons, and women who made up the canvassers working door to door in cities and small towns across the country. It was true that few of the books Bliss or other subscription publishers sold were literary or even very long-lasting in appeal.

8. Kenneth Andrews, *Nook Farm: Mark Twain's Hartford Circle* (Cambridge, Mass., 1950); see Robert D. Jerome and Herbert A. Wisbey, Jr., *Mark Twain in Elmira* (Elmira, N.Y., 1977).

9. Theodore Hornberger (ed.), *Mark Twain's Letters to Will Bowen: "My First, & Oldest & Dearest Friend"* (Austin, Texas, 1941), 16.

People from Another World, The Life of Barnum, Cuba, with Pen and Pencil, Woman's Pilgrimage in the Holy Land, were the kinds of titles to which *Innocents Abroad* would be added. But the fact that Mark Twain had a contract in hand and a commitment to deliver a manuscript in six months was enough to excite an enthusiasm for Hartford had the town nothing else to offer.

There was, importantly, something else. The trip that brought him face to face with Bliss was also one which brought him into the house of Isabella Beecher Hooker at Nook Farm. Isabella was the wife of John Hooker, direct descendant of the Thomas Hooker who is credited with founding Hartford in 1636. The connections with Mark Twain's future in that meeting are part of the workings of Providence, or circumstance, that Mark Twain pondered in a letter to Olivia Langdon. "If ever a man had reason to be grateful to Divine Providence, it is I," he wrote her during their engagement. "And often & often again I sit & think of the wonder, the curious mystery, the *strangeness* of it, that there should be only *one* woman among the hundreds & hundreds of thousands whose features I have critically scanned, & whose character I have read in their faces—only *one* woman among them all whom I could love with all my whole heart, & that it should be my amazing good fortune to secure that woman's love."[10] The facts are that, amidst too many saints and not enough sinners, too many middle-class Americans from places like Hartford, Albany, Elmira, and Cleveland, on the *Quaker City* Mark Twain had found a friend and companion in Charles Langdon, Livy's younger brother by four years and younger than Mark Twain by fourteen. The miniature of his sister that he showed to Mark Twain led to their meeting in New York at the end of 1867. On New Year's Day, 1868, he formally called upon her and also met "another beautiful girl," Alice Hooker, daughter of Isabella Beecher Hooker. Isabella was the sister of Thomas K. Beecher, the unorthodox pastor of the Park Church in Elmira and the Langdons' family pastor.[11] Thus Mark Twain established another vital connection with Hartford.

10. Wecter (ed.), *Mark Twain to Mrs. Fairbanks,* 73.
11. The maverick side of Thomas Beecher must have appealed to Mark Twain. Beecher's criticism of businessmen in his Williamsburgh pastorate led to

Mark Twain's ties with the Beechers and Hookers came about at the same time as that with the Langdons and were strengthened by his marriage into the Langdon family. Even before the marriage, he was casting about toward acquiring a newspaper that would provide support for Livy and a place for settling down. The Hartford *Courant* was one choice, but he could not arrive at satisfactory terms. The Cleveland *Herald* was another, but Mark Twain wrote that both he and Livy "would prefer the quiet, moral atmosphere of Hartford to the driving, ambitious ways of Cleveland." Petroleum V. Nasby, another platform humorist, proposed Mark Twain's coming to his paper, the Toledo *Blade*. Nearer to Elmira was the Buffalo *Express*, which, with a loan from his father-in-law, came into Mark Twain's partial possession in 1870. Mark Twain could no more refuse the situation it offered than he could the wedding gift, a surprise he describes to Bowen in a letter from Buffalo on February 6, 1870.

William, old boy, her father surprised us a little, the other night. We all arrived here in a night train . . . & under pretense of taking us to the private boarding-house . . . my new father-in-law & some old friends drove us in sleighs to the daintiest, darlingest, loveliest little palace in America—when I said, "Oh, this won't do—people who can afford to live in this sort of style won't take boarders," that same blessed father-in-law let out the secret that this was all *our* property—a present from himself. House & furniture cost $40,000 in cash, (including stable, horse & carriage), & is a most exquisite little palace (I saw no apartment in Europe so lovely as our drawing-room.)[12]

Such fortune, coming so soon upon his winning of Livy, might have claimed him for Buffalo, but Buffalo is Buffalo and in-laws are in-laws and running a newspaper is running a newspaper. The rea-

---

his walking out under threat of dismissal. Jervis Langdon was the member of the Elmira church committee to whom he defined the unorthodox conditions under which he would serve there in 1844. Eight years earlier, Langdon had led a group who broke from a local Presbyterian church because its pastor defended slavery. Beecher remained in Elmira until his death in 1900, ignoring most of the behavior expected of clergymen. Rugoff, *The Beechers*, 436–50.

12. Wecter (ed.), *Mark Twain to Mrs. Fairbanks*, 73; Hornberger (ed.), *Mark Twain's Letters to Will Bowen*, 20–21.

sons Mark Twain quickly tired of Buffalo are numerous and obvious. The death of Jervis Langdon, as much as it added to the sad fortunes that came upon the young couple there, made a move possible. And moving to Hartford would seem less like betraying a father-in-law's generosity than any other move he might contemplate. Livy and her mother were already close friends of the Hookers of Hartford, and Mrs. Langdon was to live with them in their new Hartford home. Besides, there were still ties with Elmira, and during the years at Hartford, the Clemens family regularly went back there. Susan Crane, Livy's sister, had a place at Quarry Farm that afforded a quiet place to work. On top of a hill overlooking the countryside, she had an octagonal study built for Mark Twain's use.

Hartford, to Mark Twain's eye and temperament, offered a similar kind of attraction. When he first visited it, he described it in his letters to the *Alta California* as "the best built and the handsomest town I have ever seen. . . . Everywhere the eye turns it is blessed with a vision of refreshing green. You do not know what beauty is if you have not been here." In the fall he wrote, "I have seen a New England forest in October, and so I suppose I have looked upon almost the fairest vision the earth affords." Critics who see Mark Twain as a creature molded by the social milieu around him forget his great attachment to the sensory world. Andrews justly emphasizes the contrast between the verdant Hartford landscape and the bleakness of the Washoe where Mark Twain had said, "a bird flying over the territory had to carry its own provisions." Kaplan notes Mark Twain's responsiveness to the fields of France and the Italian lakes, and he picks out *drowsing* as Mark Twain's "talismanic word to evoke the landscape of dream." His response to Hartford is like Howells' to Cambridge: both could still be regarded as villages and both were highly favorable to look upon. Hartford's population, though increasing rapidly, was given as 37,743 in the 1870 census. Moreover, it was a prosperous village. Mark Twain could ask as he would not have to ask today: "Where are the poor in Hartford? I confess I do not know."[13] But he recognized it as a friendly town and highly suited to Livy's moral nature as well as his own.

13. Andrews, *Nook Farm*, 18, 20, 21. A firsthand view of Hartford of this period is in Helen Post Chapman, *My Hartford of the Nineteenth Century* (Hart-

Mark Twain makes light of the morality of Hartford, much as he did that of Livy, and yet he adapted easily to both. For in truth, morality is at the heart of Clemens' temperament as surely as it is at the heart of Howells'. There was much morality in Hartford to observe and chide and yet live with. Clemens claimed that the ban on cards had been repealed only the year before he arrived. According to his telling, he was able to smoke in the house in which he stayed only by sneaking a cigar at night and blaming the cat. "I don't dare to do *anything* that's comfortable & natural," he writes to Mrs. Fairbanks during his first visit to the Hookers.[14] By the time he came to live in Hartford, he was no longer the California roughneck being brought by love of Livy into proving himself acceptable to her family and friends. He had passed Jervis Langdon's inspection, and Thomas K. Beecher had sanctified the marriage. The Nook Farm group in Hartford, though it offered one hard-to-digest morsel in Isabella Hooker, had more than ghosts of Puritan divines as company. When the Mark Twain house was built, it provided a gathering place for a social group remarkable for any small city in the country.

Howells came into this social group as a visitor from Boston, welcomed as much by its members as he welcomed their invitations. A telegram of March, 1874, from Mark Twain to Howells indicates that Howells and his wife, Charles Osgood, who had purchased the *Atlantic* from Fields, and Clemens were taking a train from Boston to Hartford, the Howellses to be houseguests of Charles Dudley Warner. Howells wrote to J. M. Comly, a close friend from his Columbus, Ohio, days, of this visit: "I staid with Warner, but of course I saw a good deal of Twain, and he's a thoroughly great fellow. His wife is a delicate little beauty, the very flower and perfume of *ladylikeness*, who simply adores him—but this leaves no word to describe his love for her." Evidence indicates previous visits with Mark Twain in 1873 in Boston and at least one winter visit to Hartford where he contracted a "frightful cold" at Mark Twain's house. In a letter to Howells, February 27, 1874, Mark Twain is "in a sweat" for reasons best described in the letter. "Warner's been in here swearing

---

ford, 1928); Andrews, *Nook Farm*, 20; Kaplan, *Mr. Clemens and Mark Twain*, 49; Andrews, *Nook Farm*, 20.

14. Wecter (ed.), *Mark Twain to Mrs. Fairbanks*, 15–16.

like a lunatic, & saying he had written you to come on the *4th*—& I said, 'You leatherhead, if I talk in Boston both afternoon & evening March 5, I'll have to go to Boston the *4th'*—& then he just kicked up his heels & went off cursing after a fashion I never heard of before. Now let's just leave this thing to Providence for 24 hours—you bet it will come out all right." [15]

The visit did come out all right; apparently the lecture in Boston was confined to a single appearance on March 5, and the party all took the train together from Boston and spent the weekend as planned. With his customary enthusiasm, Mark Twain wrote Howells after the visit: "You or Aldrich or both of you must come to Hartford to live. Mr. Hall, who lives in the house next to Mrs. Stowe's (just where we drive in to go to our new house,) will sell for $16,000 or $17,000. The lot is 85 feet front & 150 feet deep—long time & easy payments on the purchase. You can do your work just as well here as in Cambridge, can't you? Come, will one of you boys buy that house? Now say yes." [16]

Howells' impressions of Nook Farm, as indicated in his letter to Comly, were that it was "quite an ideal life. They [Warner and Mark Twain] live very near each other, in a sort of suburban grove, and their neighbors are the Stowes and Hookers, and a great many delightful people. They go in and out of each other's houses without ringing, and nobody gets more than the first syllable of his first name." [17] Howells was probably tempted, but his rising fortunes on the *Atlantic* and his own upward moving in Cambridge-Boston were not such as he could leave. He told Warner his true home was in Hartford, and said he would spell it *Heartford* hereafter.

Mark Twain's new home was not completed until 1874, and from the fall of 1871 the Clemenses rented the Hooker house, where Mark Twain had been a guest on his first Hartford visit. From that vantage point, the Clemenses extended their acquaintance with the Nook Farm group. By that time, the hundred-acre wooded tract that

15. M. Howells (ed.), *Life in Letters*, I, 187; Smith and Gibson (eds.), *Mark Twain—Howells Letters*, I, 14.

16. Smith and Gibson (eds.), *Mark Twain—Howells Letters*, I, 15–16.

17. M. Howells (ed.), *Life in Letters*, I, 187.

John Hooker and Francis Gillette, his brother-in-law, had bought in 1851 had been extensively but carefully developed through sales largely to friends and relatives. After Hooker and Gillette had each built houses (Gillette's son, William, grew up there and became an eminent Shakespearean actor and adapted the character of Sherlock Holmes for the stage), other houses were occupied by Thomas Perkins, lawyer and husband of Mary Beecher, Isabella's sister; John Hooker's widowed mother; Elizabeth Gillette, Francis Gillette's sister and the wife of George Warner; and Joseph Hawley, then junior partner of John Hooker. They comprised a family-related aristocracy of substance and intelligence.

The Nook Farm residents closer to Mark Twain's interests did not appear until Charles Dudley Warner, George Warner's brother, arrived just before the Civil War. Warner was a lawyer practicing in Chicago when Joseph Hawley invited him to help edit the *Evening Press*. Like many newspapers of the time—for example, the ones that Howells' father struggled with in Howells' youth—this one had been recently established as an organ of political opinion, in this instance, the views of radical Republicans. Warner was already a literary man; his essays had appeared in *Putnam's Magazine*, and he was to become Mark Twain's collaborator on *The Gilded Age* in 1873. After the war, Warner and Hawley merged the *Press* with the *Courant* (it was with them that Mark Twain had unsuccessfully dealt toward a purchase of a share in the paper). Warner became fully committed to the literary side of journalism, turning as Howells and Twain had done to travel letters and books as his chief work.

In 1862 the money brought in by the extraordinary sales of *Uncle Tom's Cabin* since its publication in 1852 enabled Harriet Beecher Stowe, now past fifty, to build a house at Nook Farm. Although she professed to be thinking of retirement and was returning to an area remembered from her childhood, she continued a very productive literary career. Howells had had some uncomfortable acquaintance with her through the outcry raised by the publication in the *Atlantic* of her article about Byron's incest. He wrote his father that he had not seen Mrs. Stowe's article, "The True Story of Lady Byron's Life," until it was in type but that he did not agree with those who condemned her. "The world needed to know just how base, filthy and mean Byron was, in order that all glamor should be forever removed from his literature." He added, however, that he did not like Mrs. Stowe's way of doing things and that "she did this particular thing wretchedly."[18] By 1896, the year of her death, her collected *Writings* numbered sixteen volumes. When Mark Twain arrived at Nook Farm, she had given up the mansion and was living in the Stowe house that now occupies the site near the Mark Twain house.

The third of the residents of Nook Farm of most interest to Mark Twain was the Reverend Joseph Twichell.[19] Howells observed as a mark of the easy life-style at Nook Farm that they even called their minister Joe. Both Howells and Mark Twain were fond of ministers. Howells' social novels include ministers as representative members of middle- and upper-class social circles. They range from bland ministers ingratiating themselves with the society they are dependent upon to a minister like Julius Peck who makes a half turn to the life of Christ only to be snuffed out by a train accident Howells borrowed from his own life. What Howells abstractly depicted in his range of minister types was the waning power and influence of the village minister that seemed to relate in some way to his becoming an accepted figure, the mark of culture and education in societies unsure of both. The theology ministers espoused similarly lost its fierceness and power and adapted itself in various ways to the need for a Christianity that rested less on theology than on social acceptance and social needs. The history of the Beecher family defines more sharply that general process, though the trial of Henry Ward Beecher for adultery in 1875 cannot be regarded as characteristic. Mark Twain was strongly attracted to Thomas Beecher, pastor of the Park Church in Elmira. Beecher commonly wore working man's clothing, played billiards, and enjoyed an occasional glass of ale. Under the pseudonym S'cat, Clemens defended Beecher in the pages of the Elmira paper when the Ministerial Union expelled him for, as

18. *Ibid.*, 150.
19. See Leah A. Strong, *Joseph Hopkins Twichell: Mark Twain's Friend and Pastor* (Athens, Ga., 1966).

Clemens put it, "being responsible to GOD for his acts instead of to the Ministerial Union."[20]

Joe Twichell came into the Nook Farm community in 1865 as pastor of the newly-established Asylum Hill Congregational Church, what Clemens called "the Church of the Holy Speculators." Clemens met him through Bliss during his early stays in Hartford while working on *Innocents Abroad*. Twichell was born twenty miles or so south of Hartford, went to Yale, volunteered for and served as a chaplain in the Civil War from 1861 to 1864. Winner of a literary prize at Yale, his journals and letters are moving accounts of his war experiences. He was twenty-seven when he came to Nook Farm, two-and-a-half years younger than Clemens, and married that year. He and Harmony and a large family remained at Nook Farm all their lives. He seems to have adapted to the mixed materialistic and spiritual interests of his congregation as he had adapted to the roughest of experiences in the Civil War. Theology had never been a preoccupation of his ministry; he was literate, tolerant, a devoted Christian with a faith lodged in brotherhood and ethics rather than doctrine, and he had a somewhat stronger optimism than even Howells in believing in the gradual movement of mankind to a higher level of humanity. At Clemens' request, he presided with the Langdon family minister, Thomas Beecher, at Clemens' wedding. Although he tried, as Livy tried, to convert Clemens to true Christianity, he succeeded no better and gave up trying early in their relationship. Howells found him to be an admirable person, though their relationship lacked the closeness that came from being a neighbor and frequent traveling companion to Mark Twain.

From the first of his residence at Nook Farm, Clemens was maintaining the friendship established with Howells in Boston and including him among the Nook Farm group. Boston and Hartford were not far apart, about two hours by train with convenient schedules for going and coming. And Howells was usually acquainted with the literary visitors who found Hartford a novel stop between Boston and New York. His position on the *Atlantic* brought him into a profes-

20. Jerome and Wisbey, Jr., *Mark Twain in Elmira*, 119.

sional relationship with Charles Dudley Warner, and the liking Clemens had for Thomas Bailey Aldrich was furthered by Aldrich and Howells' professional and personal closeness. Howells was at the welcoming end of the walk from Hartford to Boston that Twichell and Clemens embarked on in 1874. The pair made it through one day and into six miles the next before they gave out and took the train. Howells wrote his father: "I never saw a more used-up, hungrier man than Clemens. It was something fearful to see him eat escalloped oysters."[21]

H. H. Boyesen, the Norwegian-born writer whom Howells had befriended and invited into his home for a week in 1871, found that Nook Farm made Cambridge seem "pale and colorless" by comparison. As a somewhat objective observer, Boyesen identifies another essential of the friendship between Mark Twain and Howells. "The tender and considerate conduct of each toward all," which he observed in the Howells household, was carried even further into the whole family that constituted most of the Nook Farm residents. Kenneth Andrews concludes of Nook Farm that "each of the Nook Farm families conceived of a fully developed family experience as the heart of existence and devoted much energy to living up to this conception. . . . The ideal of the good life as a happy family life warmed the whole neighborhood."[22]

Family life was central to both Mark Twain and Howells, and the seventies was the period in which both were most devotedly family men. One cannot walk through the Mark Twain house today without being reminded of Mark Twain as a family man. Clara Clemens, in *My Father, Mark Twain*, is the best source of information about "the atmosphere of fairyland, kings and queens in the world of dreams," in which she grew up.[23] Dogs and ponies, tobogganing and skating, Valentines by the hundred, countless storytellings and dramatizations, games elaborately planned and invented on the spot—Mark Twain's largesse in these respects can be seen as a rich man's in-

21. William Dean Howells to William C. Howells, November 15, 1874, in William Dean Howells Papers, Houghton Library, Harvard University.

22. Andrews, *Nook Farm*, 82, 84.

23. Clara Clemens, *My Father Mark Twain* (New York, 1931), 1.

dulgence or as the overflowing of his superabundant vitality and affection.

Nevertheless, he wrote to Howells in 1886 about "the thunderstroke" that fell upon him in finding that "all their lives my children have been afraid of me! have stood all their days in uneasy dread of my sharp tongue & uncertain temper." Susy's writings during that time and Clara's later reminiscences suggest that Mark Twain exaggerated here as he was prone to do in conscience-stricken assessments of his own character. Certainly he was attentive to them; they were frequently in his correspondence and other writings, and it was only toward Jean, the last-born child, that he expressed sincere dismay that he had never understood her. He had more opportunity to observe Susy and Clara and was less under the strain of misfortunes of his later life. He wrote: "Suzy, when her spirit was at rest, was reflective, dreamy, spiritual, Clara was at all times alert, enterprising, business-like, earthy, orderly, practical." In what the family called "The Three Days," Clemens described how, on successive days, Clara was snatched from a blazing crib with her hair smoldering, Jean's baby crib caught fire while she was asleep in it, and the woodwork enclosing the fireplace began smoldering, ready to burst into flames had not the accident of Clemens' barber being sent up to the schoolroom prevented it.[24]

In Cambridge, Howells' life, too, was centered on the family, though his own demands of career and wage earning left a narrower margin for his family activities. The difference is one of both magnitude and temperament. Howells' steady movement upward into larger and more gracious family settings never came close to the grandeur and expansiveness of Mark Twain's family life almost from the start. By temperament, he could be satisfied with less. But oddly, when one reflects upon the essentially solid and stable figure Howells has come to represent, a restlessness underlies his frequent

24. Smith and Gibson (eds.), *Mark Twain–Howells Letters*, II, 575; Caroline Thomas Harnsberger, *Mark Twain Family Man* (New York, 1960), 35, 28–29. The incident of the smoldering fireplace is also related in a letter from Mark Twain to his mother, in Samuel Charles Webster, ed., *Mark Twain Business Man* (Boston, 1946), 149–150.

moves from one place to another early and late in his life. Mark Twain, for all his lecturing and traveling, had the house at Farmington Avenue and, in the summer, Quarry Farm in Elmira to return to until he left Hartford for good in 1891. During the same period of time, Howells lived in ten different residences, not counting summer boardinghouses and residences in Europe. Even the achievement of a new house in Belmont in 1878 and then one on the water side of Beacon Street in 1884 seemed to provide short-term satisfactions, though Elinor's health and the tragic illness of his daughter figured in the short stay at both places.

Nevertheless, the primacy given to family life applies as much to Howells as to Mark Twain. In large part, both measured their mature felicity by a sentimentalized remembrance of their youths, one in which both what they had and what they lacked shaped their feelings. Biographers readily relate Mark Twain's need for possessions, his creating of an opulent setting in which to lavish affection on his family, to the poverty of possessions and affection that marked his own youth. Neither his father, who died when he was twelve, or Jane Clemens, who lived until 1890, established any illusions in Mark Twain's mind about idyllic marriage and family life. What Mark Twain created was in compensation for what he had lacked, and yet his ties to the Hannibal family members who survived into his maturity remained strong in both affection and pique all his life. That family circle and Hannibal past provided characters, settings, and themes for much of his unpublished writings of the last decade of his life.[25] Howells' boyhood and youth were intensely tied to the family. It was a larger family than Clemens' and as poor. At its center was a hard-pressed but interesting, affectionate father and a conventionally anxious and ministering mother.[26] The strength of Howells' family ties was such that when financial necessity forced him into wage earning outside the home the absences were brief and traumatic.

Both Howells and Mark Twain, like Thoreau, speak of their

25. See John S. Tuckey (ed.), *Mark Twain's Which Was the Dream? and Other Symbolic Writings of the Later Years* (Berkeley, 1967).
26. See Kenneth E. Eble, *William Dean Howells* (Boston, 1982), for a brief but up-to-date account of Howells' family background in Ohio.

youths in hyperboles of remembered and lost perfection. It is a perfection lodged in the freedom that their different family circumstances allowed them, in which friendships both inside and outside
the family are a source of deepest satisfaction. It can be called romantic exaggeration, reinforced by a world in which the examples of
both family beneficence and deprivation were ever present. Orphans
abound in the popular representations of life in nineteenth-century
England and America, as do young ladies too old to be called orphans, but bereft of fathers or brothers to fend off blackguards and
seducers. Young men, and sometimes young women, seem to come
in pairs, or in groups, as in Louisa May Alcott's *Little Women* (Livy
was fond of calling Clemens "little man"). In fiction, this situation
may be attributed to the need for characters to be engaged in dialogue and to be delineated through affecting contrasts. But it was
probably also a social fact—the need for chaperonage on the part of
women, and the fact that men leaving the family earlier than women
(who, if not married, might not leave at all) needed a companion in
facing the unfamiliar world. Howells' and Mark Twain's own fiction
follows this pattern—Huck Finn and Tom Sawyer, for example, and
the young men in Howells' many novels who always seem to come in
pairs.

One other strain can be singled out from Howells' life to add to
the attractiveness he felt in Mark Twain's Nook Farm existence.
Howells was born early enough in Ohio to have experienced or
heard about the various Utopian communities attempting to establish themselves there before the Civil War. All were built upon the
idea of expanding the family as a self-sufficing social unit. Howells'
father attempted to establish such a cooperative on a small scale,
and Howells made a book of it in his late years, *New Leaf Mills*.
Elinor Mead Howells' mother was from the family who founded the
Oneida community. Howells' interest in the Shakers and other religious communities continued on into his maturity. The basis of affection and cooperation necessary to the Altrurian society that Howells in late life posed as his Utopia, has its source in the idealized
family of the nineteenth century. However deceived he may have
been in attributing so much beneficence to the family (and a work

like *A Modern Instance* shows his awareness of the other side), Howells accepted beliefs about the family quite different from those of post-Freudian times in which the family is viewed as central to most adult neuroses.

The letters Howells and Mark Twain exchanged during the seventies are full of family references. In May, 1874, Mark Twain gives Howells and Elinor a glimpse of his brother Orion and identifies Orion's wife, her older sister, and her father. In June he announces the new baby, Clara, "a gaudy thing." The answering letter notes their good fortune in having a girl, "boys wear out their clothes so fast." It was not long before the wives joined in the correspondence. In December, 1874, Livy writes to Howells thanking him for a copy of his newest novel, *A Foregone Conclusion*. Mark Twain, in a slightly later letter, observes: "My wife was afraid to write you—so I said with simplicity, '*I* will give you the language—& ideas.' Through the infinite grace of God there has not been such another insurrection in the family before as followed this. However, the letter was written, & promptly, too—whereas, heretofore she has *remained* afraid to do such things." In February, Clemens writes to Elinor thanking her for photographs of the Howells family. "I can perceive, in the group, that Mr Howells is feeling as I so often feel, viz: 'Well no doubt I *am* in the wrong, though I do not know where or how or why—but anyway it will be safest to look meek, & walk circumspectly for a while, & not *discuss* the thing.' And you look exactly as Mrs. Clemens does just after she has said, 'Indeed I do not *wonder* that you can frame no reply: for you know only too well that your conduct admits of no excuse, palliation or argument—*none!*'"[27] Such banter has given support to the notion that Livy importantly tamed Mark Twain. It is more likely that it merely reflects both Mark Twain's and Howells' acceptance of the stereotype in which otherwise dominant males became willing and loving victims of domestic servitude.

In a letter to her mother, Livy describes a visit of the Howellses in March, 1875, and gives a description of Elinor. "Mrs Howells is

27. Smith and Gibson (eds.), *Mark Twain–Howells Letters*, I, 50, 63–64.

not a bit like Mrs Aldrich. She is exceedingly simple in her dress.
. . . She is *exceedingly* bright—very intellectual—sensible and
nice. I liked her." In April she writes to Elinor explaining that she
cannot get to Boston until the baby is weaned. The letter hopes for
another visit from the Howellses soon. Affectionate and chatty as it
is, it still frames itself in the formal politeness of the times: "My
dear Mrs. Howells" and "I am affectionately yours, Livy L. Clemens."[28] As the years went on, it is fair to say, the friendship became
more confined to Mark Twain and Howells themselves, and the visits
were most often of Howells in Hartford alone or of Mark Twain's
stopping in Boston or Cambridge at the Howellses' house.

Of all the letters that document the friendship of the two families, one of November 30, 1876, from Howells to "My dear Clemens"
best expresses it. "Your visit was a perfect ovation for us: we *never*
enjoy anything so much as those visits of yours. The smoke and the
Scotch and the late hours almost kill us; but we look each other in
the eyes when [you] are gone, and say what a glorious time it was,
and air the library, and begin sleeping and dieting, and longing to
have you back again."[29]

28. *Ibid.*, 71, 75–76.
29. *Ibid.*, 165.

Three

A Friendship of Remarkable Equality

At the time of their early friendship, neither Howells nor Mark Twain was the western writer who enjoyed the greatest national fame. That honor belonged to Bret Harte, whose early stories and a piece of newspaper verse about "a Heathen Chinee" caught the public fancy to a degree even Mark Twain was not to experience until years later. Clemens had worked with Harte in San Francisco; Howells was Harte's host on his triumphant trip East. Although the three writers spent a convivial week together, the following years brought a complete end to the amicable relationship between Harte and Mark Twain. The falling-out was, in part, from frictions that can easily arise between authors. In that respect, it makes the equality and evenness of Mark Twain and Howells' friendship more remarkable.

Mark Twain's rancor toward Bret Harte has often been used as a measure of Twain's divided impulses, his insecurity, and his ability to develop and sustain grudges. The reasons for his denunciations of Harte are complex, though in any explanation Harte's own character and personality play as large a part as Mark Twain's.[1] The facts are

1. The most detailed account of the relationship is in Margaret Duckett, *Mark Twain and Bret Harte* (Norman, Okla., 1964). See also Bernard DeVoto (ed.), *Mark Twain in Eruption: Hitherto Unpublished Pages about Men and Events* (New

that Bret Harte had preceded Mark Twain in almost every aspect of the literary career he was moving toward in the 1870s. Although a year younger than Clemens, Harte had arrived in San Francisco in 1854, seven years before Samuel Clemens went to Nevada. Before Clemens ever thought of striking it rich in the Nevada diggings, Harte had already tried his luck on the Stanislaus River in California. His contributions to western journalism began in 1857 in the San Francisco *Golden Era*, and by the time he met Mark Twain, the name Bret Harte was already established as that of a promising West Coast writer.

Mark Twain met Harte shortly after he arrived in San Francisco from Virginia City in May, 1864. As editor of the new magazine the *Californian*, Harte engaged Mark Twain as a writer and may have helped develop his style. Both took a serious interest in writing even though that seriousness was deliberately covered over with an emphasis upon the natural storytelling genius that existed among the "un-literary" in the West and with a journalistic facility somewhat at odds with serious writing. Unacknowledged by either of them at the outset, a fundamental difference existed between them. The moral streak present in Clemens from his youth on, the need to reform people even while laughing at human follies, seems to have been absent in Harte. They shared a sentimentality as they shared fictional characters and locale, but Harte did not pick up, as Mark Twain did, the sobriquet "Moralist of the Main," which was as apt a designation as "the wild Humorist of the Washoe."

If moral outlook was a deep and fundamental difference between them—as it was a very strong affinity between Clemens and Howells—there were other obvious differences that arose very early in their acquaintance, differences traceable to the rivalry and jealousy that can easily grow between writers working the same vein. At the beginning of a career that was promising but not quite off the ground, Mark Twain could hardly help but find Harte's success vexing. His antagonistic feelings may have been aroused by no more than a mo-

York, 1940), 254–92, and Charles Neider (ed.), *The Autobiography of Mark Twain Including Chapters Now Published for the First Time* (New York, 1959), 294–306.

mentary irritation that some unworthy son-of-a-bitch had made it big. He might have thought differently about Howells if such a melo-dramatic poem as "The Pilot's Story"—wherein the slave's mother flings herself to her death on the steamboat paddlewheel—had been a huge success. Still, Mark Twain was not as possessive of his literary territory as, say, Ernest Hemingway was of his. And Mark Twain's dislike for Harte, setting aside specific personal grievances, was rooted in a disrespect for Harte's abilities as a writer and a moral censure of his character. His friendship for Howells, his love one can say, rests just as firmly on the twin facts that for Mark Twain Howells was both a good writer and a good man.

Mark Twain's full animus toward Harte was long in developing, coming about in large part after their collaboration on the unsuccessful play *Ah Sin* in 1876. No one knows for sure just what compounded it. But it had gained a full head when Mark Twain learned of Harte's appointment as consul to Germany in 1878 and sent Howells the following blast: "Harte is a liar, a thief, a swindler, a snob, a sot, a sponge, a coward, a Jeremy Diddler." In a long letter, again to Howells, his contempt for Harte's "slovenly shoemaker-work" is excessive but the specific criticisms just. When he read Howells' long, temperate essay on Harte in 1903, he wrote: "You have written of Harte most felicitously—most generously, too, & yet at the same time truly; for he *was* all you have said, & although he was more & worse, there is no occasion to remember it & I am often ashamed for doing it." In an indirectly stated way that often dignifies friendship, Mark Twain pays homage to Howells' steady course of trying to observe and write "truly." But his forbearance with Harte did not last long. In the dictations of 1906 and 1907 for his autobiography, Mark Twain acknowledged that "there was a charm about him that made a person forget, for the time being, his meannesses, his shabbinesses and his dishonesties. . . . Howells is right about Harte's bright wit . . . but the character of it spoiled it; it possessed no breadth and no variety; it consisted solely of sneers and sarcasms."[2]

The duality in Harte that Mark Twain remembered was probably

2. Smith and Gibson (eds.), *Mark Twain–Howells Letters*, I, 235, 261; II, 774–75; Neider, *The Autobiography of Mark Twain*, 291.

already evident in Boston in 1871 at a luncheon during which Harte
supposedly unmasked Mark Twain's coveting of eastern literary respectability. Howells compared Harte's trip East to "the progress of
a prince, in the universal attention and interest which met and followed it. He was indeed a prince, a fairy prince in whom every lover
of his novel and enchanting art felt a patriotic property, for his promise and performance in those earliest tales of *The Luck of Roaring
Camp*, and *Tennessee's Partner*, and *Miggles*, and *The Outcasts of
Poker Flat*, were the earnests of an American literature to come."
The Howellses acted as hosts for Harte. "He accepted with joy,"
Howells wrote, "the theory of passing a week in the home of virtuous
poverty, and the week began as delightfully as it went on. From first
to last Cambridge amused him so much as it charmed him by that air
of academic distinction which was stranger to him even than the refined trees and grass. It has already been told how, after a list of the
local celebrities had been recited to him, he said, 'Why, you couldn't
stand on your front porch and fire off your revolver without bringing
down a two-volumer.'"[3]

The climax of Harte's visit, as Howells remembered it, was a
luncheon for Harte with Ralph Keeler, Aldrich, Fields, Clemens,
and Howells as guests. Keeler, author of *Vagabond Adventures*, was
the host, and that in itself was something of a joke, for the impecu-
nious Keeler was known for inviting friends to lunch having neither
the cash nor the credit to pay for it. Howells' two versions of the
event, one in an essay on Bret Harte and the other in *My Mark
Twain*, do not differ materially. Neither emphasizes the lunch as
marking a breach between Harte and Mark Twain, nor does either
essay call attention to Mark Twain's repressed longing for recognition by "Boston illuminates." Inasmuch as Howells' accounts do not
single out the contributions of such a professional raconteur as Mark
Twain, he may have been, for whatever reasons, somewhat subdued
that day. Aldrich, by both Howells' and Clemens' testimony, was
particularly witty. Harte, who Howells said was "not much of a
talker, and almost nothing of a story-teller," made his most notable

3. W. D. Howells, *Literary Friends and Acquaintance* (New York, 1900),
290, 292.

contribution to the luncheon with some kind of "fleering dramatization of Clemens's mental attitude toward a symposium of Boston illuminates. 'Why, fellows,' he spluttered, 'this is the dream of Mark's life,' and I remember the glance from under Clemens's feathery eyebrows which betrayed his enjoyment of the fun."[4] There is little reason not to place Harte's remark and Mark Twain's response, whatever it exactly was, in the context of a week-long confrontation between Harte, the wild and wildly successful writer from the wild West, and the highly civilized literary Bostonians who were paying him homage.

Neither Howells nor Mark Twain, westerners themselves, could help but see their own past and present mirrored in the experience, but the incongruity provoked more joking than it did brooding about their non-Boston lineage. It is not until many pages later in *My Mark Twain* that Howells refers to Mark Twain's reception among his Cambridge acquaintances, and there the "polite learning" in America that "hesitated his praise" is contrasted unfavorably with his open acceptance in England. In America, "in proportion as people thought themselves refined they questioned the quality which all recognize in him now." Longfellow, Howells remembered, did not make much of Mark Twain, and Lowell less. The vulgar and vicious in cultivated superiority comes through in Lowell's response to both Harte and Mark Twain. Lowell's first act, according to Howells, was "the indulgence of his passion for finding every one more or less a Jew."[5] It is such a manifestation of Bostonian bigotry more than Mark Twain's supposed courting of Bostonian status that deserves emphasizing in both Howells' and Mark Twain's existence as literary men in a politely hospitable but foreign land. For their shared sense of being outsiders, however much or little they cherished acceptance, undoubtedly strengthened their friendship.

What Howells delineates at some length in *My Mark Twain* is the qualified acceptance of Mark Twain, early and late, that was forthcoming from Boston, and in the person of literary eminences like Longfellow and Lowell, whom Howells might have wished to be

4. *Ibid.*, 294; W. D. Howells, "My Mark Twain," 8.
5. W. D. Howells, "My Mark Twain," 39–40.

more knowing or generous. In the early days, according to Howells, Mark Twain liked going to Boston, preferred it over New York, but "of late years he never went there, and he had lost the habit of it long before he came home from Europe to live in New York."[6] Mark Twain and Howells came to terms with their own feelings about the values of Boston long before Boston itself did, in the abstract sense of the historically superior Boston still embodied in the attitudes of some residents of the Cambridge-Boston area. It may be hard to live down but it has to be lived with that the three great American writers after the Civil War paid their respects to Boston, and then, with various degrees of censure and disdain, disclaimed it.

Howells and Clemens' friendship may have been affected initially by a climate in which one carefully measured professional and social relationships. Certainly Clemens found Howells, as assistant editor of the *Atlantic*, a person worth knowing, but his fondness developed out of personal interest mingled with professional respect for Howells as a writer. Furthermore, while it may have been easier for a man inclined to envy to accept a fellow writer like Howells—and unlike Harte—whose success was qualified in many ways, it would not have been possible to accept a writer whose reputation and position had been fraudulently earned.

In those early years in Hartford and Cambridge, neither Howells nor Mark Twain was the writer each was to become, but each had put down the foundations upon which his major work was to be built. To some high degree, their friendship, too, was built on these foundations—of knowing early on each other's part, that they were young men of ambitions, pretensions, affectations even, for whom writing was a way of winning all those materialistic and ego-centered rewards that the greatest writers are not supposed to care about. Both seemed to recognize that in addition to the kind of talent and hard work that would win success there was within each some kind of aspiring and imagining and preaching and writing self that transcended worldly desires, transcended even the short period in which they had been granted to say whatever it was they felt most com-

6. *Ibid.*, 42.

pelled to say. And both seemed to recognize that there were personal dimensions to their lives, often at odds with their literary aspirations, that had as compelling a claim upon each as did an assured and undying fame.

By 1872, when correspondence begins to illuminate their friendship, the bond between them had become an intimacy in which one can show respect and love by making light of both. The letter from Clemens to Howells from Hartford, June 15, 1872, is both obvious jesting and a turning of the jest as only Mark Twain was capable of doing, and it must be reproduced in its entirety to make its point. To spare explanations in the text, it is necessary only to point out that Mark Twain had come upon an issue of a family magazine, *Hearth and Home*, which contained a sketch of Howells' life, written by Edward Eggleston, author of *The Hoosier Schoolmaster* and other similar books, and which featured a picture of Howells on the cover. This letter followed:

Friend Howells—

Could you tell me how I could get a copy of your portrait as published in Hearth & Home? I hear so much talk about it as being among the finest works of art which have yet appeared in that journal, that I feel a strong desire to see it. Is it suitable for framing? I have written the publishers of H & H time & again, but they say that the demand for the portrait immediately exhausted the edition & now a copy cannot be had, even for the European demand, which has now begun. Bret Harte has been here, & says his family would not be without the portrait for any consideration. He says his children get up in the night & yell for it. I would give anything for a copy of that portrait to put up in my parlor. I have Oliver Wendell Holmes's & Bret Harte's as published in Every Saturday, & of all the swarms that come every day to gaze upon them none go away that are not softened & humbled & made more resigned to the will of God. If I had yours to put up alongside of them, I believe the combination would bring more souls to earnest reflection & ultimate conviction of their lost condition, than any other kind of warning would. Where in the nation *can* I get that portrait? Here are heaps of people that want it,—that *need* it. There is my uncle. *He* wants a copy. And I want you to send a copy to the man that shot my dog. I want to see if he is dead to Every human instinct.

Now you send me that portrait. I am sending you mine, in this letter;

& am glad to do it, for it has been greatly admired. People who are judges of art, find in the execution a grandeur which has not been equalled in this country, & an expression which has not been approached in *any.*

Ys Truly

S. L. Clemens [7]

The letter does not sound like one courting the favor of a friendly and influential Boston editor either for professional or social gain. Above all, it sounds like a letter from one who finds the public aspects of careers more amusing than inflating, and who seizes upon a vehicle through which that amusement can be expressed. It is not a letter that can be sent to just anyone, only to someone for whom the sense of amusement overrules the tendency to be too proud of one's place in the world. Neither Howells nor Mark Twain undervalued their abilities and the sweetness of success, but both had ways of cutting themselves down to size. Similarly, though each was tremendously and consistently supportive and admiring of the other's work, they were capable of being critical of it if asked, and only occasionally constrained to be delicate about each other's personal idiosyncrasies and feelings. In a word, they were both humorists.

Although as each moved toward national prominence and literary and financial success, Howells began to walk more in the shadow of Mark Twain, the friendship, more closely considered, seems to be of remarkable equality. It began and prospered because of a number of similarities in background, parental families, and their own families. They had had the same kind of experiences, knew the same kind of people, and in their mutual encounters of other experiences and people, they shared recognitions and responses that brought and kept them together. And as the separation from the past left neither free from obligations to his near kin, nor free from doubts and guilts about discharging these responsibilities, that, too, was another source of shared sympathies.

Specifically at the time of their meeting, both were in their thirties, both possessing a sense of interrupted or stalled careers. Having no awareness of the long lives they were to lead, they must have

7. Smith and Gibson (eds.), *Mark Twain–Howells Letters,* I, 11–12.

felt pressed to get on with the careers that would most lead to personal as well as material satisfaction. Venice must have occupied for Howells the same sort of marking time as the Nevada-California years did for Mark Twain. Marriage had come earlier for Howells, but the realities of establishing a residence, securing a position, supporting a family, were still fresh experiences for him when he met Mark Twain in 1869; with Clemens' marriage the next year, wives and children and family life became one more shared experience. Mildred Howells and Susy Clemens were born the same year, 1872, and John Howells was only two years older then Jean Clemens, born in 1880. Howells' oldest, Winifred, was born in Venice in 1863, and Clara Clemens, the only child to survive her father, in 1874.

Their attitude toward women and domestic life and even the person and situation of the woman each married also strengthened the friendship. Both accepted the idealization of women that brought forth Mark Twain's advice to Molly Fairbanks, daughter of his Quaker City friend, Mary Fairbanks, on the occasion of her coming out: "The main thing is, to be as sweet, as a woman, as you were a maiden; & as good & true, as honest & sincere, as loving, as pure, as genuine, as earnest, as untrivial, as sweetly graced with dignity, & as free from every taint or suggestion of shams, affectations or pretenses, in your new estate as you were in the old." But both saw their wives, before and after marriage, in a more realistic light. To Joe Twichell, in December, 1868, Mark Twain wrote of Livy. "*She* don't know anything about beating the devil around the bush—she has never been used to it. She simply calls things by their right names & goes straight at the appalling subject of matrimony with the most amazing effrontery. I am in honor bound to regard her grave, philosophical dissertations as *love letters*, because they probe the very marrow of that passion, but there isn't a bit of romance in them, no poetical repining, no endearments, no adjectives, no flowers of speech, no nonsense, no bosh." Livy does not appear quite so resolutely rational in other extant letters written shortly before and after their engagement and marriage. She writes fluently and often with a knack for apt expression. "'Comfort me with apples' this warm, sultry, starchless morning" is the way one of her letters to Alice Hooker begins.[8] She appears not to spell as poorly as Clemens made out, and during the period when Mr. Clemens was stopping by, she was studying French and natural philosophy.

Elinor Mead Howells, too, seemed to possess an independence of mind, some of the no-nonsense characteristics Mark Twain attributed to Livy. Early in his engagement to her, Howells assures his father: "She's not violently intellectual, by any means. She has artistic genius, and a great deal of taste, and she admires my poetry immensely."[9] As seen projected in Isabel March, who appears in many of Howells' novels, she comes across as having a fondness for romancing about other young couples, a judging temperament, a rather stiff moral center, and a sharp tongue. Both wives were intelligent, good-looking women who ostensibly accepted the subordinate roles fixed by the culture and their husbands' professional success, and both seemed never for long to be physically well.

As their families expanded and grew older, their literary fortunes prospered. Throughout their lives, Howells and Mark Twain read each other's works, often commented upon new work in their letters, and on specific occasions set down their considered opinions of the other's achievements. *Innocents Abroad* had preceded Mark Twain's acquaintance with Howells. *Roughing It*, published in 1872, was written during a time of much adjustment, moving, and both great personal happiness and despondency. Mark Twain's marriage brought him intense personal happiness, but the confinement to Buffalo, Jervis Langdon's death, Livy's own exhaustion, the death in their house by typhoid fever of Livy's close friend, the frail condition and early death of Langdon, their firstborn, made the first years of marriage a troubling time. Nevertheless, his writing went on, and Howells' favorable review of *Roughing It* was almost as welcome as its sales, which proved that *Innocents Abroad* was not to be an iso-

8. Wecter (ed.), *Mark Twain to Mrs. Fairbanks*, 194–95; Wecter (ed.), *Love Letters*, 33; Olivia Langdon (Clemens) to Alice Day (Hooker), June 7, 1867, Katherine Day Collection, Mark Twain Library, Hartford, Conn.

9. George Arms, *et al.* (eds.), *W. D. Howells: Selected Letters* (6 vols.; Boston, 1979), I, 119–20.

lated success. On Howells' part, *Their Wedding Journey*, which he sent to Mark Twain earlier in the year, was more important to him than the book's success at the bookstores; it marked his cautious movement away from being a mere travel writer to becoming a novelist. With the appearance of *A Chance Acquaintance* in 1872, Howells' possibilities as a fiction writer were confirmed. From that point on, and for the next thirty-five years, he wrote almost a novel a year.

In their beliefs, opinions, and outlooks, Howells and Mark Twain shared much. Both were American democrats shaped by the small towns and rural areas where they grew up in which few considerations of what one person thinks of another are based chiefly on family, occupational prestige, or even wealth. Neither was a perfect democrat; Howells seemed to take on the prejudices of upper-class Bostonians against the Irish very quickly; Twain fulminated against universal suffrage as the root cause of the political and economic ills of the Gilded Age. Both experienced the actuality of slavery in the Ohio and Missouri of their youth. "No man," Howells wrote of Mark Twain, "more perfectly sensed and more entirely abhorred slavery." Mark Twain's newspaper days in the West were, in his own later reckoning, a means of moving from the bottom to the top of American society within one day's work. Clemens, like Howells, gained and enjoyed the rich man's privilege of hiring and, often with anguish, firing domestic help, and it is in this respect that both embraced the capitalism that in other respects seemed inimical to democracy. Howells tells the story of Mark Twain's being roundly and repeatedly scolded by a railway brakeman for sitting on his notebook. Asked why he took the abuse and did not report him, Mark Twain answered: "That's what I should have done once. But now I remember that he gets twenty dollars a month."[10] In their old age, the adverse effects of capitalism as an economic system and its relationship to aggressive, jingoistic political actions were deplored by both. Both harbored a romantic belief in natural goodness: man left free of the effects of society as it moved toward complexity had a

10. W. D. Howells, "My Mark Twain," 30, 37.

chance of being good. Huck Finn acts out of the goodness of his heart and against the lessons already preached to him by society. Aristides Homo, Howells' Utopian visitor, comes from an imaginary country where a just society has been built on the altruistic instincts given to all humans but held in check by most of the social systems they occupy.

Religion was a matter of great interest to both Howells and Mark Twain, though both were skeptical of religious truths, activities of established churches, and conceptions of human behavior promulgated by most churches. In their early upbringing neither escaped an acquaintance with Calvinism as the bedrock of American puritan beliefs. Howells' family had turned away from it before Howells was born, and Mark Twain faced it, defied it, made fun of it, within his own family. Paradoxically, in late life some of his fiercer fatalistic beliefs came to resemble it. The truths of religion did not seem for either to be tormenting personal questions; when such questions were asked, they were within the framework of personal anguish, such as the death of Mark Twain's son, and were not resolved either in God's power or His mystery.

Their respect for Christianity as beneficently shaping moral and social conduct was severely qualified. Missionaries were a particular target of Mark Twain's satire, and Howells' depictions of ministers in his novels have among them those true men of the cloth who are drawn to living the life of Christ rather than merely preaching it. The urbane ministers found in Howells' novels, though not ideal figures, are still on the right side. Their attitudes and activities are probably not much different from those of Joe Twichell, Mark Twain's close, lifelong friend. Mark Twain and Howells shared a suspicion of organized charities, ministerial unctuousness, certainties about immortal life, and the general effectiveness of religious beliefs loosely and tolerantly held. The admiration that Mark Twain felt for Joan of Arc coexisted with horror toward the atrocities that could arise from fanatically held beliefs. The best book of Howells' very late years is *The Leatherwood God*, a novel based on a true story of the career of Joseph Dylks, who set himself up as God and temporarily gained a body of adherents in Ohio in 1828. In the end, more disbelief marked their religion than belief. Although in his fiction and his personal writing Howells could repeat variants of a character's avowal that he does not know what it all means but that it must mean good, his marginal optimism was not too far from a pessimism as dark as Mark Twain's about man's prospects. And yet, a complete pessimism would not have found either so persistent in castigating mankind for its collective and individual follies and in urging upon his readers reforms of many kinds.

Both were very much children of their age in response to intellectual currents and the formal philosophies of the period. Darwinism and determinism, to take two of the most important, greatly engaged the attention of both. Circumstances and temperament, Mark Twain said, were the determinants of his own life. He spelled out the details of that belief in 1909 in "The Turning Point of My Life." In *The Quality of Mercy* (1893), Howells has one of his characters pronounce his judgment on the embezzling protagonist: "His environment made him rich, and his environment made him a rogue." The previous year, *The World of Chance* showed how the workings of an economic chance world ruled over the man of letters as much as over the man of finance. Almost all of the fiction he was writing between 1890 and 1910 in one way or another worked out the powerful forces of temperament and circumstance shaping the characters involved. Although it may be as much a response to their common old age as to a common philosophy, both Mark Twain and Howells ended up pessimistic about the prospects of a just democratic society. Howells' confession to Henry James in 1888 could stand for a reflection that came upon both Mark Twain and Howells in their middle and late years: "After fifty years of optimistic content with 'civilization' and its ability to come out all right in the end, I now abhor it, and feel that it is coming out all wrong in the end, unless it bases itself anew on a real equality. Meantime, I wear a fur-lined overcoat, and live in all the luxury my money can buy."[11]

Lest this misanthropy of conscience create too strong an impres-

11. Robert C. Leitz III (ed.), *W. D. Howells: Selected Letters* (6 vols.; Boston, 1980), III, 231.

sion, it is well to remember that both Mark Twain and Howells embraced with delight much that was progressive in the late nineteenth century. Mark Twain was enthusiastic about the explosion of big and small inventions that so dazzled people of the age. He called James Paige, the unfortunate genius whose typesetting machine could never be brought to economic feasibility, "a poet . . . the Shakespeare of mechanical invention." Although Howells deplored the coming of motorboats to Portsmouth Bay, he lived long enough to buy a Model T Ford himself. The typewriter and telephone were both welcomed and cursed. "I DONT KNOW WHETHER I AM OGING TO MAKE THIS TYPE-WRITING MACHINE GO OR NTO," Mark Twain wrote to Howells in 1874 on a newly purchased machine having only capital letters. Six months later the machine was still defying him, and he wrote: "You just wait a couple of weeks & if you don't see the Type-Writer come tilting along toward Cambridge with the raging hell of an unsatisfied appetite in its eye, I lose my guess." Eventually Howells ended up with the typewriter, and in 1877, he wrote Clemens, "The wretch who sold you that typewriter has not yet come to a cruel death." By 1891, Howells had not only adapted to the typewriter but was urging the merits of the dictating machine on Mark Twain: "I talked your letter into a fonograf in my usual tone, at my usual gait of speech. . . . the whole expense, cylinders and all, is only $115." As it turned out, Mark Twain was able to adapt to dictation and Howells was not. "I was amused when I was in London last fall," he wrote to Clemens in 1898, "to have James tell that he had taken to dictating all his fiction because he had heard that I always dictated. He makes it go, but if there could be anything worse for me than a typewriter, it would be a human typewriter."[12] Nevertheless, the generalization holds that both Howells and Mark Twain were quickly and enthusiastically receptive to most of the scientific and technological wonders that came into being in the late nineteenth century. Although Mark Twain could project apocalypse in that remarkably prescient and ambiguous work, *A Connecticut Yankee*, his personal response to invention and technology was often that of a child confronting magic, like Howells at seventy-five leav-

12. Paine, *Mark Twain: A Biography*, II, 904; Smith and Gibson (eds.), *Mark Twain–Howells Letters*, I, 51, 89, 181; II, 638–39, 681.

ing Shakespeare's plays at Stratford-on-Avon to indulge himself with a crowd of children in watching cowboys and Indians through the magic of the moving picture.

Above all else, Mark Twain and Howells were American romantics whose lives happened to come after that first upwelling of European and American romanticism. Howells defines it well. "At heart Clemens was romantic, and he would have had the world of fiction stately and handsome and whatever the real world was not; but he was not romanticistic, and he was too helplessly an artist not to wish his own work to show life as he had seen it."[13] Almost everything about their shared experiences and perceptions could be developed as revealing their basic romantic temperaments. The artificialities of literary distinctions in which realism is made to oppose romanticism and is attached to Howells as if he invented it stand in the way of perceiving that Howells was almost as much a romantic as Mark Twain. Mark Twain's indignation toward the "literary offenses" of Cooper, his animus toward Scott, are not rejections of the romantic outlook; they are rejections of a made-up literature to fit a made-up conception of romance, and of faulty literary technique. So, too, with Howells; even though he became the creator of "literary realism" by emphasizing the real life from which literature comes, his main work as a critic was to attack the sentimental, the *falsely* romantic.

What has been said is not meant to deny the fact that both Mark Twain and Howells can be numbered among those writers whose bias is to write from life and experience rather than from previous literature, and for whom the powers of precise observation and the ability of rendering that observation with precision in words are paramount. If that were all there was to their literary practice, we would end up with more works like Howells' *Their Wedding Journey* and Mark Twain's *Life on the Mississippi* and fewer like *A Hazard of New Fortunes* and *A Connecticut Yankee*. We might have been exposed to the precision of language and effects that is in *Huckleberry Finn*, but would not have had *Huckleberry Finn* at all if Mark Twain had been denied the animating power of a romantic temperament.

13. W. D. Howells, "My Mark Twain," 42.

After the Civil War, romanticism suffered a severe diminution of its great animating principles: the belief in spirit as superior to matter, in freedom as the means toward spiritual fulfillment, and in the passions as certifying the primacy of both. The waning of these powers of belief to compel appropriate action was the crux of the crises in social conditions that seemed to mock the promise of the American revolution. On the one hand was an obsession with materialism that provoked both Mark Twain's *The Gilded Age* and all of Howells' economic novels. On the other was a dissolution of passion into sentimentality and a shifting of religious emphasis from the spiritual to the social. Facing such conditions and the literature that reflected them, those who still believed in romantic premises were forced into taking the offensive. As romanticism had seemed to describe the literature of the past, so was it assumed to be (and in part was) the enemy of those seriously interested in literature after the Civil War. But the realistic position Howells espoused is much closer to the reality that Thoreau said we must confront and plumb than it is to the reality offered by popular fiction either of a romantic or realistic kind in Howells' time and after. For popular fiction took the courses most open to a society that strips reality of all but its physically verifiable sensations: one in the direction of a conspicuously acknowledged departure from reality of place, characterization, motivation, and outcomes; the other in the direction of adherence to fact and an accumulation of detail. Mark Twain's work inclined toward the former as Howells' to the latter, but neither would let life be so stripped to its mere physical terms as to limit the power of imagination and language.

Realism and romanticism are unfortunate as opposing terms, as if they are sharp contraries by which one measures the other. Reality and romance move in and out of our lives, the one claiming our attention at one time, the other at another. If they are opposites, then we are compelled by our human natures to move back and forth between them all our lives. If they are but parts of the mixed whole that we perceive imperfectly, then we similarly respond realistically or romantically as our circumstance and temperament incline us to perceive and choose. A marked condition of friendship is how friends help fill us out in this choosing, mirroring what we already feel but putting before us angles of vision outside our ordinary perspectives, both confirming our shared perceptions, and respecting the un-shared choices we make despite our friend's example or advice.

Some time in 1874, while installments of *Old Times on the Mississippi* were appearing in the *Atlantic*, Clemens proposed to Howells that they take a trip down the Mississippi. "Mrs. Clemens dreads our going to New Orleans," he wrote Howells, "but I tell her she'll have to consent this time." On December 19, Howells replied: "Mrs. Howells has sprung back from it with astonishing vigor and is saying that I ought not to go to New Orleans without her." In a January 10 letter Howells reveals that the idea had been his in the first place and that he had included the wives in the original plan. Now he is ready to back out altogether, "more sorry and ashamed than I can make it appear."

"We *mustn't* give up the New Orleans trip," Clemens answers promptly. "Mrs. Clemens would gladly go if her strength would permit, but can't Mrs. Howells go anyway? . . . You just persuade her." On January 14, Howells writes: "About New Orleans, I can't tell. Mrs. Howells is behaving very handsomely about it, and so am I." February 10, Clemens writes to Howells, "Mind you try *hard*, on the 15th, to say you will go." But on February 16, Howells' letter begins, "I can't manage the trip, this winter." And on February 20, Clemens responds: "I find I cannot go to Boston. And what grieves me as much, is, that I have to give up the river trip, too." Apparently Clemens revived the idea, offering to pay Howells' expenses, but again, sadly, Howells refused. A letter of April 27, following a visit of Clemens to Cambridge, said: "Now Clemens, it really hurts me . . . to say that I can't. It would be the ruin of my summer's work. . . . I haven't the courage to borrow any more of the future, when I'm already in debt to it."[14]

Howells and Mark Twain never did make such a trip, though both did, out of the need to write about the locale, make separate

14. Smith and Gibson (eds.), *Mark Twain–Howells Letters*, I, 55–58, 61, 65–67, 79.

trips on the Mississippi and the Ohio. If the incident says anything about their early careers, it is that the romantic impulses of each were kept in check by their own ambitions as well as by the presence of wives and families. Elinor and Livy and the children and the exigencies of childhood ills and the separations and distances occasioned by professional preoccupations limited the opportunities to respond to friendship's urgings as might have been possible in bachelor days. Howells seems to have had the press of duty, self-imposed as well as by family obligations, more heavily upon him. It comes as no surprise to find that Howells was the original spokesman in Henry James's *The Ambassadors*, when Strether tells Little Bilham: "Live all you can. It's a mistake not to." For, as James pointed out, that was the gist of an actual conversation between a middle-aged Howells and a young Jonathan Sturges in Paris in 1884.[15]

Within the Mark Twain–Howells correspondence is the equally revealing account Howells sent Clemens on August 15, 1908. "The other morning, after first waking, I dreamt of talking with a girl in Bermuda. I said that as it was coming spring, I supposed she would be going north, but she said, 'No, we are going further into the tropics,' and I made the reflection how perfectly natural that was, when she added, 'We want to see some Pepper Trees, and hear a pigeon sing.' Then it occurred to me that I had never heard a pigeon sing, and that it must be very nice."[16]

15. F. O. Matthiessen, *The James Family: Including Selections from the Writings of Henry James, Senior, William, Henry, & Alice James* (New York, 1948), 511–12.

16. Smith and Gibson (eds.), *Mark Twain–Howells Letters*, II, 834.

Four

Author to Author

Through forty years, Howells and Mark Twain's friendship was little marred by their relationship as writers. Howells' great admiration for Mark Twain's work is well known; Mark Twain's admiration for Howells' work, though not as well known, is strong and genuine. From the first, they read and commented upon each other's work, and both proposed writing schemes in which they might collaborate. As editor of the *Atlantic* Howells had an official responsibility to review books, Mark Twain's among others, and a further responsibility to solicit and edit manuscripts for the magazine. Clemens had no official duty of reading Howells' works or those of any other novelist, but the records show he was a far more faithful reader of Howells' works than of any others. Mark Twain was an eclectic reader, and fiction was only one of his interests and not a very strong one at that.

From the start, Howells and Mark Twain recognized the differences in each other's work, but more than that, they recognized what each was trying to do. Howells' course, from the writing of *Their Wedding Journey* through the seventies, was to write an honest domestic fiction that would not falsify itself with either sentimentality or sensationalism. Such fiction would not only be entertaining but useful to white, educated, middle- and upper-class families and of particular interest to wives and daughters, who constituted one of the most powerful civilizing agents for the vigorous, ambitious, business-oriented American male. Literate husbands and brothers were not excluded from this audience, especially if they were in academic or ministerial positions that fostered reading and a respect for polite literature. In a splenetic attack on both writers and readers of such fiction, Ambrose Bierce noted Howells' move in 1892 from *Harper's Magazine* to the *Cosmopolitan.* That "diligent insufferable," as Bierce called him, has taken "his factory of little wooden men and women on wheels" and "his following of fibrous virgins, fat matrons, and oleaginous clergymen" with him. Not-yet-married ladies and men, like clergymen, who had the time and inclination to read, were very much an important part of Howells' audience. Howells believed that young women provided the largest audience for fiction in America and that a novelist's power was to be tested largely by his success in dealing with feminine nature. We cannot be sure if he is expressing fact or preferences in his praise of the eighteenth-century English women novelists Fanny Burney, Maria Edgeworth, and Jane Austen when he writes: "They forever dedicated it [the novel] to decency; as women they were faithful to their charge of the chaste mind, and as artists they taught the reading world to be in love with the sort of heroines who knew how not only to win the wandering hearts of men, but to keep their homes pure and inviolable. They imagined the heroine who was above all a Nice Girl; who still remains the ideal of our fiction."[1]

How life and literature intermingle! Howells is describing a time he never knew except through literature, just as he is describing the kind of novels he and his friend Henry James were writing and the lives he and his peers were living. At the center is the coming together of the young man and woman in holy matrimony; preceding it are the months or years of courting; beyond is a future in which they live happily ever after. It is the timeworn but not worn-out theme of

1. Ambrose Bierce, "W. D. Howells, Artificer, Dispatch from San Francisco, May 22," *Literary Digest,* V (May 28, 1892), 110; William Dean Howells, *Heroines of Fiction* (2 vols.; New York, 1901), I, 12.

romance, though romance customarily plays itself out against a backdrop or is intermingled with other human conflicts that help catch and hold our interest. A great writer, Chaucer for example, can expand the convention to portray a wife of many husbands and marriages and an old man trying to rekindle his lust with a young wife. Howells' focus enlarges as he develops as a writer, but in his early work, he seldom strays outside comfortable, safe bounds in which he could establish a reputation and learn the fiction-writer's art.[2] Courting and marriage fell within the range of emotional experiences that Howells had recently had. It satisfied an audience for whom getting a young woman safely married was a foremost concern. It fit both Howells and Clemens, not so much because they were both fathers of future brides, but because both were very conscious of just having won away from the parental family a young, virginal, protected woman.

For all their realistic details, Howells' domestic novels surely left out many of the realities of the time. For all its banality, popular fiction had a wider range. Mindful of literary traditions of the past, Howells' early novels were animated by a desire to confront the falsity and immorality of popular fiction. Charles Dudley Warner, Mark Twain's collaborator, commented upon current novels in the June, 1872, *Scribner's*, in the form of a dialogue among individuals, undoubtedly drawn from members of the Nook Farm circle. Arguing that women dominate the writing of popular novels, the main spokesman calls attention to the "two sorts" of novels that women writers

2. Howells and his work need to be seen in relation to the conventions of his own time and the literary market upon which his livelihood depended. Twentieth-century critics continue to impose present-day standards and attitudes even while attempting to reconstruct Howells' past. A recent example is a published Ph.D. dissertation, "The Circle of Eros," in which the author "greedily" seizes on psychoanalytic techniques to "simultaneously expose the hidden sexual threads in the novels, and weave them with the rest of Howells' history" (xiii). Although, here and elsewhere, I offer my own arguments against the image of an excessively genteel and prudish Howells, I am not much taken with claims of his "long search for an affirmative sexuality" (184), his digging up "the dark truth of American sexuality," (184), his reintroducing "demonic sexuality (clarified by personal history)" (9), and the like. See Elizabeth Stevens Prioleau, *The Circle of Eros: Sexuality in the Work of William Dean Howells* (Durham, N.C., 1983).

write: "the domestic story, entirely unidealized, and as flavorless as water-gruel; and the spiced novel, generally immoral in tendency." Warner goes on to deplore these latter novels, perhaps indicative of "a social condition of unrest and upheaval." The character who probably represents Mark Twain in the dialogue closes out the discussion by saying, "We are living, we are dwelling, in a grand and awful time; I'm glad I don't write novels."[3]

Mark Twain accepted the kind of novels Howells wrote, tame as they may seem to us, but he showed no disposition toward writing novels along those lines. The novel attracted Mark Twain as the prevailing literary form for a sustained narrative, but the burlesquing of the popular novel was much more appropriate to his talent. Judged by the forms that define long fictional narratives, all of his works are seriously flawed. It is easy to perceive his early works, *Innocents Abroad* and *Roughing It*, for what they are, elaborations of the humorous travel narrative that needs no literary substance so long as the journeys themselves are interesting and the teller of them engaging. Such works escape judgment by literary standards. The writer, as Howells noted, has not embraced all the literary virtues, but the appeal of the work is somewhat independent of that. The obvious appeal of both works is the extension of view each provides for the reader, whether he is an American in one of the many guises Mark Twain describes or a more generalized American with some interest in the Europe from which he had come and in the West to which so many of his numbers were drawn. If the writer of such a narrative conveys the humor and irony of the adventures, so much the better, but what the writer succeeds at is not dependent upon its fitting a literary form or its being "literary" at all.

Mark Twain rarely enunciates any literary principles except the fundamental ones of being true to experience and of finding the exact language for conveying the writer's truth. In his early development, his theorizing probably was tied almost entirely to making effects, and the application to writing came directly from the shrewd observations he was making about affecting live audiences from the lecture platform. Mark Twain shares with most of the platform hu-

3. Charles Dudley Warner, *Backlog Studies* (Boston, 1872), 157, 158, 161.

morists of his day the idiosyncrasies of delivery that were part of their effects, which each developed by magnifying the distance between actuality and expectations. The westerner was assumed to be a buffoon and a vulgarian, and enough of both were retained to let the audience enjoy the stereotype. But, by a manipulation of individual effects, the audience was led to recognize that the buffoon possessed an extraordinary aptness of act and expression, a wisdom even that belied his appearance. He appeared to be anarchic and yet showed up on time to deliver his promised entertainment. He was flagrantly impious, yet wrestled with pieties that might be superior even to our own conventions. He was sentimental and cynical enough (but not too much of either) to permit the audience to indulge its own propensities toward sentimentality and cynicism. And all the while, he made audiences laugh by carefully manipulating incongruities, the chief of all being that this audience would gather at this time to spend an evening listening to him.

There is much evidence of how carefully Mark Twain polished the performances he gave. In part he did it for money. Although momentary popularity of a subject or person could win a successful lecture season or two, only a polished and professional performer could demand high fees over a longer period of time. It is probably fair to say that Mark Twain's lecture appearances were as carefully contrived and polished as Hal Holbrook's re-creations of Mark Twain as lecturer. Paul Fatout, editor of *Mark Twain Speaking*, calls attention to his "professional" approach to speechmaking. "There was nothing offhand about his concern for a craft to which he gave his best attention as lifelong student of the spoken word. He was a conscious artist, alert to nuances, sensitive to meaning and arrangements of words, and persistent in attempts to make speech serve his purposes."[4]

The fastidiousness that Mark Twain exercised in his lectures carried over to his writing. Many illustrations could be given; one of the simplest to describe is his attitude toward dialect. Among other faults Clemens found with Bret Harte's writing was Harte's use of dialect. "The man who attempted to wield a dialect which he has not been actually bred to is a muggins," he recorded in his notebook

4. Paul Fatout (ed.), *Mark Twain Speaking* (Iowa City, 1976), xxiii.

while in England in 1873. "Neither Bret Harte nor Dickens nor anybody else can write a dialect not acquainted with . . . Bret Harte is not acquainted with Pike County dialect . . . he mixes about 7 dialects, put them all in the one unhappy Missouri mouth."[5] If a writer were going to use dialect at all, Twain insists, he ought to get it right. Getting it right is not only a matter of hearing it in the ear and being able to reproduce it in the mouth, but of spelling it out on paper so a reader has a chance of hearing it to some degree approximated in the mind's ear. It is a complicated business. Even a trained linguist has to take on faith Mark Twain's assertion as to the fidelity with which the dialect of Pike County, Missouri, is reproduced. But even the linguistically unsophisticated reader can see the difference between the rendering of vernacular speech in the dialogue of Mark Twain and that of any of his contemporaries. The plain and vital difference is that Mark Twain's dialect is readable as almost all other attempts to reproduce a dialect accurately were not. When dialect was used for humorous effect, as it often was, its unreadability was compounded.

Consider, for example, the familiar Joel Chandler Harris tale, "Tar-Baby Story": "'Youer stuck up, dat's w'at you is,' says Brer Rabbit, sezee, 'en I'm gwineter kyore you, dat's w'at I'm a gwineter do,' sezee." Or the opening sentence of the story "Rare Ripe Garden-Seed" by George Washington Harris, creater of Sut Lovingood: "I tell yu now, I minds my fust big skeer jis' as well as rich boys minds thar fust boots, ur seeing the fust spotted hoss sirkis." Or this random bit of dialogue from a story by George Washington Cable, with whom Mark Twain shared the lecture platform one season: "'Old Charlie he been all doze time tell a blame *lie!* He ain't no kin to his old grace-granmuzzer, not a blame bit!" What may have been a listener's delight was certainly a typesetter's and a reader's nightmare. Howells, in a far-ranging essay about dialect in *Harper's Weekly* in 1895, concluded that the general reader "has got tired of dialect" and that the "conscientious artist" should consider "how little di-

5. Frederick Anderson, Michael B. Frank, and Kenneth M. Sanderson (eds.), *Mark Twain's Notebooks & Journals* (3 vols.; Berkeley, 1975), I, 553–54.

alect he can get on with, and how much can be done by suggestion, without actual representation."[6]

Howells found the "best and realest kind of black talk" in "A True Story," Mark Twain's first contribution to appear in the *Atlantic*. Mark Twain's reply to Howells' specific praise indicates the care he took to reproduce dialect, though it sheds no particular light on exactly what he did to reproduce it on the printed page: "I amend dialect stuff by talking & talking & *talking* it till it sounds right—& I had difficulty with this negro talk because a negro sometimes (rarely) says 'goin' & sometimes 'gwyne,' & they make just such discrepancies in other words—& when you come to reproduce them on paper they look as if the variation resulted from the writer's carelessness. But I want to work at the proofs & get the dialect as nearly right as possible."[7] Another example of Mark Twain's attention to the small but vital details of his craft comes from an appreciation of Howells that Mark Twain wrote in 1906. Although written later, it links with this early period, in which both Howells and Mark Twain were young writers improving their natural gifts through painstaking attention to details.

There is another thing which is contentingly noticeable in Mr. Howells' books. That is his "stage directions"—those artifices which authors employ to throw a kind of human naturalness around a scene and a conversation, and help the reader to see the one and get at meanings in the other which might not be perceived if entrusted unexplained to the bare words of the talk. Some authors overdo the stage directions. . . . Other authors' directions are brief enough, but it is seldom that the brevity contains either wit or information. . . . In their poverty they work these sorry things to the bone. They say:

". . . replied Alfred, flipping the ash from his cigar." (This explains nothing; it only wastes space.)

". . . responded Richard, with a laugh." (There was nothing to laugh about; there never is. . . .)[8]

6. Edwin H. Cady, *W. D. Howells as Critic* (London, 1973), 242.

7. Smith and Gibson (eds.), *Mark Twain–Howells Letters*, I, 26.

8. Samuel Clemens [Mark Twain], "William Dean Howells," in *What is Man? and Other Essays* (New York, 1917), 235–36.

And Mark Twain continued with a parade of bad examples, followed by contrasting examples of the skillful way in which Howells provides such stage directions.

Praising a writer for his handling of the "he saids" and "she saids" may seem to be faint praise, a singling out of small virtues where nothing more substantial appears. But Mark Twain's attention here is the same as his insistence on getting dialect right, an attention to the details of writing that escape most readers and careless writers. Mark Twain established a way of handling dialect that made it unnecessary for later writers, if they were aware of the problem and schooled themselves in how he solved it, to repeat their predecessors' mistakes. As Howells was a master of stage directions, that lesson, too, was transferable to future fiction writing.

Attention to the details of their writing was a part of the link between Howells and Mark Twain during the early years, years in which each had the primary task of developing his literary skills. Far from exercising a restraining hand over Mark Twain's work, Howells was a contributor to the give-and-take between writers by which each perfects a complex art. Robert Jack Lowenherz, who examined closely the literary relationship between Howells and Mark Twain, "found it impossible to discuss the literary relationship of the two writers without dealing at considerable length with their personal relationships." Of the question of direct influence, good and bad, of Howells on Mark Twain, he concluded that "purely literary problems concerned Howells more than Mark Twain's occasional transgression in respect to God, sex, or swearing." Lowenherz finds Howells, despite his personal bias in favor of Mark Twain, "a clear-sighted and intelligent critic."[9]

Fully as important was the general support each gave to the other's work. There is little specific guidance in Mark Twain's re-

9. Robert Jack Lowenherz, "Mark Twain and W. D. Howells: A Literary Relationship" (Ph.D. dissertation, New York University, 1954), ii, 185, 223. Another student of the relationship, Teresa Buxton, concludes: "Howells exerted practically no positive influence on Clemens and but little negative influence." See Teresa L. Buxton, "A Study of the Relationship of William Dean Howells and Samuel L. Clemens" (Ph.D. dissertation, Bucknell University, 1930), 55.

sponse to Howells' *A Foregone Conclusion* (1874), but there is a great deal of appreciated encouragement. "I should think that this must be the daintiest, truest, most admirable workmanship that was ever put in a story. The creatures of God do not act out their natures more unerringly than yours do. If your genuine stories can die, I wonder by what right old Walter Scott's artificialities shall continue to live." Howells replied: "I was proud as Punch to hear that you liked my story. I shall yet make immortality bitter to the divine Walters—as the French would call the Waverley man."[10]

Howells and Mark Twain's developing professional relationship is disclosed in the forthright but tactful response Howells made to the first two contributions Mark Twain sent him for the *Atlantic*.

My dear Clemens: I'm going to settle *your* opinion of the next installment of *A Foregone Conclusion* by sending back one of your contributions. Not, let me hasten to say, that I don't think they're both very good. But The Atlantic, as regards matters of religion, is just in that Good Lord, Good Devil condition when a little fable like yours wouldn't leave a single Presbyterian, Baptist, Unitarian, Episcopalian, Methodist or Millerite *paying* subscriber—all the dead-heads would stick to it, and abuse it in the denominational newspapers. Send your fable to some truly pious concern like Scribner or Harper, and they'll extract it into all the hymnbooks. But it would ruin *us*.

A curious reader can find the sketch printed in the appendix to the *Mark Twain–Howells Letters* and become usefully informed about the kind of material that might offend nineteenth-century pieties. The rejection did not damage their friendship, though it was offset by Howells' accepting the other piece, "A True Story," with great enthusiasm. When he sent Clemens proofs, he added, "This little story delights me more and more: I wish you had about forty of 'em!"[11]

Although Howells seems not to have been driven by the same need as Mark Twain to live like a pocket-miner who has struck it rich, he steadily moved to a scale of living that only continuing popular success as a writer could support. Both men were typically

10. Smith and Gibson (eds.), *Mark Twain–Howells Letters*, I, 21, 33.
11. *Ibid.*, 24. 25.

influenced by the Gilded Age and victims of the same drive that made many other Americans of humble origins accumulate goods well beyond their needs. Ultimately, it made neither of them happy, though it seemed to provide a great deal of happiness along the way. Despite their own need for the comfort that wealth provides and despite the spirit of American materialistic ambitions working in them, neither Mark Twain nor Howells allowed the marketplace to control his writing. Although the work of both is characterized by the unevenness which is inevitable in the great volume each produced, neither wrote merely and carelessly for money.

The relationship between both writers' work and the literary marketplace is complex throughout their careers. Looking at two of their earliest works, *Their Wedding Journey* and *Roughing It*, may be instructive in that and other respects. The two books, published within two months of each other in 1871 and 1872, were important confirmations of their authors' literary and financial prospects. Many of the buyers of *Their Wedding Journey*, one can guess, bought it because they had read a portion of it or heard it spoken of as a serial in the *Atlantic Monthly*. It carried the imprint of a respectable Boston publishing house, and it could be purchased in bookstores. *Roughing It* was a follow-up to *Innocents Abroad*, with which subscription book agents had established a large and less literary audience for Mark Twain. Henry Adams reviewed the Howells book. "Our descendants will find nowhere so faithful and pleasing a picture of our American existence, and no writer is likely to rival Mr. Howells in his idealization of the commonplace." Howells reviewed *Roughing It* in two paragraphs. "Merely the personal history of Mr. Clemens during a certain number of years. . . . It is singularly entertaining and its humor is always amiable, manly, and generous." [12]

The Clemenses were among the buyers and readers of *Their Wedding Journey*. From Elmira in March, 1872, Mark Twain thanked Howells for a copy of the book. "We bought it & read it some time

12. Henry Adams, *"Their Wedding Journey* by W. D. Howells," *North American Review*, CXIV (1872), 444–45; William Dean Howells, "Recent Literature," *Atlantic Monthly*, XXIX (1872), 754–55.

ago, but we prize this copy most on account of the autograph. I would like to send you a copy of *my* book, but I can't get a copy myself, yet, because 30,000 people who have bought & paid for it have to have preference over the author." Three months later, he reported that 62,000 copies of *Roughing It* had been sold and delivered in four months. Howells was saying much the same thing to his father, but on a greatly reduced scale. "I meant to have sent you before this a copy of *Their Wedding Journey*, but I had great difficulty to get any of it, not being at the store in person, and only secured 8 copies on Friday out of the last lot of the 1st edition. The book was published Tuesday, and on Wednesday noon more than the whole 1500 were ordered from the publishers."[13] During its first year the book went through six printings, adding up to about 6,000 copies.

Today it is as difficult to see anything new about Howells' first novel as it is to reconstruct an audience that would respond enthusiastically to a slightly fictionalized description of a young couple's wedding trip to Niagara Falls. Yet, it is indisputable that such an audience existed and that Howells earned a part of his income by furnishing novels for that audience year after year. The favorable reception of *Roughing It* indicated that a body of readers also existed for books that dared to be personal in shades other than those adopted by literary New Englanders, that played upon the curiosity aroused by the West, and that tapped some of the raw energy and vitality that still seemed to be at odds with Anglo-European culture. Although Mark Twain had a surpassing talent along these lines, the necessity to accommodate that talent to the conventional literary culture must bear some responsibility for the varied and often flawed nature of his many works. Both writers' development was aided by a friendship in which they could be frank about their larger views of literature and generously critical of each other's individual books. As each achieved stature as a distinctive kind of writer, their works became strong forces in the cultural acceptance of the new realistic writing.

13. Smith and Gibson (eds.), *Mark Twain–Howells Letters*, I, 9–10; M. Howells (ed.), *Life in Letters*, I, 163.

The idealization of the commonplace met with a responsiveness over the next three decades that made Howells' successful career as a novelist possible. The core of that audience, however, was not the more widely representative American audience that bought Mark Twain's books and came out to his lectures. Nor, for that matter, was either author's audience the one that supported the best-selling novelists of the day. The three most popular novelists in 1872, according to librarians of the Boston Public Library, were Mrs. E. D. E. N. Southworth, Caroline Lee Hentz, and Mary Jane Holmes. Although Hentz was dead before Howells and Clemens had fairly begun their own literary careers, the other two continued to write through the end of the nineteenth century, their dozens of novels selling in the aggregate of millions of copies. Their names and books are forgotten today. The closest a general reader may have come to such books is through T. S. Arthur's *Ten Nights in a Barroom* or more likely by seeing a beer-hall version of a temperance melodrama. The output and total sales of sentimental fiction were enormous; the literary value of the works was negligible, and yet they passed as literature for a large part of the reading public. Sentimentality was mated with morality in those novels, as they were in the popular novels, novelettes, and lectures of J. G. Holland, a newspaper favorite who earned both Howells' and Mark Twain's contempt independently of their acquaintance with each other. One of Howells' earliest reviews in the *Nation* was a demolishing of Timothy Titcomb, the name Holland assumed for much of his work. "He loves to say 'Now, mark you,' when there is nothing to mark," Howells wrote, "and is fond of the sort of metaphor which, like bear's meat, grows as you chew upon it, and can neither be swallowed nor ejected. Nothing daunts him, and he does not hesitate to electrify you with the idea, for example, 'that hate is not so good a motive as love, and, thank God! it is not so powerful a motive as love!'" Mark Twain had a passing acquaintance with Holland as a lecturer, but he did not arouse Mark Twain's full wrath until he became editor of *Scribner's* in 1871. There he editorialized against the new lecture bureaus that had deposed edifying lecturers like himself in favor of "literary jesters and mountebanks . . . buffoons and triflers." Mark Twain's characterization of Holland was that "he moves through the lecture field a remorseless intellectual cholera."[14]

In addition to the sentimental and pious, another large body of fiction flourished outside the family- and religious-oriented weeklies and the dime novel. Sensationalist fiction, in its general condemnation of vice, took the opportunity to describe vice in great and vivid detail. The popularity of this fiction leads Bryant Morey French, the most thorough student of Mark Twain's *The Gilded Age*, to argue that Mark Twain and Warner were motivated to write the novel in large part as a burlesque of popular fiction. French's thesis is convincing. Mark Twain, despite his own success with a mass audience, was an accomplished writer and virtuoso lecturer. And Howells, though he began writing fiction with the same feminine audience in mind as supported the sentimental novel, had nothing but contempt for the false characterizations, situations, and emotions of that genre. Howells' avowal of "realism" as his main critical principle is best understood as an attack upon the "unreal" of the sentimental novelist. Mark Twain was just as vexed by the claptrap of such novels as *Robert Falconer* by George McDonald, or *The Enemy Conquered, or Love Triumphant* by S. Watson Royston. The latter provoked a printed piece that sums up what Howells and Mark Twain found fault with: "The reader must not imagine that he is to find in it wisdom, brilliancy, fertility of invention, ingenuity of construction, excellence of form, purity of style, perfection of imagery, truth to nature, clearness of statement, humanly possible situations, humanly possible people, fluent narrative, connected sequence of events—or philosophy, or logic, or sense. No; the rich, deep, beguiling charm of the book lies in its total and miraculous *absence* from it of all these qualities."[15]

Ludicrous as popular fiction often is, its nature and popularity

14. Cady, *Howells as Critic*, 20; Wecter (ed.), *Mark Twain to Mrs. Fairbanks*, 146.
15. Bryant Morey French, *Mark Twain and the Gilded Age: The Book that Named an Era* (Dallas, 1965), 25–58; Mark Twain, *A Cure for the Blues with "The Enemy Conquered; or Love Triumphant" by G. Ragsdale McClintock* (Rutland, Vt., 1964).

suggest a rough division in the general human response to literature, particularly the novel. One response is to those stories that take the reader outside ordinary life; the other is toward a fiction in which one can see the actualities of life mirrored. The one is the province of the romance; the other of the realistic novel. The sentimental novel was marketed for both responses, purporting to mirror reality but catering to a reader's wish to have situations and emotions and outcomes other than they really were. A large part of the American populace after the Civil War was on the edge of an actual romance of epic proportions: the movement West and its promise of a new and exciting life. Another large part was immersed in the realities of reconstruction, economic instability, urbanization, and industrialization from which romance seemed very distant. Howells' and Mark Twain's lives embraced both the romance of the West and the actualities of a developing American civilization in which attention to the materialistic was foremost. Critics still fuss over precisely what Mark Twain intended in the ending of *Huckleberry Finn* when Huck says: "But I reckon I got to light out for the territory ahead of the rest, because Aunt Sally she's going to adopt me and sivilize me, and I can't stand it. I been there before." Whatever else it may mean, it clearly expresses the contrary pulls of romance and reality, adventuring and civilizing, that are so thematic in the novel.

Literature, Howells and Clemens recognized, was importantly involved in the tremendous task of "civilizing" that was undertaken in America between the Civil War and World War I. The sentimental novelists, the Hollands, the newspapers and magazines, the lecturers, even the dime novels, were engaged in it. The denial of the honest claims of romance and realism upon a developing adult's attention offended Clemens and Howells at the point of their own dualistic natures and experiences. The shoddy way it was presented to a public offended them as writers. Each, in different ways, took the fashioning of literature as a high and serious endeavor.

Howells' path to becoming a successful writer independent of his being a salaried editor was different from Mark Twain's, but there was an important similarity. Howells, no more than Mark Twain, came to the writing of fiction by following a proper literary line, though he deepened his youthful interest in writing and developed skills by studying languages and literature. Compared with Clemens' self-education, Howells' education was amazingly literary. He schooled himself in Heine and Longfellow, in Goldsmith and Cervantes, and went in pursuit of Spanish and German so that he might grasp the literature of those languages firsthand. Thackeray was one of his early literary passions, as was Dickens, but by the time he came to write and seriously consider the novel, he had developed reservations about both. His chief objection was that they let their artifice show; indeed, in the instance of Thackeray, he deliberately paraded "literary" skills. "You are always aware in Dickens," Howells wrote, "how he is 'making it up.'"[16] Being an intensely literary young man himself, Howells was attracted in his youth to the display of literary virtuosity he found in Thackeray, but the same "literosity" later made him place Thackeray much below Dickens and to share Mark Twain's disdain for the even greater artificialities of Scott. As Howells developed his skill as a novelist and as his critical views of American society became more compelling, he began to see the novel in terms of its social function. Although Thackeray was adept at satirizing English society, Howells increasingly saw past the satirical effects and envisioned the novel as dealing precisely and truthfully with real, commonplace human life. His later ideal he found in Tolstoy, "a man without any artifice at all."

"Fenimore Cooper's Literary Offenses," one of Mark Twain's few extended pieces of literary criticism and one of the most engaging to be found, suggests how much Mark Twain shared Howells' mature views.[17] For both, successful literature came directly from life and conveyed a true sense of life. Literature was not the same as life; if one must choose, life was superior, that is, an excessive valuation of

16. Cady, *Howells as Critic*, 269.
17. Samuel Clemens [Mark Twain], "Fenimore Cooper's Literary Offenses," *Literary Essays*, Author's National Edition: The Writings of Mark Twain, (25 vols.; New York, 1899), XXII, 78–96. See Sydney Krause, *Mark Twain as Critic* (Baltimore, 1967). Krause observes: "Over all, the record seems embarrassingly lean, yielding not so much as a fully rounded book review. . . . He both read and wrote criticism primarily as a writer would," 13, 15.

or preoccupation with literature may cause a writer to play false with both life and literature. Both men realized that the transformation of life into literature and back into imagined life was dependent upon the writer's mastery of language. Both showed an extreme hostility to fakiness in literature, to falsification in the creation of character or plot or detail of action or setting designed to arouse an equally false response in the reader. Both insisted that the writer be true to actuality and get the thing right.

Cooper was an easy target for Mark Twain, but through his derision run two consistently urged and serious criticisms: that Cooper was an inaccurate observer and that his "word-sense was singularly dull." Not all literary virtues are summed up in acuteness of sensory perception and precision in use of language, but no great writer can be deficient in either. Mark Twain's well-known aversions to Jane Austen, George Eliot, and Henry James—despite Howells' contrary opinions—suggest limitations in his literary sensibilities. "I never did have the fullest confidence in my critical penetration," he wrote Howells in 1875.[18] Nevertheless, his casual comments about literature, his responses to new writers as well as to established ones, and his idea of doing a book of critical essays document the continuing presence of his critical sense. The author to author aspect of Mark Twain and Howells' friendship was important to the literary development of both.

18. Smith and Gibson (eds.), *Mark Twain–Howells Letters*, I, 65.

Five

The False Scoundrel Is Myself

All writers project some portion of themselves into their characters; the great writers project some vital parts of every man and woman into characters that become as much a part of our lives as the actual persons who share our time on earth. Huckleberry Finn and Tom Sawyer are such creations, endearing themselves to readers because they represent the anarchy that exists beneath social conformity, the lawlessness of youth as contrasted with the law-abiding acceptances of maturity. The fullness of freedom, its terrors as well as joys, comes forth more clearly in Huck; the beginnings of compromise with social conventions and restraints are more evident in Tom. No one misses the Huck and Tom in Mark Twain; deeper examination may be necessary to see these characters in Howells.

Mark Twain's first oblique mention of *Tom Sawyer* as "another book for Bliss," is in a letter of February 20, 1875, the first of an exchange lasting several months that conveys much of the warmth of the Howells–Mark Twain friendship. The book had begun the previous summer at Quarry Farm and carried on until Mark Twain "ran dry." At this point he tells Howells that he will "trim up & finish 2 or 3 more river sketches for the magazine (if you still think you want them), & then buckle in on another book for Bliss, finish it the end of May, & then either make the river trip or drop it indefinitely." His work does not get in the way of looking forward to a visit from the Howellses. "We want you to give us just as many days as you can. We shall be utterly out of company, & you can choose your own rooms, & change & take *ours* if they don't suit."[1]

Howells replied with some caution but agreed to a brief visit setting the time of their arrival at March 11. "As Mrs. H. and Mrs. Clemens are both tearing invalids, don't you think it would be better not to give that ball *this* visit? Let us just have a nice sit-down, quiet time." Clemens assures him that he will close the door against all visitors if Howells chooses, except that Twichell "will no more hesitate to climb in at the back window than *nothing*." He went on with other assurances: "You shall go to bed when you please, get up when you please, talk when you please, read when you please. Mrs. Howells may even go to New York Saturday if she feels that she must . . . I do wish she & Mrs. Clemens could have a good square chance to get acquainted with each other. But first & last & all the time, we want you to feel untrameled & wholly free from restraint, here. The date suits—*all* dates suit." The Howellses stayed from Thursday to Saturday, and Howells wrote of the visit to his father: "The Clemenses are whole-souled hosts, with inextinguishable money, and a palace of a house, to which, by the way I really prefer ours." In response to Howells' letter of thanks, Twain replied March 16, 1875, "Well, all that was necessary to make that visit perfect was to know that you & Mrs. Howells enjoyed it. . . . My most secret reason for not going to the Aldrich lunch was that I had got intellectual friction enough out of your visit to be able to go to work Monday. Which turned out to be correct—I wrote 4000 words yesterday. To-day I am proposing to bang away again."[2]

It is not certain whether Mark Twain is banging away at *Tom Sawyer* or finishing the sixth and seventh installments of "Old Times on the Mississippi," which were to be printed in the June and Au-

1. Smith and Gibson (eds.), *Mark Twain–Howells Letters*, I, 67.
2. *Ibid.*, 67–69; William Dean Howells to William C. Howells, March 14, 1875, in William Dean Howells Papers, Houghton Library, Harvard University; Smith and Gibson (eds.), *Mark Twain–Howells Letters*, I, 70–71.

gust issues of the *Atlantic*. We do know from a letter of June 21 that Howells had seen and commented on the story by that time. That letter hints at an earlier response from Howells, which, unfortunately, is not a matter of record. *Tom Sawyer* must have been part of the discussion during the Saturday evening and Sunday Howells spent with Clemens in Hartford, June 12 and 13. "Thank you ever so much for the praises you give the story," Mark Twain writes in a June 25 letter. "I am going to take into serious consideration all you have said, & then make up my mind by & by. Since there is no plot to the thing, it is likely to follow its own drift, & so is as likely to drift into manhood as anywhere—I won't interpose."[3]

The letter gives some clarification of problems Howells and Mark Twain may have discussed. Mark Twain acknowledges he might have made a mistake in not writing it in the first person (he was to adopt the first person for *Huckleberry Finn*); he avows: "It is *not* a boy's book at all. It will only be read by adults. It is only written for adults"; and he indicates a need to finish "'working up' vague places." He goes on to indicate that he would "dearly like" to serialize it in the *Atlantic*, but thinks he could not be paid enough for it. (Howells, perceiving it as a boy's book, had some reservations about *Atlantic* serialization, too. But he wrote in a later letter: "Give me a hint when it's to be out, and I'll start the sheep to jumping in the right places.") The rest of Mark Twain's letter, as it is concerned with *Tom Sawyer*, follows.

You see I take a vile, mercenary view of things—but then my household expenses are something almost ghastly.

By & by I shall take a boy of twelve & run him on through life (in the first person) but not Tom Sawyer—he would not be a good character for it.

I wish you would promise to read the MS of Tom Sawyer some time, & see if you don't really decide that I am right in closing with him as a boy— & point out the most glaring defects for me. It is a tremendous favor to ask, & I expect you to refuse, & would be ashamed to expect you to do otherwise. But the thing has been so many months in my mind that it seems a relief to snake it out. I don't know any other person whose judgment I could venture to take fully & entirely. Don't hesitate about saying no, for

3. Smith and Gibson (eds.), *Mark Twain–Howells Letters*, I, 87–88.

I know how your time is taxed, & I would have honest need to blush if you said yes.

Howells' reply was prompt—the next day—and as unfailingly receptive as always: "Dear Clemens: Send on your Ms when it's ready. You've no idea what I may ask you to do for *me* some day. I'm sorry that you can't do it for the Atlantic, but I succumb. Perhaps you'll do Boy No. 2 for us. . . . I count it a pleasure and privilege to read your story. There!"[4]

Howells did not read the manuscript until November, chiefly because Clemens thought twice about imposing on Howells and did not send it until months later, and partly because both were energetically busy during the summer. Howells was taking a working vacation outside of Boston, worried over Elinor's wretched health and much caught up in his own varied writing. Among much other work, he reviewed *Mark Twain's Sketches, New and Old*. The Clemenses vacationed briefly in Newport in the summer, and in early October visited the Howellses in Cambridge, provoking Clemens to catalog the crimes he had committed while there:

Of course I didn't expect to get through without committing some crimes & hearing of them afterwards, so I have taken the inevitable lashings & been able to hum a tune while the punishment went on. I "caught it" for letting Mrs. Howells bother & bother about her coffee when it was "a good deal better than we get at home." I "caught it" for interrupting Mrs. C. at the last moment & losing her the opportunity to urge you not to forget to send her that MS when the printers are done with it.—I caught it once more for personating that drunken Col. James. I caught it ⟨like everything for confessing, with contrition⟩ for mentioning that Mr. Longfellow's picture was slightly damaged; & when, after a lull in the story, I confessed, shamefacedly, that I had privately suggested to you that we hadn't any *frames* & that if you wouldn't mind hinting to Mr. Houghton, &c., &c., &c., the madam was simply speechless for the space of a minute. Then she said:

"How *could* you, Youth! The idea of sending Mr. Howells, with his sensitive nature, upon such a repulsive er————"

"Oh, *Howells* won't mind it! You don't know Howells. Howells is a man who—"

4. *Ibid.*, 91–92, 111, 92, 94.

She was gone. But George was the first person she stumbled on in the hall, so she took it out on George. I was glad of that, because it saved the babies.[5]

Howells' review of Mark Twain's *Sketches* came out in the *Atlantic* in December, 1875. He promptly sent a copy to Mark Twain, somewhat concerned that he had not found enough to praise among the uneven collection of early works. Clemens found the notice "perfectly superb," and took the opportunity to contrast the value he attached to Howells' opinion with that which he placed on favorable reviews by others. "Yours is the recognized critical Court of Last Resort in this country; from its decision there is no appeal; & so, to have gained this decree of yours before I am forty years old, I regard as a thing to be right down proud of." Although Twain seems to have responded favorably to Howells' finding "a growing seriousness of meaning" coming into his work, their relationship is still full of jesting and drolleries. The typewriter appears again as a source of mutual frustration and joking. "I have begun several letters to My d ar lemans, as it prefers to spell your respected name," Howells wrote. "It's fascinating, in the meantime, and it wastes my time like an old friend."[6]

On November 21, Howells gave his verdict on *Tom Sawyer*. "I finished reading Tom Sawyer a week ago, sitting up till one A.M., to get to the end, simply because it was impossible to leave off. It's altogether the best boy's story I ever read. It will be an immense success." Mark Twain was later to agree, despite his earlier contrary opinion, that Howells and Livy were right in seeing it as a boy's story. Howells indicates he has made some corrections and suggestions, mostly in the first third, and suggests he cut the last chapter (apparently a continuation of Huck's life, which found its proper place in *Huckleberry Finn*). Howells' letter closes with a P.S.: "Took down Roughing It, last night, and made a fool of myself over it, as usual."[7]

5. *Ibid.*, 103–104.
6. *Ibid.*, 107, 109.
7. *Ibid.*, 110–111.

The matter of Howells' specific corrections of *Tom Sawyer* have been too much discussed to be detailed here. The overwhelming testimony of Howells and Clemens' long friendship is that Howells' reservations, his sensitivity to vulgarities of a scatological or sexual kind, his literary bent as displayed in his own kind of fiction, were accepted by Mark Twain as one accepts differences in respected and loving friends. We can accept Mark Twain's response to the returned manuscript just as he wrote it on January 18, 1876. "There [never] was a man in the world so grateful to another as I was to you day before yesterday, when I sat down (in still rather wretched health) to set myself to the dreary & hateful task of making final revisions of Tom Sawyer, & discovered, upon opening the package of MS that your pencil marks were scattered all along. This was splendid, & swept away all labor. Instead of *reading* the MS, I simply hunted out the pencil marks & made the emendations which they suggested."[8]

A similar mingling of their personal and professional relationship went on during the writing of *Huckleberry Finn*. Mark Twain kept Howells informed of the "astonishing way" manuscript pages piled up, and Howells saved him more hateful drudgery by carefully reading the manuscript. Huck Finn had a depth and complexity and moral dimension absent from Tom Sawyer and flattering to the image of themselves that both men saw in the characterization. But equally as interesting is the likelihood that both responded to the outlaw side of Huck, to the unwashed, even scoundrelly, Huck seemingly so much in tune with their natures but so at odds with their acquired respectability. When Howells, some fifteen years later, was to write about his own boyhood in *A Boy's Town*, the freedom and anarchy and fears and longings expressed there are not unlike those found in Mark Twain's two books. And in *The Flight of Pony Baker*, Howells created characters like Tom and Huck, the one a properly reared, somewhat dutiful son of a conventionally anxious mother, but seduc-

8. See Charles A. Norton, *Writing Tom Sawyer: The Adventures of a Classic* (Jefferson, N.C., 1983), Walter Blair, *Mark Twain and Huck Finn* (Berkeley, 1960), 77–90, and Henry Nash Smith, *Mark Twain: The Development of a Writer* (Cambridge, Mass., 1962), 71–91; Smith and Gibson (eds.), *Mark Twain–Howells Letters*, I, 121.

tively attracted to his wilder and freer companion who always threatens to lead him astray.

The image of being a scoundrel at heart is difficult to square with the public image of either Howells or Mark Twain, and yet it is one both men recognized and even smiled upon. "You didn't intend Bartley for me," Mark Twain wrote Howells after he had finished reading the serialization of *A Modern Instance* in the summer of 1882, "but he *is* me, just the same, & I enjoy him to the utmost uttermost, and without a pang. Mrs. Clemens indignantly says he doesn't resemble me—which is all she knows about it." When Howells happened to reread the novel in 1911, he wrote to Brander Matthews, "yesterday I read great part of *A Modern Instance*, and perceived that I had drawn Bartley Hubbard, the false scoundrel, from myself."[9] Livy Clemens had a right to be indignant about her husband's seeing himself in Bartley Hubbard, for the plot of the novel, the "modern instance" of its title, is Bartley's marrying and deserting his wife Marcia, their divorce, and Bartley's being shot down by a slandered husband in Whited Sepulchre, Arizona—all of which may have well fit Mark Twain's penchant for fastening guilt upon himself, and Howells' own harboring of a chronically guilty conscience.

Bartley Hubbard, the hero/villain of Howells' seventh published novel, is a provincial journalist, poor but talented, possessed of a ready wit, ingratiating manners, and with an eye out for the main chance. He had been orphaned early in life, made his way through college, and arrived in a New England village as editor of the local paper and dazzler of the local girls. Howells describes him as having "a yellow mustache, shadowing either side of his lip with a broad sweep, like a bird's wing; his chin, deep-cut below his mouth, failed to come strenuously forward; his cheeks were filled to an oval contour, and his face had otherwise the regularity common to Americans." His eyes, Howells writes, and here most directly draws upon his own appearance, were his most striking features, "a clouded gray, heavy-lidded and long lashed." But it is in the nature of Bart-

9. Smith and Gibson (eds.), *Mark Twain–Howells Letters*, I, 412; William C. Fischer and Christoph K. Lohmann (eds.), *W. D. Howells: Selected Letters* (6 vols.; Boston, 1983), V, 361.

ley's ambitions and in his fitfully active conscience that greater identification lies. "'Chicago,' he said, laying the book on the table and taking his knee between his hands, while he dazzled her by speaking from the abstraction of one who has carried on a train of thought quite different from that on which he seemed to be intent,— 'Chicago is the place for me. I don't think I can stand Equity much longer.'"[10]

Equity is Equity, Maine, the northern New England village that frames the story. Bartley is there only long enough to arouse the passions of Marcia Gaylord, to get into a mild scrape with another young woman, and to flee Equity with Marcia after a mild tongue-lashing by Marcia's father. Married by a justice of the peace, the Hubbards settle in Boston where Bartley's talent, brashness, and lack of scruples gain him a salaried "basis" on a Boston newspaper. Like Silas Lapham in Howells' next significant novel, Hubbard's material success seems to ordain his moral decline. Despite his genuine love for Marcia and his doting fondness for their baby, Flavia, Bartley degenerates. He quarrels with Marcia, gets drunk on whiskey (Mark Twain wrote, "How very drunk, & how recently drunk, & how altogether admirably drunk you must have been to enable you to contrive that masterpiece!"), goes in debt, plays the stock market, and appropriates the literary material of a friend.[11] He repents almost as often as he sins, and at a crucial point in the story, after a quarrel reflecting Marcia's jealousy and temper as much as his own moral flabbiness, he packs his bag (actually it is *her* bag, one he had given her the previous summer) and leaves for Chicago.

In the late fall of 1881, when Howells had reached this climactic desertion scene, he suffered "some sort of fever," which put him in bed for five weeks. Mark Twain wrote Elinor from Hartford on the twenty-fifth of November, apparently in response to her informing him of Howells' serious illness: "Dear Mrs. Howells—How you startle me! Can a man so near by, fall sick, & linger along, & approach death, & a body never hear of it?" Two weeks later, Howells wrote Mrs. James T. Fields that he had been in bed nearly four

10. William D. Howells, *A Modern Instance: A Novel* (Boston, 1881), 7, 11.
11. Smith and Gibson (eds.), *Mark Twain–Howells Letters*, I, 408.

weeks, with "fever, and a thousand other things." Initially, at least, he had attributed his illness to long worry and sleeplessness from overwork, but a later letter to his father explains that he has moved into Cambridge to be close to "the doctor at all hours," and suggests that he was being treated for a recurrent cystitis.[12]

Whatever the exact cause and complications of Howells' illness, it interrupted his work on *A Modern Instance* and may have brought back memories of the debilitating psychic ills of his youth. In January while still recovering, he wrote Mark Twain: "There isn't anything I should like so much as the sight of you. . . . I'm *not* myself, by any means. I'm five years older than I was. . . . I may young up again, but that is the present fact. The worst of it is that I work feebly and ineffectually." A letter two weeks later comments upon the interruption and resumption of work on the novel. "I find that every mental effort costs about twice as much as it used, and the result seems to lack texture."[13]

Critics are probably not justified in relating Howells' illness to his struggling with desertion and divorce in the novel he was writing. There were other facts that may have caused Howells to feel psychically drained as well as physically ill. Writing to Horace Scudder earlier in 1881, he explained his recent resignation from the *Atlantic*: "I have grown terribly, inexorably tired of editing. I think my nerves have given way under the fifteen years' fret and substantial unsuccess." In addition, since the summer of 1880, he and Elinor had been under the strain of a mysterious wasting illness that had come upon their daughter Winny, then sixteen. The undiagnosed illness, seemingly psychic in origin, manifested itself in periods of both crises and remission until her death, apparently of organic causes, in 1889. Just before Howells' own illness, he could write his father of "rejoicing over the rapid restoration of Winny to health," and the doctors had apparently given the Howellses very recent indications of her probable recovery. Nevertheless, the pressing fact was that she had been in bed and uncertainly responsive to

12. *Ibid.*, 379; George Arms and Christoph K. Lohmann (eds.), *W. D. Howells: Selected Letters* (6 vols.; Boston, 1979), II, 301–302.
13. Smith and Gibson (eds.), *Mark Twain–Howells Letters*, I, 385, 391.

treatment of something vaguely called "nervous prostration," and the Howellses' future plans were to take her to Europe in hopes of rejuvenation.[14]

What Howells' illness brings out are the tensions in his life at odds with the image of personal ease and professional productivity that he conveyed to even as close a personal friend as Mark Twain. Howells' "neuroticism" has been acknowledged by scholars since at least 1945, when Edwin Cady brought it to their attention.[15] To readers of his autobiographical writings, the facts had always been there, and his account of his morbid fears in the summer of 1856 is the main source of what we know about it. He had been troubled earlier by the fear of dying, but his most severe obsession was triggered by a village doctor's remark about the nature of hydrophobia. "Works around in your system," Howells reports him as saying, "for seven years or more, and then it breaks out and kills you." Childhood fears of dogs and an outdated dog bite combined with hypochondriac fears incapacitated him for months and left him with fears of a recurrence of "the old hippo" for several years to come. Such fears unite with youthful romantic melancholy in letters to his sisters and brother in the late 1850s. "In the morning I get up in a stew, and boil and simmer all day, and go to bed sodden, and ferociously misanthropical. . . . I know myself, and I speak by the card, when I pronounce myself *a mistake*," he wrote in October 1857, to Victoria. In May, 1858, he told Aurelia: "Up till to-day I have been very well; but a fit of indigestion has brought on my old troubles of the head. I hope it will soon pass off." And to Joseph in August, 1859: "For two months, my familiar devil, Hypochondria, had tormented me, so

14. Arms and Lohmann (eds.), *W. D. Howells: Selected Letters*, II, 274; see also John W. Crowley, "Winifred Howells and the Economy of Pain," *Old Northwest*, X (1984), 41–75.

15. Edwin H. Cady, "The Neuroticism of William Dean Howells," *Publications of the Modern Language Association*, LXI (March, 1946), 229–38. See also Cady, *The Road to Realism: The Early Years of William Dean Howells* (Syracuse, N.Y., 1956), 54–60, and Kenneth S. Lynn, *William Dean Howells: An American Life* (New York, 1971), 253–54. Mark Twain has also not escaped being labeled neurotic. Henry Seidel Canby, *Turn West, Turn East: Mark Twain and Henry James* (Boston, 1951), has a section on Mark Twain, "A Neurotic Genius," 251–54.

that I sometimes thought that death would be a relief. Yesterday, I could bear it no longer, and went [to] Dr. Smith, telling him my trouble, and receiving for answer that there was nothing the matter with me."[16]

In a general way, both Howells and Mark Twain, despite the positive images their lives project, were almost stereotypes of the chronically guilty husband, perhaps manifesting in adult life the fears and anxieties of youth. Such guilts may have existed because their careers separated them from both wife and children in various ways, because writing necessitated a drawing upon personal situations and feelings that might be better left private, and because of the many specific neglects that busy, ambitious men living so much in their own minds can be charged with. For the most part, such guilts were worked off, some shared with their wives and later their children, some elaborated upon, usually in a comic way, in their writing, some minimized and some exaggerated, and undoubtedly some exchanged between the two of them as part of what bound them together as friends. But the two also shared moments of severe depression. In the midst of a June letter to Mrs. Fairbanks in 1876, for example, Mark Twain responds to news of the death of a mutual friend. "What a curious thing life is. We [toil] delve away, through years of hardship, wasting toil, despondency; then comes a little butterfly season of wealth, ease, & clustering honors,—Presto! the wife dies, a daughter marries a spendthrift villain, the heir & hope of the house commits suicide, the laurels fade & fall away. Grand result of a hard-fought successful career & a blameless life. Piles of money, tottering age, & a broken heart."[17]

Something of that same grimness seems to enter into Howells' writing of *A Modern Instance* at about the point at which he had been forced to break off. As the novel goes on there is a relentlessness in damning Bartley Hubbard that seems excessive within the novel and which may be a means of castigating himself for real or imagined

16. Arms, *et al.* (eds.), *W. D. Howells: Selected Letters*, I, 14, 15; William Dean Howells to Aurelia H. Howells, May 19, 1858, Howells Papers; Arms *et al.* (eds.), *W. D. Howells: Selected Letters*, I, 40.

17. Wecter (ed.), *Mark Twain to Mrs. Fairbanks*, 199–200.

shortcomings. Howells and Mark Twain probably saw in the character of the wretched Hubbard, fleeing from his careless nature, shadowy reflections of some of their own inclinations. As regards Clemens, he came to his courting of Livy trailing a past harder to disavow than Bartley's. His attempts to convince Livy and the Langdons that he was worthy of her are both comic and touching. Having won her—openly and manfully, unlike Bartley's stealing her away—he still had to face some feeling that he was taking away the treasure of Jervis Langdon's life. Moreover, Livy's father had been uncommonly accepting and generous, responding to the lukewarm letters Mark Twain could produce as testimony to his character: "I'll be your friend, myself. Take the girl, I know you better than they do." [18] Howells' voluminous correspondence gives but the barest details of his wooing Elinor, though his letters as a young husband contain such words of endearment as "darling," "sweetest girl," "my dear good sweet wife," "duck," and "ducky." Like his going to Venice, his decision to marry was a kind of desertion of the parental family to which he had been extremely attached. His letters to his Ohio family members, which continued through most of his life, convey a sense of the successful son who feels some guilt in leaving his family and their continuing cares behind. As to his relations with Elinor's family, he was like Mark Twain, a provincial outsider of ill-defined prospects come to take a daughter away.

Conflicts between husband and wife, not so much personal ones for which we have little evidence, but in the conventional roles Victorian society placed upon male and female, are a strong part of Howells' novel. His writings of the seventies and eighties take a serious interest in the plight of women in a masculine-dominated society. In his reading of *Medea*, the literary source for *A Modern Instance*, he could be expected to pause over a passage such as this:

Of all things that have life and sense we women are the most hapless creatures; first must we buy a husband at a great price, and over ourselves a tyrant set which is an evil worse than the first; and herein lies the most important issue, whether our choice be good or bad. For divorce is not

18. Wecter (ed.), *Love Letters*, 62.

honourable to women, nor can we disown our lords. Next must the wife, coming as she does to ways and customs new, since she hath not learnt the lesson in her home, have a diviner's eye to see how best to treat the partner of her life. If haply we perform these tasks with thoroughness and tact, and the husband live with us, without resenting the yoke, our life is a happy one; if not, 'twere best to die. But when a man is vexed with what he finds indoors, he goeth forth and rids his soul of its disgust, betaking him to some friend or comrade of like age; whilst we must needs regard his single self.[19]

The general public impression we have of both Howells and Mark Twain as husbands and fathers is Victorian in the extreme. They exemplify every married virtue: fidelity, patience, respect, devotion, a love of home and children, and a commitment to steady work sufficient to provide a life of reasonable comfort and religiously sanctioned decency. No one has questioned the devotion of Mark Twain to Livy; indeed almost all of the emphasis has been upon the supposed price devotion forced him to pay in the alleged adverse effects Livy had on his work. Precisely comprehending their love is even more difficult than ascertaining her exact effects upon Mark Twain's writing. Howells' devotion to Elinor is seemingly as complete, but there is little personal testimony on either side that suggests an intensity of shared feelings like that between the Clemenses. Clearly *A Modern Instance* questions the premise that marriages were made in heaven; if they were, it was perhaps because good ones were so few on earth.

The ideal Victorian marriage was such as to arouse guilt in all less-than-perfect males, as it seemed to arouse faintings and palpitations in the less-than-perfect women. Howells may expose a fundamental guilt in writing of Bartley: "Perhaps such a man, in those fastnesses of his nature which psychology has not yet explored, never loses, even in the tenderest transports, the sense of prey as to the girl whose love he has won." When Howells wrote *A Modern Instance*, he had been twenty years married, and the details of his own domestic life, however unruffled it might appear to posterity, could

19. In Whitney J. Oates and Eugene O'Neill, Jr. (eds.), *The Complete Greek Drama* (2 vols.; New York, 1938), II, 728.

hardly have failed to furnish some of the specifications for the conflicts between Marcia and Bartley.

Although the central theme of the novel is concerned with the
Hubbards as man and woman, husband and wife, the depiction of
Bartley as a journalist mirrors the uneasy regard with which Howells
and Twain held themselves as journalists:

> He was a poor, cheap sort of creature. Deplorably smart, and regret-
> tably handsome. A fellow that assimilated everything to a certain extent,
> and nothing thoroughly. A fellow with no more moral nature than a base-
> ball. [Said of Bartley by his pious college friend]
>
> . . . .
>
> He had the true newspaper instinct, and went to work with a motive
> that was as different as possible from the literary motive. He wrote for the
> effect which he was to make, and not from any artistic pleasure in the
> treatment. [This from Howells' authorial voice]
>
> . . . .
>
> "I'll get my outlines, and then you post me with a lot of facts,—queer
> characters, accidents, romantic incidents, snowings-up, threatened star-
> vation, adventures with wild animals,—and I can make something worth
> while; get out two or three columns, so they can print it in their Sunday
> edition. And then I'll take it up to Boston with me, and seek my fortune
> with it." [Bartley Hubbard about "working up" a story]
>
> . . . .
>
> At the same time he wrote more than ever in the paper, and he discov-
> ered in himself that dual life of which every one who sins or sorrows is
> sooner or later aware: that strange separation of the intellectual activity
> from the suffering of the soul, by which the mind toils on in a sort of ironi-
> cal indifference to the pangs that wring the heart; the realization that, in
> some ways, his brain can get on perfectly well without his conscience.
> [Howells' voice again, describing Bartley][20]

On occasion, Hubbard turns a phrase that sounds like Mark
Twain, and the banter between Marcia and Bartley in the best moments of their courtship and marriage must have reminded both
Howells and Clemens of their own courting repartee. In Kinney, an
up-country logger, Howells creates a character endowed with Mark

20. Howells, *A Modern Instance*, 243, 193, 128, 96.

Twain's facility for colorful storytelling and original turns of speech. In one scene, Kinney is speaking to Bartley, but it might well be Howells revealing some of his own early reactions to Mark Twain's love of "style":

"I found out some time ago that a fellow wa'n't necessarily a bad fellow because he had money; or a good fellow because he hadn't. But I hadn't quite got over hating a man because he had style. . . . But I tell you, I sniffed round you a good while before I made up my mind to swallow you. And that turnout of yours, it kind of staggered me, after I got over the clothes. Why, it wa'n't so much the colt,—any man likes to ride after a sorrel colt; and it wa'n't so much the cutter; it was the red linin' with pinked edges that you had to your robe; and it was the red ribbon that you had tied round the waist of your whip. When I see that ribbon on that whip, dumn you, I wanted to kill you."[21]

The feeling behind the scene surely comes from such feelings as Howells must have had when first confronted by Mark Twain in his sealskin coat. Their friendship was not only that of shared traits and inclinations but of accepting differences that broadened each one's general sympathies. Both were also fond of seeing themselves as worse than they were; Mark Twain made a professional asset of it in drawing upon self-disparagement as a source of humor in his stage appearances. In his dimmer perceptions of himself he was gauche, crude, a buffoon. The outward signs by which Howells tried to blacken Bartley's character—smoking, drinking, and talking with the boys—were those which Mark Twain tried to forswear to please Livy. Howells was less given to these vices, but he was the one who had to fight against growing fat, a sign of Bartley's moral flabbiness as well as a consequence of drinking too much Tivoli beer. Both men recognized a selfishness in their characters, a selfishness in all human character, which defied the higher moralities they, and other humankind, set for themselves. As writers, both may have felt the proddings of ego more sharply, simply because ego was necessary to a writer's work. Their moralizing selves that neither could escape viewed selfishness as the worst of man's sins, whether it manifested

21. *Ibid.*, 123–24.

itself in petty meannesses or in an utter disregard for others. Their morality had a common source in the cultivation of the inner sense of right and wrong and acting by that sense when and if one could. Both were tolerant of human weaknesses, even as they could despair of the loftier prospects of human society because of these weaknesses. Both were generous men and yet troubled over not being generous enough. And yet, like Bartley Hubbard before Howells gave him three chins and a tallowy pallor, neither thought too badly of himself.

There is little excoriation in either Mark Twain's or Howells' identification with Howells' villain, partly because Bartley is not very villainous and partly because both treasured some small bit of villainy in themselves. Clara writes of the trait in Clemens that all biographers have noticed: "He tortured himself according to his habit, with self-accusations of imaginary shortcomings and self-ishness."[22] Yet, both Mark Twain and Howells could understand Thoreau's assertion in *Walden*: "I never knew, and never shall know, a worse man than myself." At the end of a letter to his brother Joseph in 1909, after recounting fifty years of vexations over his feckless younger brother, Sam, Howells concludes, "In one way or other we are all Sams."[23]

Howells' and Mark Twain's self-perceptions are complicated by how they saw themselves and each other with respect to New England social and literary aristocracy. In the fall of 1877, the *Atlantic Monthly* staff decided to give a dinner honoring Whittier's seventieth

22. C. Clemens, *My Father, Mark Twain*, 175. A letter from Mark Twain to Howells in April, 1882, goes on and on about some "crime" Mark Twain had committed: "But oh, hell, there is no hope for a person who is built like me;—because there is no cure, no cure." According to a postscript added by Livy, the "discourtesy" was toward Mr. Howells. Smith and Gibson comment about the incident: "It was doubtless trivial. Clemens had all his life a tendency toward rather melodramatic self-accusation" (Smith and Gibson (eds.), *Mark Twain–Howells Letters*, I, 400–402). Another example is in a letter from Mark Twain to Charles Fairbanks, June 25, 1890: "I have never seen an opinion of me in print which was as low down as my private opinion of myself" (Wecter (ed.), *Mark Twain to Mrs. Fairbanks*, 265).

23. Fischer and Lohmann (eds.), *W. D. Howells: Selected Letters*, V, 279.

birthday and the *Atlantic*'s twentieth, both of which fell on December 17. It was at Howells' suggestion that Mark Twain was invited to be the main speaker. Although Mark Twain's reputation was established in Boston as it was elsewhere, he became known to the readers of the *Atlantic* with "Old Times on the Mississippi," serialized in 1875. For most of that decade, Howells had been widening the literary horizons of *Atlantic* readers with works of other authors outside the New England circle. Mark Twain had previously appeared as one of the after-dinner speakers at an *Atlantic* dinner in 1874, but Howells, nevertheless, recognized a certain distance between Mark Twain's customary manner and the literary sensibilities of New England men of letters. "Don't write *at* any supposed Atlantic audience," he had advised Clemens in regard to the Mississippi pieces, "but yarn it off as if into my sympathetic ear."[24]

Mark Twain worked up something very special for the Whittier dinner, probably with some sense of doing it for Howells as well as for the occasion. The fall before the event was full of correspondence between the two men. In late October the Howellses were at Nook Farm visiting the Warners and Clemenses. In December, Howells gave two lectures in Hartford, one on Gibbon and the other on Venice, and he and Winny stayed several days with the Clemenses. Mark Twain introduced him at the Gibbon lecture, saying: "The gentleman who is now to address you is the editor of the Atlantic Monthly. He has a reputation in the literary world which I need not say anything about. I am only here to back up his moral character."[25]

The dinner at the Brunswick Hotel four days later was everything such a dinner might be imagined to be. The meal began with oysters on the shell and ran through soups, fish, potatoes, smelts, capon, rice, cauliflower, saddle of mutton, string beans, turnips, filet of beef, epinards, Vol au Vent of Oysters à l'Américane, squabs, terrapin, sorbet au kirsh, partridge, duck, watercress, sweet potatoes, dressed lettuce, charlotte russe, gelee au champagne, vari-

24. Smith and Gibson (eds.), *Mark Twain–Howells Letters*, I, 46.
25. *Ibid.*, 210.

ous candies, fruit, dessert, coffee, and flowing through the courses, sauterne, sherry, chablis, champagne, claret, and burgundy. The three guests of honor were Longfellow, Emerson, and Holmes (Lowell would have been the fourth, but he was in London at the time). Fifty-three *Atlantic* contributors and other invited guests made up the audience. There were a number of after-dinner responses and then Howells came forth to introduce Mark Twain. Henry Nash Smith, the scholar who is to be thanked for reconstructing the dinner, observes that Howells' introduction was unusually long and syntactically involved.[26] It suggests to him that it was a kind of prayer to Clemens not to do something out of keeping with the occasion. Perhaps Howells did have an idea Mark Twain might do something inappropriate. Although they had just seen each other, and Clemens might have revealed his plan, chances are that he did not. He would have spoiled a surprise, and Mark Twain loved surprises. Then, too, if Howells had had any genuine apprehensions, he must have known he was praying in vain. He knew Mark Twain was a professional performer who prepared well whatever he had to say and was not likely to be diverted at the last moment. A more plausible explanation of the orotundity of Howells' introduction is the quantity of food and drink that had been consumed. Only a professional performer of Mark Twain's caliber could have gotten round the thirteen courses and six wines and still retained control of his delivery.

In print, the speech Mark Twain delivered seems to be as engagingly worked up as any of his inventions from his Nevada mining days. It purported to be a true incident in which Mark Twain had visited a lonely miner's cabin and had been scoffed at for introducing himself as the author, Mark Twain. The miner said that just three days before three other chaps had wandered by claiming to be Longfellow, Holmes, and Emerson. He described each of the three: Emerson, a "seedy little bit of a chap—red-headed"; Holmes, "fat as a balloon"; Longfellow, "built like a prizefighter." All had been drinking and each began to recite from his poetry. Here Clemens

26. Henry Nash Smith, "That Hideous Mistake of Poor Clemens's," *Harvard Library Bulletin*, IX (1953), 145–80. Also in Smith, *Mark Twain*, 97–112.

made comic use of lines from the authors' most familiar poems. The snapper at the end was when Mark Twain tried to tell the miner that those vagabonds were obviously imposters. "Ah—imposters, were they?" the miner responded; "are *you*?"

Both Howells and Mark Twain, writing long after the event, magnified the audience's response to the speech. Mark Twain noted his "gradually perishing hope—that somebody would laugh, or that somebody would at least smile, but nobody did." Howells said the silence was broken "only by the hysterical and bloodcurdling laughter of a single guest."[27] Newspaper reports did not single out the speech as the disaster it seemed to be to Clemens and Howells, though not long afterwards some newspapers did use the speech as a means of attacking Mark Twain's lack of taste and respect. Nor did Howells spirit Mark Twain away immediately to brood upon his mistake. The dinner went on, though by the time it was over and in the days following, Clemens displayed to Howells and other friends all the contriteness he was to remember, albeit inaccurately, the rest of his life.

Mark Twain's "sense of disgrace," as he reported to Howells from Hartford a week later, "does not abate. It grows. I see that it is going to add itself to my list of permanencies—a list of humiliations that extends back to when I was seven years old, & which keep on persecuting me regardless of my repentances." Howells' reply from Cambridge on Christmas day was soothing. He assured him he would not be dropped from the *Atlantic*, that Emerson, Longfellow, and Holmes would see it as the human and well-intended mistake it was, and that a fastidious Bostonian had *read* the speech and found no offense in it. He went on: "But I don't pretend not to agree with you about it. All I want you to do is not to exaggerate the damage. You are not going to be floored by it; there is more justice than that even in *this* world. And especially as regards *me*, just call the sore spot well."[28] It is of interest here that Howells, and probably rightly, attributes some of Mark Twain's chagrin to a feeling that he had hurt Howells, had jeopardized their friendship as well as their profes-

27. Smith, *Mark Twain*, 97; W. D. Howells, "My Mark Twain," 52.
28. Smith and Gibson (eds.), *Mark Twain–Howells Letters*, I, 212–13.

sional relationship. It is also to be said that, however Mark Twain may have delivered the speech as an unconsciously recognized hostile act toward the respectable literary world, he also may have perceived it as a favor being done a friend. It had backfired and was humiliating not only to him but to Howells as well.

Mark Twain seized upon Howells' commonsense suggestion that he write to each of the men explaining that no offense was meant. "I wrote a letter yesterday," he wrote back to Howells; "& sent a copy to each of the three." He ends the letter with one of his best known self-denigrations: "Ah, well, I am a great & sublime fool. But then, I am God's fool, & all His works must be contemplated with respect."[29]

Dixon Wecter's comment on the affair may be the wisest words said of it: "The saints and sinners alike took the incident with a gravity that attests to the massiveness of New England's genteel tradition." Mark Twain himself went back and forth about the merits of the speech during much of the rest of his life. To Mrs. Fairbanks shortly after, he vowed that he was not going to sell his powers short: "Very likely the Atlantic speech was in ill taste; but that is the worst that can be said of it. I am sincerely sorry if it, in any wise, hurt those great poets' feelings—I never wanted to do that. But nobody has ever convinced me that that speech was not a good one—for me; above my average considerably." Much later, as he remembered the incident in his *Autobiography*, he claimed he had lived with the meaning of the speech as "coarse, vulgar, and destitute of humor." In reviewing the speech for a reprinting of it in 1910, however, he found "there isn't a suggestion of coarseness or vulgarity in it anywhere."[30]

The images of themselves that Howells and Mark Twain saw in their fiction and in events that activated often guilty consciences identify them with their age. The morality they lived by and espoused, the manners to which they adapted, even the roles of husband and father and friend, were subject to dispraise or ridicule or hostility by a later generation that found "all Gods dead, all wars

29. *Ibid.*, 214–15.

30. Wecter, *Mark Twain to Mrs. Fairbanks*, 215, 217; Mark Twain, *Mark Twain's Speeches* (New York, 1910), 1–16.

fought, all faiths in man shaken." Hard as it is to see in Howells, less so in Mark Twain, the scoundrel that was part of their self-image was a betrayer of the age in which they lived. Both were as questioning of Victorian gods and wars and faiths as were their successors. And in their personal lives, there is a restlessness that is at odds with the image of affluent stability.

Six

Travelers

"I wish *I* had been on that island," Howells wrote of *Tom Sawyer*, and that same wistful feeling has captured generations of Americans wishing to move back to a simpler past or trying to move on to a more richly endowed future. Huck Finn, even more than Tom Sawyer, stirs sentiments of youthful anarchy and adventure in the adult reader. Howells placed it "with the great things in picaresque fiction. Still, it is more poetic than picaresque and of a deeper psychology."[1] Both books appealed greatly to Howells' poetic nature, the opposite of that relentless adherence to duty and the realities of both his fictional and real worlds. Mark Twain's divided nature has long been apparent in his works and his life, though many admirers are still surprised to find that such a comic genius could have such a deeply serious side.

A restlessness beneath the surface appears in the lives of both men. Curiously, it manifests itself in the many years that Mark Twain, that quintessential American, lived abroad. And it is to be discovered in Howells' moving from house to house while he lived in the Boston area and his continuing to move seasonally and year after

1. Smith and Gibson (eds.), *Mark Twain–Howells Letters*, I, 111; W. D. Howells, "My Mark Twain," 150.

year most of his life. His last novel, left uncompleted at his death, was called *The Home Towners* and was about the aging northerners, like himself, who had gone south to live out their lives. But the portion of the novel he finished clearly indicates that it was more than that, that it was about the universal homelessness that besets many human beings and the search to find a home that characterizes many lives.

Being at home in the world is more than a matter of place and time, though literature often dramatizes it in just those terms. The greatest achievements of Howells and Mark Twain during their most productive years of the eighties were *Huckleberry Finn* and *The Rise of Silas Lapham.* Huck's journey out of youth and innocence, the contrasts Mark Twain makes between life on the river and on the shore, the cycle that brings Huck and Jim back but with the prospect of Huck's setting out again, lie close to the author's deepest feelings. *Silas Lapham*, too, centers around a journey, one that takes Silas away from an up-country New England village, places him in Boston where he is never quite at home, and moves him back to the village at the end. Part of the richness of these stories is in how a central character faces the world, finds it not to his liking, and retreats to the past or sets out again for a better territory.

The inner conflicts of Howells and Mark Twain have that larger character. Their comic side as well as their desire to live well took the world pretty much as it came, but another side would not let them leave the world alone. That serious side would badger it and mock it and rant at it and even try to change it. Their personal lives, too, took on that character, the one side building up stately mansions not just for the soul, another side backing away from or protesting against being an author and a father and a householder.

No argument is being made here that a single reason lies behind the going to and fro that marked both men's lives. There are too many immediate reasons for the many years Mark Twain lived abroad and for the many houses Howells occupied to make such an argument defensible. Nevertheless, it can be observed that the establishing of themselves, in literary reputation as in financial success, paralleled a moving away from the actual establishments each had built up and maintained.

Nook Farm was truly an establishment, and together with Quarry Farm in summers, was the center of Mark Twain's life until Susy's death in 1896. But long before that, the Clemenses began lengthy periods of residence abroad. The first extended stay was in Hamburg in April, 1878, and the next year in Germany, Italy, Switzerland, Paris, and London. In inviting the Howellses to visit before his family's departure for Europe, Mark Twain observes, "This is a pretty big concern to tear up, disband & put in order for a year or two's absence."[2] In the weeks of preparing to go abroad, they turned to the Howellses as the experienced advisers about living in Europe. Their years in Italy were a dozen years in the past, however, and the only specific advice Howells gave was to be sure to stay at the Sign of the Savage in Vienna, the locale and title of a story he had written for the *Atlantic* in 1877. Howells' own circumstances were such as to preclude a European trip until 1882, the year after his resignation from the *Atlantic*. And though he had not planned it that way, the trip became in part one of recuperation from his own illness at the end of 1881 and one that held out some hopes of assisting Winny in wrestling with her anguishing condition.

Like other American writers both before and after his time, Mark Twain justified his first long stay in Europe by the necessity to live more cheaply and escape the social obligations that cut into his time for writing. Howells and Clemens were both victims of a self-deception that distorted their financial position: both might have lived more frugally and less socially at home. Although Clemens was probably not exaggerating when he said his expenses in Hartford were "something fierce," the cost of going to and returning from Europe and living abroad as the Clemenses lived must have been fierce, too. When they sailed first-class on the *Holsatia*, on April 14, 1878, the party included not only Clara and Susy, but Clara Spaulding, an Elmira friend who was both an aid to Livy and tutor for the children, a nursemaid, who gave the children instruction in German, and George, the Clemenses' butler. In addition, when Joe Twichell joined them for a two-months stay, Clemens took care of expenses, though he could rightly claim that these were a necessary

2. Smith and Gibson (eds.), *Mark Twain–Howells Letters*, I, 218.

investment in the travel book he was working on. The financial pinch he felt was fairly short-lived. In June, 1878, he could write to Howells from Heidelberg, barely three months after they had left America, the good news that "*we've quit feeling poor!* Isn't that splendid. . . . Yesterday we fell to figuring & discovered that we have more than income enough, from investments, to live in Hartford on a generous scale."[3]

Europe, however, did not prove to be a place where he could work without interruption. His pattern of work was not much different from what it had been in America: periods of intense and prolific writing and periods barren of inspiration or production. Mark Twain could honestly claim, as he often did, of being both the laziest and busiest of men. The desire to escape work altogether may have been part of his deeper desire to escape being an adult, to return to the anarchic freedom of an imagined childhood or into the ultimate freedom of death. To Mrs. Fairbanks, who in 1878 was still a confidante, he gave both reducing expenses and getting a chance to work as the primary reasons for going abroad. "The only chance I get here to work is the 3 months we spend at the farm in the summer. A nine months' annual vacation is too burdensome. I want to find a German village where nobody knows my name or speaks any English, & shut myself up in a closet 2 miles from the hotel, & work every day without interruption."[4]

Heidelberg, Munich, and Paris were hardly villages, and his writing in Europe was a combination of gathering material and bursts of writing at various intervals of their long stay. In Heidelberg, he found an "airy perch" high above Heidelberg Castle and the Neckar River, with "two great glass birdcages (enclosed balconies)" which provided a view, which, he told Howells, "is my despair." The long physical description he provides makes the place seem not far different from his octagonal study on the hilltop at Quarry Farm, or, in some aspects, from the pilot house on a Mississippi River steamboat. At night, Heidelberg's "curved & interlacing streets are a cobweb, beaded with lights." His seriousness of intent, however, led

3. *Ibid.*, 237.
4. Wecter (ed.), *Mark Twain to Mrs. Fairbanks*, 222.

him to rent a workroom in a house across the river, and though he admitted to being idle for some six weeks after he arrived, the "'call' to go to work" came and he plotted a steady course through summer until Twichell was to join him for their walking trip. Although he tore up a good deal of what he wrote of *A Tramp Abroad* and referred to it as "this confounded book," it moved steadily along. A "rattling set-back in Munich" in April, 1879, shows how methodically he could and did work. The setback was that he discovered, at the point when he thought he was half done, that he had been writing only 65 to 70 words per page rather than his usual 100. Robbed, by his logic, of a third of what he thought he had written, he worked out a simple and strenuous corrective. "I had been writing 30 pages a day, & allowing myself Saturdays for holidays. However, I had 8 clear days left before leaving Munich—so I buckled in & wrote 400 pages in those 8 days & so brought my work close up to half-way."[5]

Considering the obligations to Livy and the children that he continued to carry out, his struggles to learn German (Howells wrote, "You always seemed to me a man who liked to be understood with the least possible personal inconvenience"), and the professional and personal need to experience life abroad, Mark Twain's professional discipline demands increased respect. The expressed longings not to be working as he was are a measure of how hard he did work and how much he resisted the sensory appeals of the locales he found himself in. Switzerland, for example, which he saw only in passing, made an overpowering impact. Writing to Twichell in January, 1879, he said: "Well, time and time again it has seemed to me that I *must* drop everything and flee to Switzerland once more. It is a *longing*—a deep, strong, tugging *longing*—that is the word. We must go again, Joe." Another response to the Alps was his firing off a letter to his London publishers asking, "Can't you send me *immediately* Mr. Whymper's book?"[6] Edward Whymper had first as-

5. Smith and Gibson (eds.), *Mark Twain–Howells Letters*, I, 229; Wecter (ed.), *Mark Twain to Mrs. Fairbanks*, 226.

6. Smith and Gibson (eds.), *Mark Twain–Howells Letters*, I, 233; Paine (ed.), *Mark Twain's Letters*, I, 351; S. L. Clemens to Chatto & Windus, London, April 25, 1879, in Mark Twain Papers, Bancroft Library, University of California, Berkeley.

cended the Matterhorn in 1865, and his *Scrambles Among the Alps* had been immensely popular since its publication in 1869, the same year that *Innocents Abroad* appeared.

The Neckar was another locale that fed his imagination even as it threatened to pull him away from writing about it. On an impulse stimulated by his gazing for days and nights down upon the river, he chartered a raft and he and a companion pushed into the stream and let themselves be carried along as Huck and Jim were to be and as Mark Twain's psyche often longed to be throughout his life. But once again, at the end of the journey, Clemens faced reality. For what must have been other strong psychic reasons, he took great satisfaction in getting safely off the raft and watching it smash itself against a bridge abutment shortly after. He later observed that the entire European trip had gone pretty much according to plan. In the same letter in which he had expressed his desire to get back to Switzerland, he wrote, "I haven't the slightest desire to loaf, but a consuming desire to work, ever since I got back my swing."[7]

Howells was probably too busy to be envious of Mark Twain's travels abroad. He had, as usual, a number of diverse writing tasks going forward and was fretting through delays in the completion of the Howellses' new house in Belmont. "In fact," he expressed to Clemens, after naming their mutual acquaintances—Osgood, John Hay, Bret Harte—who would be in Europe that summer, "I find that I have outlived all longing for Europe: you are now the principal attraction of that elderly enchantress, as far as I'm concerned."[8] Clearly, the two friends missed each other when they were either out of touch by correspondence or at such a distance that they could not make plans to visit. In fact, Mark Twain and Howells were together no more than a dozen times in the five years between the Clemenses' departure for Europe in early spring, 1878, and the Howellses' return from Europe in late summer, 1883. Most of these visits found Mark Twain staying with the Howellses while he was in Boston or Howells coming alone to Hartford. Family ill health, the ages of their children, obligations to other family members or friends, and

7. Paine (ed.), *Mark Twain's Letters*, I, 350.
8. Smith and Gibson (eds.), *Mark Twain–Howells Letters*, I, 233.

the press of work caused visits to be set aside or delayed on both sides.

"How forlorn Hartford will seem without you!" Elinor had written to Livy just before the Clemenses' departure for Europe in 1878. They had visited the Clemenses in Hartford two weeks before at a time when the house was already being emptied and only friends as close as the Howellses could be entertained. Clemens' letters from Europe are spaced at intervals of several weeks or a month. Some letters are lost now, and some of Howells' must have miscarried at the time. But Mark Twain found more time to write and had more to write about than Howells. As much as Mark Twain himself complained about having to write letters, he excluded those to Howells from that complaint. His own obligations to correspondents may have made him more sensitive to the obligations he was placing on Howells through his own letters. From Heidelberg in June he repeats a concern he had expressed earlier: "Look here, Howells, when I choose to gratify my passions by writing great long letters to you, you are not to consider anything but the briefest answers necessary—and not even those when you have got things to do. Don't forget that. A lengthy letter from you is a great prize & a welcome, but it gives me a reproach, because I seem to have robbed a busy man of time which he ought not to have spared."[9]

Whether Howells took him at his word or because some letters have been lost, Howells' letters are infrequent during this period. Mark Twain's next extant letter, September 27, 1878, begins by asking if he has offended Howells in some way. Although we have no indication of what the offense might have been and no letters from Howells until September, 1879, there are clear indications in the long letters of Clemens that the offense, real or imagined, was quickly put aside. Howells did keep in touch, though fitfully, and not as often as Mark Twain wished. Mark Twain's first letter from Elmira, September 8, 1879, five days after arriving in New York, begins, "Are you *dead*—or only sleepeth?" Howells replied promptly, "Sleepeth is the matter—the sleep of a torpid conscience."[10] The

9. *Ibid.*, 225, 237.
10. *Ibid.*, 268.

string of questions Howells asks suggests he has not heard from
Clemens very recently nor written to him.

With Howells' confession of bad conscience, and the two now
back within visiting distance, the friendship resumed on its old
terms in the period before the Howellses themselves departed for
Europe. They probably did not see each other until December in
Boston. Howells proposed that Clemens come to the breakfast to be
given Oliver Wendell Holmes on the third and to be the Howellses'
guest as long as he could. Clemens replied: "Will I come? O *hell-*
yes!" Before that visit, the first chance to have a face-to-face conversation with Howells in almost two years, Clemens had had a
grand week of "solid dissipation" in Chicago attending the meeting
of the Society of the Army of the Tennessee. He had wanted Howells
to go along, and gave him a full account of what had transpired. "I
doubt if America has ever seen anything quite equal to it." Four
speeches almost carried away his wits, a reflection both of the admiration he felt for General Grant and the sentiment aroused by the
occasion. The grand style of Bob Ingersoll, quite apart from the agnosticism that was to make him notorious, caught Mark Twain's attention forcibly. "Lord," he concluded, "there's nothing like the human organ to make words live & throb, & lift the hearer to the full
altitudes of their meaning."[11]

The memory of the Whittier dinner may have caused Mark
Twain to hesitate when Howells invited him to speak at the breakfast
for Holmes to be held in December, 1879. But in late November
Mark Twain wrote that he finally had *A Tramp Abroad* off his hands
(he had said that before and was to say it once more before the book
was actually finished), and he did go. That time he let Howells read
his speech in advance, giving him leave to strike out whatever he
wished. After the visit, he wrote that the time at Belmont was intol-
erably short. By January 24, Howells was seemingly out of touch
once again, causing Mark Twain to write, "Say—are you dead
again!" Howells was merely loaded with work and further weighed
down with Elinor's care, since she had apparently been in bed since

11. *Ibid.*, 276, 279.

Clemens' visit. In March, Mark Twain reckoned Howells was dead again, making him decide to "heave a line at the corpse" anyway. Despite the Clemenses' urgings, the two families did not get together until April, 1880, in Boston. In the intervening months, there was some jesting about the Howellses' expressed obligations to visit the Warners in Hartford before they could, in good conscience, accept the Clemenses' invitation. The visit in Boston was, as always, too short. "I have thought of upwards of a million things I wanted to say to you—but that is always the way. Probably there *is* an eternity."[12]

The Howellses passed up a May visit in Hartford to spend a week with President and Mrs. Rutherford B. Hayes, relatives of the Meads, whom Elinor Mead had visited in Ohio twenty years before when she first became acquainted with William Dean Howells. Clemens found the excuse adequate, but missed their company anyway. On Howells' part, he hoped to see Clemens at Ashfield, Massachusetts, where C. E. Norton held an annual seminar in late summer. But the birth of Jean Clemens in July and Livy's long recovery put off visiting for much of that year, though Clemens was able to stop at the Howellses in October on a trip to Boston. Winny's illness, coming in the fall of 1880, required much care, and the Howellses' next visit to Hartford was not until March of the next year, at the time they were making their plans for Europe. Clemens made a "fat visit" in August 1881, but when Elinor informed him of Howells' serious illness in November, it came as a great shock. When Howells had recovered sufficiently after the first of the year to have visitors, he was prompt in asking Mark Twain to come: "I can't offer you a bed, because I haven't a house, (only a boarding-house,) but here is a room to smoke in, and I can place three meals a day at your disposal."[13] Howells was in Hartford in March, and Clemens in Boston and Belmont in late spring. The summer intervened, with each in their separate summer places, before the Howellses departed for Europe, not to return until August, 1883.

12. *Ibid.*, 288, 300.
13. *Ibid.*, 385.

When they did return, the intentions of seeing each other continued and the collaboration on a script for a play made it possible to combine pleasure and business. As expressed in their letters and reflected in their public writing, both men's attitudes toward traveling and living abroad were equivocal. They clearly missed each other's stimulation, though their personal visiting was not as frequent as the short distance between Hartford and Boston might have made possible. Letters helped to fill in, and many had to do with the writing each was doing, Clemens' letters often in part those of writer to editor, since he was making frequent contributions to the *Atlantic*. Mark Twain continued to lecture, though he often professed a hatred of doing it. Still, the power to move across the land, to bring a crowd of strangers under his sway, to begin as a stranger himself and end as a hero, had enough of an appeal to offset the dreary spaces between. Howells resisted Mark Twain's urgings to lecture, even to becoming part of a Mark Twain–Howells–Cable lecture circuit "circus." Although he made individual lecture appearances earlier, he waited until he was sixty to appear on the lecture circuit, and though he experienced some of the thrills he mostly suffered from the dreariness and strain.

What both experienced in lecturing can be related to their other travel experiences. Both writers had begun as travel writers, and a sensitivity to landscape and an ability to depict different places and peoples remained among their great skills. And though it might seem that either could have settled for becoming a writer who spun his substance from his own bowels, as Emerson had advised, each profited from the exposure to actual incidents and characters that travel provided. Writing in 1909 about the earlier period, Mark Twain speaks of "his hungry desire to travel," but also of the forty sea voyages and numberless land trips that seemed to him to be a hard fate. "I made all those journeys because I could not help myself—made them with rebellion in my heart, & bitterness." In the midst of his European trip, from Munich on January 30, he expressed his envy of Howells for being able to write sharp satires on European life. "I *hate* travel, & I *hate* hotels."[14]

14. *Ibid.*, 242, 248.

In the early eighties, Howells' and Mark Twain's European travels had barely begun—Mark Twain was to spend almost half of the next twenty years abroad, and Howells' travels in later years took him to Europe eleven times. Faced by financial losses and Livy's ill health in 1891, Mark Twain decided to live in Europe once again. He wrote Howells: "Travel has no longer any charm for me. I have seen all the foreign countries I want to see except heaven & hell, & I have only a vague curiosity as concerns one of those." Howells' trip with Mildred to Europe in 1894 provoked his own wan response, not just to travel, but to the sojourning of life itself. "My wife and I had expected to stay, and spend the winter in Italy, but . . . we lost courage and came home; that is, *I* lost courage first, as mostly happens in these cases, and then she did."[15]

Howells and Mark Twain were probably not much different from other affluent Americans with respect to transatlantic travel and in their relationship with Europe. Their books, from Mark Twain's *Innocents Abroad* through Howells' many fiction and nonfiction volumes, helped define and shape the attitudes and actions of Americans abroad. They lived through the first great age of Atlantic crossings, beginning with the replacement of sails by steam, paddle wheel by screw propeller, and wooden hulls by iron. Howells sailed to Venice in 1861 on the *City of Glasgow*, one of the ships of the Inman line that established post–Civil War passenger travel. The trip from New York to Liverpool took fourteen days, most of them uncomfortable if not miserable. By 1900, the travel time had been cut in half, and the level of comfort provided cabin passengers had been even more remarkably enhanced. In 1871, the White Star line's *Oceanic* was described in this way: "Among her other more distinctive features were an especially elegant main lounge with two coal-burning fireplaces, marble mantels, and a Broadwood piano; individual chairs in the dining saloon in place of the usual long benches; a ladies' boudoir and a bridal suite; and fresh and salt running water in the staterooms."[16]

15. Smith and Gibson (eds.), *Mark Twain–Howells Letters*, II, 645; M. Howells (ed.), *Life in Letters*, II, 85.

16. Foster Rhea Dulles, *Americans Abroad: Two Centuries of European Travel*

Speed and comfort were two reasons for the expansion of tourist travel after the Civil War, but the bulk of Atlantic travelers continued to be immigrants, over 2.25 million from 1861 to 1870 and over 5.25 million in the decade of the eighties, 80 percent coming by ship from European ports. By comparison, cabin passengers numbering 100,000 a year in 1900 and perhaps half that in the 1880s were but a small fraction of the total passenger travel. Nevertheless, the improvements in and catering to tourist travel increased greatly from the time in 1842 when Dickens could compare a cabin berth to a coffin and decide to return to England by sailing ship rather then endure the vibrations of the paddlewheel. Despite the increases in speed and comfort, costs did not rise sharply. Cabin passage (later called first-class) on the *Sirius* in 1840 was $140 to England. After the Civil War, $100 to $200 remained a standard fare, though increasingly more expensive accommodations became available. (As a comparison, Howells' consulship at Venice in 1861 was offered him at $1,000 per year, and in entertaining the possibility of his sister, Aurelia, visiting them, he said she would need no less than $500 for passage and an extended stay with them.) By 1895, a guidebook for the American and White Star lines said an American tourist could obtain passage and travel in Europe for three months for $500 inclusive.

The catering to tourists may, with some accuracy, be dated from Mark Twain's *Innocents Abroad*, for the *Quaker City* voyage in 1867 was one of the first planned tourist travel packages. By the time of the sinking of the *Titanic* in April, 1912, which, with the advent of World War I, signaled the end of the first great transatlantic tourist age, ships were taking on a European luxuriance matched only by the pillaging of European castles and palaces by American millionaires. Although Mark Twain, and to a lesser extent, Howells, acquired home furnishings to be shipped back from Europe, neither followed the fashion of disassembling and shipping back for reconstruction whole dwelling places. Probably the most engaging re-

---

(Ann Arbor, 1964), 50. This book affords an excellent account of both transatlantic passage and travel abroad. See also Terry Coleman, *The Liners: A History of the North Atlantic Crossing* (London, 1976).

minder of Mark Twain's European travels in the Hartford home is the ornately carved bed purchased from an antique dealer in Venice in 1878. He had it made up foot to head so he could enjoy the ornate headboard, so the story goes, and the Clemens children found the carved figures on the bedposts to be among their favorite dolls.

At the level of the abstract and ongoing quarrel between Europe and America that is so much a part of Henry James's life and work, both Mark Twain and Howells contributed to the definition of Americans in Europe in both fiction and nonfiction. Their works, too, offered a comparison of European and American cultural values. For the most part, both valued Europe as a place for travel, were often vexed with the discomforts that such travel entailed, were most often gratified by what they found there. "I ask why J[ames] or I, even," Howells wrote to his friend C. E. Norton in 1905, "should not live forever out of America without self-reproach?" A decade earlier, when the illness of his father had called him home, Howells wrote to his son John: "Perhaps it was as well I was called home. The poison of Europe was getting into my soul. You must look out for that. They live much more fully than we do. Life here is still for the future—it is a land of Emersons—and I like a little present moment in mine."[17]

A year later, Mark Twain began the most ambitious trip that either of them was to undertake. He was not the first to circumnavigate the globe, but his progress from August, 1895, to August, 1896, was celebrated almost as if he were. Nor was it kept from the public that the trip had a grand motive, to pay off his creditors instead of resorting to bankruptcy. The correspondence between Mark Twain and Howells, however, leaves the trip a mystery. No letters, though there must have been some, survive the year of his actual tour, though Mark Twain wrote three days before leaving Vancouver and five days after arriving in England.

Before and after that trip, the two writers' correspondence expresses a longing for a settled existence. "We are drifting about from one place to another, this summer," Howells wrote Norton, "trying to discover some spot within a few hours of New York where we might

17. Fischer and Lohmann (eds.), *W. D. Howells: Selected Letters*, V, 133; M. Howells (ed.), *Life in Letters*, II, 52.

pitch our ragged tent for the few summers that yet remain to us."
Eventually, the Howellses bought a house at Far Rockaway, Long
Island, but occupied it for only the summer of 1896 before selling it.
From Southhampton, England, shortly after finishing his tour, Clemens wrote Howells, "We hope to get a house in some quiet English
village away from the world & society, where I can set down for six
months or so & give myself up to the luxury & rest of writing a book
or two after this long fatigue & turmoil of platform-work & gadding
around by sea & land." Susy's sudden death in Hartford before any
of the family could reach her brought the two families close together
in grief ("Yes, you two know what we feel—but no others among our
friends"), but the Clemenses returned to Europe after Susy's funeral
and remained until October, 1900. The Howellses were in Germany
and Holland in the summer of 1897, but apparently did not see the
Clemenses. "I stupidly hoped some chance would bring us together," Howells wrote Mark Twain later, "and we might talk out all
that was in us, as we used to do in those glorious days when I went to
Hartford or you came to Cambridge. But it did not happen, and now
the ocean is between us again."[18]

By this time, the weariness of travel is also the weariness of old
age, and the immense sadness of the losses that have come upon
them. Clemens recovered slowly from Susy's death. "I am a mud
image," he wrote Howells six months later, "& it puzzles me to know
what it is in me that writes, & that has comedy-fancies & finds pleasure in phrasing them." After the Howellses had returned home the
following fall, Elinor had a complete nervous collapse, and Howells
wrote Mark Twain: "She enjoyed Europe like a child, and perhaps
overdid; at any rate she faces the fact in this merciless clear air that
we are two elderly people, whose margin of hoping and doing is reduced to something very narrow, and she can hardly bear it."[19]

Both turned again to work. "I bury myself in it up to the ears,"
Mark Twain records. And Howells: "Of course, I am tugging away at
the old root." He also undertook a short eastern lecture tour in

18. Thomas Wortham (ed.), *W. D. Howells: Selected Letters*, IV, 78, 107;
Smith and Gibson (eds.), *Mark Twain–Howells Letters*, II, 661, 662, 667.
    19. *Ibid.*, 664, 667.

1897, and, encouraged by Clemens—"*Of course*, go lecturing, if you can stand the travel"—undertook a more ambitious trek as far west as Kansas in 1899. "It was worse, far worse," he told Mark Twain after he had finished, "than you ever said in your least credible moments."[20] It was the last lecture tour he ever attempted, and it was appropriate, if coincidental, that he should come upon York Harbor as an attractive summer place among the many he and Elinor had known through the years. Before long, he was to buy the place at Kittery Point, just down the coast, which became the place he most clearly identified as home. Mark Twain could not bear to return to Hartford, so strong was his attachment to Susy and to the past he identified with her. The house was sold for a fraction of its worth, and only by good fortune was it saved and restored. It now stands as more of a permanent residence for Mark Twain than he enjoyed during his life. Appropriately, his last residence at Stormfield, which was designed by Howells' son, burned after his death, leaving him free to roam heaven and hell as whatever Providence there might be should decide.

As for Howells, with Elinor's death his last decade found him "as ever a nomad."[21] For the years immediately after her death, his memory of her was too compelling to permit his occupying either his New York apartment or the summer place at Kittery Point. He went to England and Spain in 1911 and to England again in 1913. In America, various addresses at Cambridge, Boston, and New York were usual stopping places during the year, and York Harbor, Maine, and Kittery Point in summer. Winters often found him going south, to Bermuda first and later chiefly to St. Augustine, Florida, or Savannah, Georgia.

"From childhood up to the 'Innocents Abroad' excursion," Mark Twain wrote in 1909, "I was a natural human being, with a natural human being's desires; one of them being a hungry desire to travel— but the Excursion, with its five or six months of ceaseless & exhausting gadding around, surfeited me, surfeited me thoroughly, &

20. *Ibid.*, 670, 667, 703, 712.
21. Van Wyck Brooks, *Howells: His Life and World* (New York, 1959), 284.

for good & all." In light of Mark Twain's later travels and his often expressed responsiveness to landscape and to the adulation he received, one reads the passage with skepticism as well as acceptance. Howells looked back on his own travels with fondness despite the risks and discomfort and trouble. Setting aside his early residence in Italy, he seemed to see his transatlantic journeyings as beginning late and therefore valued more. Had the war not intervened, he probably would have taken more European trips in his last years. At it was, he wrote to Brand Whitlock in 1913, shortly after returning from what was to be his last trip abroad: "It stirs my blood to think of your going to Italy; I wish I could go with you! . . . In that thin, clear Italian air you can see American things distinctly."[22]

22. Smith and Gibson (eds.), *Mark Twain–Howells Letters*, I, 242; William M. Gibson and Christoph K. Lohmann (eds.), *W. D. Howells: Selected Letters* (6 vols.; Boston, 1983), VI, 164, 41.

Seven

Working Together

Mark Twain seemed to suffer more than Howells from the isolation necessary for working—not the isolation that forced itself on him when a story was boiling, but that which was a daily necessity for a gregarious man who needed to earn a handsome living by writing. A need to talk, to be with others, is surely behind the schemes he pursued for working with someone else—with Charles Dudley Warner on *The Gilded Age*, Bret Harte on the play *Ah Sin*, Howells on *Colonel Sellers as a Scientist*. As an editor as well as a writer, Howells had a more social professional life. He made friends with other writers easily, and his duties brought him into acquaintance with many. Nevertheless, he as well as Mark Twain devised schemes for their collaborating as writers.

Both Howells and Mark Twain were compulsive writers, and probably because of their years as journalists, they could write anywhere. Neither could have produced the enormous amount of work he did without both traits. The Nook Farm house with its splendid library, spacious study, billiard room, and vistas all around provided everything for writing. But more than anything else it was a social and family place. Mark Twain's writing space, as it is shown to visitors today, is not in the library, but the billiard room. At times, he escaped the house altogether and worked in a room above the carriage house. Even then, lecturing and traveling took him away from Nook Farm, and he, like Howells, wrote as he traveled. In the summers at Quarry Farm outside Elmira, he found conditions most congenial to his work. "Susie Crane has built the loveliest study for me, you ever saw," he wrote Joe Twichell in July, 1874, just after Clara ("the great American Giantess—weighing 7 3/4 pounds") was born. "It is octagonal, with a peaked roof, each octagon filled with a spacious window, and it sits perched in complete isolation on top of an elevation that commands leagues of valley and city and retreating ranges of distant blue hills. It is a cozy nest, with just room in it for a sofa and a table and three or four chairs—and when the storms sweep down the remote valley and the lightning flashes above the hills beyond, and the rain beats upon the roof over my head, imagine the luxury of it!"[1]

Although Twain's splendid life at Hartford and Nook Farm loomed over Howells' own social ascent in Cambridge and Boston, Howells' rising affluence enabled him to move into a new house in 1873, fitted out as a writer's house should be. He described it to his father in detail.

This is the first letter I write in my beautiful new library, which is more charming than I could make you understand by the longest description. The ceiling is richly frescoed; below the cornice, and down to the chairboard running the room is a soft buff paper and then dark red to the floor. The book-casing, drawers and closets are heavily chestnut; the hearth is of tiles, and the chimney-piece rises in three broad shelves almost to the cornice. This is the glory of the room, and is splendidly carved, and set with picture-tiles and mirrors; on either jamb of the mantel is my monogram, carved, and painted by Elinor, who modified and improved the carpenter's design of the whole affair.[2]

The Howellses' residence at Belmont was brief, and both before and after, much of Howells' writing went on in settings quite bereft

---

1. Paine (ed.), *Mark Twain's Letters*, I, 220.
2. Arms and Lohmann (eds.), *W. D. Howells: Selected Letters*, II, 31.

of frescoed ceilings and his own monogram. He did his salaried work in the *Atlantic* offices, and he carried proof sheets, manuscripts, and the like to his summer vacation places, doing his salaried and his own work wherever he could find space to sit and write. During his nonvacation times, he established regular habits almost as demanding as those of his youth when he was getting up before dawn so that he might read and write before beginning his work in the print shop. Describing his work habits to an inquirer in 1884, he wrote: "I am lazy, and always force myself more or less to work . . . I often work when dull or heavy from a bad night, and find that the indisposition wears off. I rarely miss a day from any cause. . . . For a lazy man I am extremely industrious."[3]

As Mark Twain could only be lazy for brief periods, so Howells could only break away from paid journalistic positions briefly during his life, despite much vexation that such work tied him down both physically and psychically. A closely related conflict within both men was that of reconciling social life with their work. Editing must have been attractive to Howells in part because it enabled him to meet and work among many acquaintances and friends. Mark Twain's many efforts at collaborating with others, his reading of his work to the family circle, and his close literary relationship with Howells were ways of tempering the essentially solitary work of the writer.

It is not surprising to find that Howells and Mark Twain made various proposals to collaborate on writing projects, usually with an eye toward great profits at the end.[4] It is more surprising that little came of these schemes. Of three substantial efforts at collaboration—a play based on Colonel Sellers of *The Gilded Age*, a collection called *The Library of Humor*, and a novel by many hands, "The Blindfold Novelettes"—the first has the most interesting history. Howells is very little remembered for his work as a playwright. Yet his collected plays fill a fat scholarly volume, including one-act farces and other comedies (his most popular works) as well as adap-

3. Leitz (ed.), *W. D. Howells: Selected Letters*, III, 102.
4. A detailed discussion of each of these collaborations is in Lowenherz, "Mark Twain and W. D. Howells: A Literary Relationship," Chap, 2, "We can do anything together," 81–122.

tations of his own works and translations or adaptations of serious works of others.[5] Mark Twain on the lecture platform was Samuel Clemens' most successful dramatic creation, though his novels led to various dramatizations by both himself and others.

Very early in their friendship, Mark Twain was able to secure Howells a $500 commission for translating Ippolito d'Aste's play, *Samson*, which had a long and successful run. At the time, Mark Twain had already taken Colonel Sellers out of *The Gilded Age* and turned him into the central character of a five-act play. Soon after, he urged Howells to undertake a play of his own, and also turned over to him the opportunity to develop a play idea an actor and stage manager had proposed to Clemens. While *Tom Sawyer* was still in manuscript, he proposed sending it to Howells with the following instructions. "If you will do as follows: dramatize it if you perceive that you can, & take, for your remuneration, half of the first $6,000 which I receive for its representation on the stage. You could alter the plot entirely, if you chose. . . . Come—can't you tackle this in the odd hours of your vacation?—or later, if you prefer?" Howells responded, "It's very pleasant to have you propose my working in any sort of concert with you." Nevertheless, he declined, giving as his chief reason that he "couldn't enter into the spirit of another man's work sufficiently to do the thing you propose."[6]

The idea of collaborating on a play with Howells did not come up again until after the failure of *Ah Sin*, through which Mark Twain and Harte had hoped to capitalize on the immense popularity of Harte's "heathen Chinee" character. The play appeared to enlist more of Mark Twain's energies than Harte's, and though it got off well in New York in late summer, it failed quickly; by November, 1877, Mark Twain admitted that it was "an abject & incurable failure." Nevertheless, he completed another full-length play, *Simon Wheeler, Detective*, which, revealing its deficiencies before it ever reached the stage, was left unpublished during Mark Twain's life. Howells' modest success with *A Counterfeit Presentment*, which Clemens saw in Hartford in 1878, revived the idea of their collabo-

5. See Walter J. Meserve (ed.), *The Complete Plays of W. D. Howells* (New York, 1960).

6. Smith and Gibson (eds.), *Mark Twain–Howells Letters*, I, 95–96.

rating on a play. Clemens' trip to Europe made a close-at-hand collaboration impossible, though Howells noted two months before the Clemenses' departure, "We shall yet write a play together." Before he left, Mark Twain had apparently planted the notion with Howells of developing a play around Clemens' brother Orion and his many impractical schemes and inventions. Howells mentions such a possibility with the title of "The Steam Generator" in June, 1878, but neither seems to have pursued the idea strenuously. A letter to Clemens from Orion in February, 1879, ignites all of Clemens' enthusiasm anew. He wrote to Howells immediately. "You *must* put him in a book or a play right away. You are the only man capable of doing it. You might die at any moment, & your very greatest work would be lost to the world. *I* could write Orion's simple biography & make it effective, too, by merely stating the bald facts—& this I will do if he dies before I do; and *you* must put him into romance. This was the understanding you & I had the day I sailed." Mark Twain was truly respectful of Howells' technical mastery of dramatic dialogue, and he may have believed that Howells' comic touch had the deftness that might provoke both laughter and sympathy. Certainly he was aware of what Howells was to bring out openly—that exposing Orion to ridicule was inevitable if he were to be made the vehicle for a popular comedy. At any event, the idea persisted, its attractiveness lodged in Mark Twain's mixed vexation and pity for his brother's ambitious flounderings. It is, he wrote Howells, "a field which grows richer & richer the more he manures it with each new top-dressing of religion or other guano."[7]

Within two weeks of his return from Europe, September 15, 1879, Mark Twain reminded Howells of "*our* old projects. . . . don't you think you & I can get together & grind out a play with one of those fellows in it?"[8] Howells' reply admits to reservations he has long held about subjecting poor Orion to ridicule, but falls back upon the press of other work as an excuse for not being able to take up the project. Mark Twain continued to be fascinated by Orion's shifting ill fortunes. It was not, however, until the fall of 1881 that

7. *Ibid.*, 216, 253, 269.
8. *Ibid.*, 269.

the long discussed plans began to take the form of *Colonel Sellers as a Scientist.*

In the meantime, both had become committed to another collaboration, the compiling of *Library of Humor*, a collection originated by George Gebbie, a Philadelphia publisher. Gebbie dropped out of the scheme early; Osgood was to be the publisher before his firm folded, and eventually the Charles Webster Company, Mark Twain's publisher, issued the book in 1888 as *Mark Twain's Library of Humor*. By that time, Howells had signed an exclusive contract with Harper's that required payment for the use of his name in a work issued by another publisher. In addition, his "textbook" idea of a thorough and judicious sampling of nineteenth-century American humor was at odds with Clemens' freer-handed version of a book that would be bought and read by a large public. Some of the work of getting the material together was hired out, some was done by Howells, and some, toward the end of the process, by Mark Twain. Howells received an agreed-upon settlement for his work, but his name did not appear on the cover, nor did the work constitute a very real collaboration.

On the eve of the Howellses' departure for Europe, July 14, 1882, Howells wrote Clemens from Toronto telling him of a cash offer he had received for their projected comedy. The producers offered Howells $4,000 for it with $1,000 more to go to Clemens for the idea. He flatly rejected the offer and left the matter with Mark Twain to negotiate as he might wish. His letter to Clemens in October expressed great enthusiasm for the project, as well as for the Clemenses to come to Europe to work on it.

What you want to do is pack up your family, and come to Florence for the winter. I shall have my story [he was finishing *A Woman's Reason*] as good as done when I get there early in December, and shall be ready to go to work with you on the great American comedy of "Orme's Motor" which is to enrich us both "beyond the dreams of avarice." Its fate needn't rest with the Madison Squarers. We can get it played. We could have a lot of fun writing it, and you could go home with some of the good old Etruscan malaria in your bones, instead of the wretched pinch-beck Hartford article that you're suffering from now.[9]

9. *Ibid.*, 415.

In February, Howells admits that he has been so busy with other matters that he has not "put pen to paper yet on the play." Clemens has been at least as busy, chiefly in bringing *Life on the Mississippi* into book form, which he seemed to be having as much difficulty with as he had had with *A Tramp Abroad*. The producers continued to pursue Howells, and Howells, in turn, referred them to Mark Twain. Clemens settled the matter temporarily with the forthright common sense Howells always praised him for. "Said I did not wish to bind myself to write a play. Next October you will come here and roost with me, and we will lock ourselves up from all the world and put the great American comedy through."[10]

Early in November, 1883, almost as soon as the Howellses had returned from Europe, Howells went to Hartford to work on the play. "Mrs. Howells nobly declared," he had written Mark Twain in October, "that she would do anything for money, and that I might go to you when I liked." Recalling this period in *My Mark Twain* in 1910, Howells refers to "a jubilant fortnight in working the particulars of these things out. It was not possible for Clemens to write like anybody else, but I could very easily write like Clemens, and we took the play scene and scene about, quite secure of coming out in temperamental agreement. . . . We would work all day long at our several tasks, and then at night, before dinner, read them over to each other. No dramatists ever got greater joy out of their creations." After that period of work together in Hartford, the two continued to work separately at the play during the next months. Much of 1884 they were involved in negotiations to produce the play. John T. Raymond, the actor who had appeared in the previous Sellers play, offered the most promising negotiations. The negotiations were prolonged and cumbersome, the cause of some misunderstandings between the two authors, but in September, 1884, Raymond rejected the play with finality. Mark Twain used some of the material and ideas in his novel *The American Claimant*, which was published eight years later. Howells wrote: "Never mind about the play. We had fun writing it, anyway."[11]

10. *Ibid.*, 431.
11. *Ibid.*, 444; W. D. Howells, "My Mark Twain," 22; Smith and Gibson (eds.), *Mark Twain–Howells Letters*, II, 507.

Their collaboration is remarkable in displaying both writers' ability to sustain professional careers, family responsibilities, and personal friendships, for it was going on during a period when both had young families, with the attendant onslaughts of childhood diseases, and when both were otherwise occupied with books now recognized as among their highest literary achievements. *Tom Sawyer* was still in manuscript when the idea for collaboration first came up. *Life on the Mississippi* was making its way from a series of *Atlantic* articles in 1875 into a book, and *Huckleberry Finn*, begun in 1876, was being completed in 1883. Howells, meanwhile, was seeing *A Modern Instance* appear in its final installments in 1882, completing two other novels and most of *The Rise of Silas Lapham* before 1885. In addition to other separate projects, both were engaged sporadically from 1881 on in *Mark Twain's Library of Humor.* Passing the age of forty was scarcely noticed by either writer in the midst of this sustained period of shared excitement and creativity.

The subsequent history of the Sellers play provoked the only documented quarrel between Howells and Mark Twain in their long years of friendship, though there were periods in their respective travels when they were out of touch and periods in their later life when they saw relatively little of each other. Although it played no part in their later clash, Mark Twain and Howells had differed sharply in support of political candidates for the 1884 presidential election. Grover Cleveland's having a mistress was too much for Howells' moral sensibilities, and he gave support to the Democrat James Blaine, despite Blaine's alleged dishonesty. "Besides," he wrote to Clemens about Cleveland, "I don't like his hangman-face. It looks dull and brutal." Mark Twain was the one to take the higher moral ground. He accepted the charges of dishonesty against Blaine, and loyalty to the Republican party was not enough for him to support Cleveland. He lectured Howells: "A man's *first* duty is to his own conscience & honor—the party & the country come second to that, & never first. I don't ask you to vote *at all*—I only urge you to not soil yourself by voting for Blaine."[12]

12. *Ibid.*, 503, 508.

That was the difference of opinion; it apparently put no great strain on their friendship. Both were busy with other matters when the election was held: Mark Twain was out on the road again with George Washington Cable; *Huckleberry Finn* was soon to be published; Howells' *The Rise of Silas Lapham* was being serialized; and Osgood was asking about their *Library of Humor*. Howells heard Mark Twain read in Boston on November 14 and wrote: "You were as much yourself before those thousands as if you stood by my chimney-corner grinding away to the household your absence bereaves here. You *are* a great artist, and you do this public thing so wonderfully well that I don't see how you could ever bear to give it up."[13]

In the spring of 1886, the idea of doing the Sellers play resurfaced and led to the sharpest recorded clash between the two friends and collaborators. This time, the actor A. P. Burbank proposed to do the Sellers part. Clemens at first backed away from the proposal. He wrote to Charles Webster on March 19. "Burbank is a personal friend and a first rate fellow, but I won't allow the play to be played this year or next, upon *any* terms." His hesitation, as he expressed to Webster, had to do with his doubts about the play—"isn't worth a damn and is going to fail"—and the effects such a failure would have on his publishing firm.[14]

Nevertheless, by May the two of them were ready to plunge in again. "Let's be *private*," Mark Twain wrote, "& let nobody know, till the work is finished. Interruptions would be fatal." They chose Howells' house as the place for getting together, but even before they did, Howells had reread the play and had begun to doubt that it would hold up. He attached the term *lunatic* to their characterization of Sellers and predicted certain failure if they could not "shade Sellers' lunacy." The two apparently worked over the play on a Sunday and Monday, and Mark Twain left for New York with some assurance that he might now negotiate firmly with Burbank. Howells' earlier reservations welled up during the night and he fired off a

13. *Ibid.*, 513.
14. Hamlin Hill (ed.), *Mark Twain's Letters to His Publishers 1867–1894* (Berkeley, 1967), 196.

letter and telegram the next day proposing to Clemens that they either withdraw the play absolutely or keep the commitment with Burbank in the form of a *reading* of the play after further revisions. The messages did not reach Mark Twain in time to forestall his negotiating an agreement with Burbank that resulted in Burbank's leasing the Lyceum Theatre for two weeks. It was the financial obligation to buy off the play—at a cost eventually amounting to $700—which was responsible for Mark Twain's wrath. "There—," he wrote Howells, "what I'm jumping on top of, & taking by the neck, hair and ears . . . is your gentle & even almost Christlike ⟨admission⟩ concession that 'the folly was mine as much as yours.'"[15]

The precise provocation was Howells' expressed willingness to share with Clemens the blame in the affair and "to pay for it too, in money as well as misery." Mark Twain's reply began, "No, no, *sir*—I'm not going to let you shoulder a solitary ounce of the 'folly' onto *me!*" Then he listed the facts that put the blame where he thought it belonged—squarely and wholly on Howells. Having established that, Mark Twain recounted his negotiations with Burbank that extricated all parties.

A P.S. followed Mark Twain's long exposition by two days. "Mrs. Clemens has condemned this letter to the stove—'because it ⟨well⟩ might make Mr. Howells feel bad.' *Might* make him feel bad! Have I in sweat & travail wrought 12 carefully-contrived pages to make him feel bad, & now there's a bloody *doubt* flung at it? Let me accept the truth: I am grown old, my literary cunning has departed from me. I purposed to shrivel you up; & the verdict is as above. However, I don't care; I couldn't have enjoyed it more than a couple of minutes, if I had succeeded."[16]

Mark Twain's anger was as brief as he declared it to be. Al-

15. Smith and Gibson (eds.), *Mark Twain–Howells Letters*, II, 554; see Smith and Gibson (eds.), *Mark Twain–Howells Letters*, II, 554–63, letters and notes, for a more detailed account of these events.

16. Smith and Gibson (eds.), *Mark Twain–Howells Letters*, II, 559, 562. Lowenherz comments, "But characteristically, by the time he reached the end of his tirade, his sense of humor and his affection for Howells got the best of him, and he concluded mildly enough." Lowenherz, "Mark Twain and W. D. Howells: A Literary Relationship," 119.

though there is one further exchange concerning the details of the incident, Howells' check for his share of the reparations brought an end to the matter. The whole flare-up of interest in the play and the scrape it got them into occupied scarcely three weeks. Howells gives an entire chapter of *My Mark Twain* to the incident, passing over both his own culpability and Mark Twain's wrath. By that time, memory had enhanced the quality of the play so that he could write, "I still believe that the play was immensely funny."[17]

Although Howells had his own dreams of making big money in writing for the stage, his attraction to the Sellers play must be attributed to Mark Twain's greater enthusiasm and their friendship. One of the defects of their close collaboration lies in the great pleasure they both received from entertaining each other's outrageous notions. While the mood was on them, the Sellers play must have seemed extremely funny, as funny perhaps as Mark Twain's "unfinished sketch of Elizabeth's time," which he had sent Howells in 1876, about the time they were entertaining the collaboration scheme for "Blindfold Novelettes." The humor of *1601* is similar to much that went into the Sellers play, though the latter had a wider range of effects than the earlier's emphasis on flatulence in Elizabethan times as its main joke.

Left alone, Howells' caution and critical sense reasserted themselves. In 1890, when he and Mark Twain were once again wrestling with the remains of the play with a view to maintaining James Herne's expressed interest, Howells wrote, "Herne is immensely pleased with main points of play—fire extinguisher, phonograph, telephone scene, drunken scene; but we both think the materialization must all come out, and Sellers kept sane."[18] Whatever his reasons, Herne did not produce the play. Howells was a careful manager of his own writing talent (he published virtually everything he wrote), and it was his caution with respect to collaboration that was to be both praised and blamed.

The one other collaboration Howells and Mark Twain attempted was as two writers of a proposed dozen enlisted to write separate

17. W. D. Howells, "My Mark Twain," 22.
18. Smith and Gibson (eds.), *Mark Twain–Howells Letters*, II, 630.

stories based on a common plot. The idea apparently sprang up during a visit Howells and his son John made to the Clemenses in March, 1876. The "Blindfold Novelettes" were to be written "blindfolded," each author not knowing what the others had written. The idea so pleased both authors that Mark Twain did a sketch for the basic plot and envisioned attracting such "big literary fish" as James, Holmes, and Lowell in addition to Harte, Warner, Aldrich, John Trowbridge, Howells, and himself—"it would make a stunning book to sell on railway trains."[19] Although the idea never came to completion (and the manuscript of Mark Twain's skeleton plot affirms the notion that their pleasure in collaborating dulled both men's critical sense), it remained a possibility for a number of years.

Throughout their lives, both Howells and Mark Twain complained of what Howells called "an uncontrolled way of living," a self-imposed necessity that bent them to both the literary project at hand and the social life that they found as necessary and often as demanding. Nevertheless, their careers did not get in the way of their friendship, even though it did not afford them the opportunities for collaboration that may have seemed apparent. What each was doing still provided opportunities to write to each other or meet together or observe one another in print when personal association was not possible. Each had a stake in the career of the other. The naïve criticism that Howells had a baneful influence upon Mark Twain's writing has been largely set aside, and it is nearer the mark that each influenced the other toward developing his distinctive talents, the one not measuring the other according to his own inclinations and practices. Although in their later years each may have paid less attention to the other's work, the more remarkable fact is that over so many years the strong mutual attention and interest persisted.

19. *Ibid.*, I, 160.

Eight

Dark Times

From Munich in 1878, Clemens told Howells about Susy's recurring dream in which she is being eaten by bears. One morning after such a dream, she told her mother, "But mamma, the trouble is, that I am never the *bear*, but always the *PERSON*." The story is Susy's but the mood of it is pure Mark Twain. He later used it in *Which Was the Dream?*, putting it in the mouth of Bessie Sedgewick, daughter of Major General "X" and Alison Sedgewick, whose rise and abrupt fall is one of a number of self-lacerating narratives written in the late 1890s. Howells shared with him a view of the world in which there are bears and persons, and in which most of us seldom get to be bears. As a figure in American literature, Howells will probably always be identified with his pronouncement that "Our novelists . . . concern themselves with the more smiling aspects of life, which are the more American."[1] His judgment, in this instance, was a relative one, American freedom and prosperity against political repression and poverty elsewhere in the world. For a large part of his later life, however, he viewed America dimly. Central to his personal life was

---

1. Smith and Gibson (eds.), *Mark Twain–Howells Letters*, I, 242; William Dean Howells, *Criticism and Fiction* (New York, 1891), 128.

the baffling and eventually fatal illness that blighted almost a decade of what should have been the great time of his daughter's coming of age. Mark Twain's last years are so well-known for their misanthropy that there is no need to emphasize the tragic side of his nature. The literary work of both men did not directly reflect the moods and circumstances of their personal lives. They were both too professional as writers and too complex as human beings to permit that simple a response. In their best works, they drew upon all they had experienced and felt for which the comic and tragic are only two ways of defining the extremes.

Shared adversity strengthened the friendship of Howells and Mark Twain as it strengthens many friendships. An underlying pessimism toward their personal lives as toward the possibility of a better society was another affinity between the two. Howells was neither as smug nor Mark Twain as unfailingly comic as is often supposed. Nor, in the instance of Mark Twain, do the facts quite support the image of the sad face beneath the clown's mask. Both were whole men who fully embraced the common human experience of growing up within a family and of establishing families of their own and living out lives past three score and ten, through times of ecstasy and satisfaction and boredom and intense pain.

What Bacon said about a man's wife and children being hostages to fortune has particular force for the family-oriented society of the nineteenth century. Few escaped the harsh slap of fortune as it worked among wives and husbands and the large numbers of sons and daughters, sisters and brothers, cousins and aunts and uncles, parents and grandparents. The most intense periods of anguish to both Howells and Mark Twain came from fates visited upon their children, and the longest period of having to sympathize and support and care came from the attachments to members of their parental family.

Stated bluntly, the record for both Howells and Mark Twain is bleak enough to account for a morbid strain in their old age. Of Samuel Clemens' four children only one survived him. Langdon died in infancy, the victim of a commonplace respiratory illness, but in Mark Twain's memory, a victim of his own neglect. Susy died young, out of sight and hearing of both father and mother. Jean suffered from the effects of epilepsy during most of the youth that made up her brief life. Clara, who lived a long life, struggled to overcome anxieties that crippled her for long periods while her father was still alive. Viewed simply and in light of Mark Twain's great fondness for his children, it is an awful record. Viewed in light of the families of the time, it appears less stark. Mark Twain, in one of his mildly mordant moments, described to Howells the winter of 1883: "Pneumonia is slaughtering people right and left. . . . The death rate of Hartford for the month of January, was twenty-eight to the thousand. This is thirty or thirty-five per cent bigger than it ought to be. Ninety-nine people died of pneumonia alone in New York last week." Pneumonia was only one killer. Any one of the contagious childhood diseases—scarlet fever, measles, diphtheria and croup, mumps, and cholera infantum—diminished the chances of living unimpaired into or past the teens. Pneumonia and tuberculosis, typhoid, malaria, and tetanus threatened child and adult alike. Tuberculosis had something of the actual and symbolic power over the times that cancer has today. In Amherst, Massachusetts, not far in place and time from Mark Twain's Hartford, Emily Dickinson's intense response to death was not at all strange; death was an omnipresent fact. In Massachusetts in 1855, only about 68 percent of the population survived to age ten, and by the end of the century that figure had risen to only about 75 percent.[2] If later readers reject Howells' seemingly optimistic assessment of American life, how much more smiling are our times than his as measured by the chance of one's surviving, or surviving unscarred, into adulthood.

Howells' greatest anguish arose from the death of his oldest

2. Smith and Gibson (eds.), *Mark Twain–Howells Letters*, I, 428; William B. Bailey, *Modern Social Conditions: A Statistical Study of Birth, Marriage, Divorce, Death, Disease, Suicide, Immigration, Etc., with Special Reference to the United States* (New York, 1906), 346. The contrast with today's childhood diseases is startling. "Today's youngsters are spared most of the infectious illnesses—smallpox, scarlet fever, dysentery—that carried off so many in the past. Of the 10 leading causes of death in infants and young children in 1850, every one has been brought under control." René Dubos, Maya Pines, and the editors of *Life, Health and Disease* (New York, 1965), 9. See also Sam Shapiro, Edward R. Schlesinger, and Robert E. L. Nesbitt, Jr., *Infant, Perinatal, Maternal, and Childhood Mortality in the United States* (Cambridge, Mass., 1968), for recent statistics.

daughter, Winny, at twenty-five, from an illness that remains as mysterious today as it appeared to Howells then. Beginning in the summer of 1880 as something vaguely called a nervous breakdown, it affected her physical movement, her eating, and sleeping, and was either in itself or a cause for pronounced depression. The first treatment was a forced-feeding regimen that increased her weight but did little else to change her condition. For the better part of two years, Winny was incapacitated, then in the spring of 1882, she recovered markedly and was able to accompany her parents to Europe, where a period of relapse in Florence was followed by a remarkable recovery in Venice, the city of her birth. By 1884 she was falling back into the pattern again, and by the fall of 1885 she had become so seriously affected that the Howellses moved to quieter surroundings in Auburndale to have her cared for. That summer and the following one she was much in Howells' care, and in the early fall of 1886 she was placed in a sanitarium in Dansville, New York, where the Howellses kept vigil near her until the doctors judged it would be better for them to be away. In February they took her first to a specialist in New York City and then to Dr. S. Weir Mitchell, one of the best-known experts in nervous disorders. Again, she was placed on a rest and forced-feeding regimen. On March 3, 1889, she died suddenly. Although records show that an autopsy was performed and the cause of death was determined to be organic, the sources give no more information than that.

The Clemenses knew Winny well; they were first informed of her condition in February, 1881, when Howells writes that she is "quite broken down" and that she has not been in school for five months. By August he writes, "Our dear girl has to lie *abed* now all the time—rest cure." At first, Elinor had taken her into Boston, leaving Howells and John at Belmont, to try to divert her from the apparent depression into which she had fallen. The Clemenses were particularly solicitous in trying to relieve some of the burden falling on the Howellses and did get them to visit in March, 1881. The following Christmas, Mark Twain sent Winny one of the fourteen special copies of *The Prince and the Pauper*, for which she thanked him "for remembering me in such a lovely way." Her responsiveness to the details of the story indicated the kind of verbally gifted, thoughtful, and serious person she was. Howells wrote his sister Aurelia in 1889, "Up to the time Winny's health began to break, her life was radiantly happy."[3]

Howells' own breakdown the next year found explanation enough in the incessant strain and anxiety of facing an inexplicable and incurable disease in a child he loved. Mark Twain's letters during Howells' convalescence are tender and respectful of the family's prolonged pain: "I won't fret you & worry you by insisting & insisting that you and Mrs. Howells come down here, for nothing is quite so utterly hellish as one of those bowelless & implacable insisters— but I shall *yearn* for you just the same." Six weeks later, Howells had recovered sufficiently to make a business trip to New York with Clemens with regard to extending Howells' father's consulship at Toronto. They returned via Hartford, leaving Clemens off there; a letter that followed suggests the burden of family care Howells had been carrying from which any person might have wished to escape. "You can't think what a sneaking desire I had to get into the carriage, that day, and drive home with you and Mrs. Clemens."[4]

As if the prolonged and mysterious illness could bear only so much mention, few references to Winny's condition appear in writing after the Howellses returned from Europe in 1883, though her condition grew increasingly grave in 1885. The family moved to Washington briefly at the end of winter, 1886, as a consequence of her health, and subsequent residences in Auburndale, near Dansville, New York, and New York City were directly connected with her condition and treatment. Correspondence between Howells and Mark Twain is scant between the summer of 1887 and Winny's death on March 3, 1889. A letter from Howells to Mark Twain in May, 1889, apprises him of their whereabouts for the coming summer. "We shall be just beyond Cambridge, not far from Winny's grave, beside which I stretched myself the other day, and experienced what

3. Smith and Gibson (eds.), *Mark Twain–Howells Letters*, I, 348, 366, 383; William Dean Howells to Aurelia H. Howells, April 28, 1889, in William Dean Howells Papers, Houghton Library, Harvard University.

4. Smith and Gibson (eds.), *Mark Twain–Howells Letters*, I, 389, 395.

anguish a man can live through." When Mark Twain next wrote in July, it was after the death of Susan Crane's husband in Elmira "after ten months of pain & two whole days of dying." He was especially fond of Susan Crane, and her grief reminded him of "the desolation which uttered itself in the closing sentence of your last letter to me." He added, "I do see that there is an argument against suicide: the grief of the worshipers left behind, the awful famine in their hearts, these are too costly terms for the release."[5]

The lives of Howells and Mark Twain while their children were prey to childhood diseases for which primitive and ineffectual treatments were prescribed can be imagined and are not a part of the past anyone would wish for. Mark Twain urges the Howellses to visit in fall, 1875, "before children's diseases get fashionable again, because they always play such hob with visiting arrangements." From Munich in 1879 he laments to Joe Twichell: "I work *every* day that some member of the family isn't sick. This does not give me a great deal of time, but I make the most of what I *do* get. . . . We thought our youngest child was dying, three days ago, but she is doing pretty well, now."[6] Susy, then four, had diphtheria in the spring of 1876, Clara, only three, a severe fever in the summer of 1877; Susy and Jean, barely two, were both down with scarlet fever in the spring of 1882, Susy with mumps (George Washington Cable had been confined in the Clemens house with them first) in March, 1884; Clara was very ill in October, Jean, probably with the first manifestations of epilepsy, in 1890.

Fewer childhood ills marked the Howellses' lives during that same period, probably because their children were somewhat older. Measles struck the two Howells children in 1881, and scarlet fever came upon John in 1884. Mark Twain lets himself go in sympathy and advice for Howells. "Money may desert you, friends forsake you, enemies grow indifferent to you, but the scarlet fever will be true to you, through thick & thin, till you be all saved or damned, down to the last one." He also passed on a tip picked up from Lily Warner that putting Vaseline on metal fixtures during the mandatory

5. *Ibid.*, II, 603, 604–605.
6. *Ibid.*, I, 107; Hill (ed.), *Mark Twain's Letters to His Publishers*, 110–111.

fumigation that followed scarlet fever could save hundreds of dollars in ruined metal fixtures. Howells called fumigation a "ridiculous incantation"; it went on in his house for seventy hours with brimstone and five hours thereafter. In the spring of 1884, Clemens filled almost seven pages of his notebook with names like Diphtheria Marsh, Influenza Smith, Rectum Jones, Convulsion Wheeler, "& last of all, the hero—Scrofula St. Augustine," apparently for a never-completed sketch. In August he made the notation: "I think we are only the microscopic trichina concealed in the blood of some vast creatures' veins, & that it is that vast creature whom God concerns himself about, & not us," which did become the thesis of the unpublished fantasy "Three Thousand Years Among the Microbes," written in 1905.[7]

Insofar as Howells and Clemens had the means to cope with these ills in ways then available and to provide assistance for their wives, they were better off than most families. Nevertheless, pregnancies and confinements, ordinary child care, respiratory ills of their own, and the increased care and anxiety from illnesses had adverse consequences on the health of both Livy Clemens and Elinor Howells. Neurasthenia was a general term given to "women sicknesses" of the times. Insufficiently understood even now, despite a considerable body of careful investigation, neurasthenia must in part be attributed to the general wasting effects of coping with illnesses of a physical kind in a harsh climate.[8]

With full acknowledgment of the love shared between each couple, one might say that both Howells and Mark Twain had bad luck with their wives. Livy's infirmities began with a fall suffered at sixteen that left her bedridden until a faith healer induced her to walk. Mark Twain's care and encouragement sustained the cure, but

7. Smith and Gibson (eds.), *Mark Twain–Howells Letters*, II, 460–464; William Dean Howells to Aurelia H. Howells, January 13, 1884, in Howells Papers. Robert Pack Browning, Michael B. Frank, and Lin Salamo (eds.), *Mark Twain's Notebooks & Journals* (3 vols. completed; Berkeley, 1979), III, 50–53, 56.

8. See F. G. Gosling, "American Nervousness: Medicine and Social Values in the Gilded Age, 1870–1900" (Ph.D. dissertation, University of Oklahoma, 1976), and John S. and Robin M. Haller, *The Physician and Sexuality in Victorian America* (Urbana, 1974).

she was never a vigorous woman who could keep pace with the physical energy Mark Twain possessed. From the first, he accepted her limitations, one consequence of which was to throw more of a burden on the friendships that went on largely outside the home. His devotion to Livy was manifest, and yet the persistence of her ills, like those of the children's, must have tried his patience. In the summer of 1882, he lamented the effects of Jean's scarlet fever, which interrupted his work and robbed him, so he wrote to Howells, of "the very most valuable 6 weeks of my entire life." His letters to Howells, though they often refer to specific as well as chronic conditions, contain few remarks like that of January, 1880, in which he refers to the desirability of their being "two husbands, so one could stay here & give the medicine."[9]

While Livy was still going through pregnancies and childbirths, there was scarcely a period of six months without some disabling illnesses.[10] Her confinements usually lasted a month or more. A near miscarriage accompanied Clara's birth in March, 1874. In August a trip to visit Mark Twain's mother in Fredonia rendered her "dreadfully broken down." In February, 1875, she must lie abed all day; Mark Twain's own sickness forced him to be in bed for the first time in twenty-one years, causing him to write, "How little confirmed invalids appreciate their advantages." In June and July Livy is "only tolerably well." In September both have terrible colds. In October they might visit the Howellses if Livy is strong enough. In April, 1876, she is in bed with sore throat and rheumatism. In June Mark Twain writes for her "from the habitual sick bed." Abroad from 1878 to 1879, she remained well except for a sore throat contracted aboard ship and a near collapse on returning home. Through most of 1880 her condition was periodically alarming, with confinement following Jean's birth in July. The year 1881 shows no mention of illnesses, but the scarlet fever of 1882 brought Livy down again. In 1883 Mark Twain mentions "many and rather alarming distempers,"

9. Smith and Gibson (eds.), *Mark Twain–Howells Letters*, II, 460; I, 288.

10. Livy's illnesses are mentioned on the following pages in Smith and Gibson (eds.), *Mark Twain–Howells Letters*: I, 16, 22, 58, 62, 66, 67, 88, 90, 95, 103, 108, 129, 141, 286, 318, 324, 406, 408, 432, 435; II, 496, 506, 511, 616, 623, 645.

which keep her confined to bed for weeks. In 1884 she had to contend with *his* being in the dental chair for ten days, followed by another spell of her own sickness in the fall. So it went through these years, relieved, to be sure, by periods of normal health, and grimly taking a new turn with an attack on her eyes in February, 1889, which persisted throughout the year. In May, 1891, the Clemenses left for Europe, largely because "Mrs. Clemens must try some baths somewhere."

All the while, Mark Twain's own health, while it did not continue unblemished as in the twenty-one years preceding 1874, was often so hearty as to be "ridiculous." That did not prevent him from exaggerating his own occasional illnesses, as in July, 1882, when scarlet fever struck the family. He wrote a Hannibal friend, "Next, I myself was stretched on the bed with three diseases at once, and all of them fatal." He was ill four weeks straight in midwinter 1875–1876, occasionally struck down with colds, "half dead with malaria" in September, 1882, down with gout in 1884, "in the doctor's hands" in the summer of 1884, "the first summer which I have lost," and almost disabled with rheumatism in his right arm by 1891. A letter to Fred J. Hall, head of his publishing company, from Berlin in 1891 concludes: "I must stop—my arm is howling."[11] Nevertheless, he enjoyed vastly better health than did Livy, as Howells enjoyed compared with Elinor.

Justin Kaplan summarizes the family's chronic ill health and Mark Twain's reaction to it. "Susy was to die of meningitis; Jean's pattern of physical and emotional disturbance was diagnosed finally as epilepsy; Clara had nervous breakdowns, and Livy had hyperthyroid heart disease." He comments that "in the early 1880s, even though he often felt he was running a hospital in his home, he was still able to find a kind of humor in it all." By the later years of his life, Kaplan adds, "he had developed, with considerable justification, a sense of horrible nemesis."[12]

11. Paine (ed.), *Mark Twain's Letters*, I, 423. Smith and Gibson (eds.), *Mark Twain–Howells Letters*, I, 118–19; Hill (ed.), *Mark Twain's Letters to His Publishers* (Berkeley, 1967), 157, 179, 285.

12. Kaplan, *Mr. Clemens and Mark Twain*, 247. Mark Twain's illnesses are mentioned on the following pages in Smith and Gibson (eds.), *Mark Twain–*

Some of Elinor Howells' earliest health problems were attributed to nerves; her later disabilities are attributed to some injury to the spine, and throughout her life a principal manifestation of her ill health was that of losing weight, seemingly a foreshadowing of Winny's fatal condition. By 1865 Howells notes that while Elinor has never been sick in Venice, she "has grown very delicate in the Venetian climate." In March, 1873, he found Elinor's health improved, but she "went into Boston in the horse-cars for the first time *in eight months.*" In March, 1875, they went south for her health, at least as far as Bethlehem, Pennsylvania, since they had spent the summer in Newport and found it very helpful to her condition.[13] The visits between the families were curtailed or put off as much by Elinor's illnesses as by Livy's. In fact, visiting throughout their lives was predominantly Howells' visiting with the Clemenses or Clemens' visiting the Howells family in Cambridge or Boston, partially because of the reluctance of both wives to leave the children and the assumption that mothers were the ones to remain at home. Then, too, Mark Twain's travels made it possible for him to stop in at the Howellses more often alone. Nevertheless, the visits between families were relatively rare; the common expectation of one or the other visitng is

Howells Letters: I, 118–19, 417; II, 474, 483, 495–96, 637. Smith and Gibson observe of Mark Twain: "His teeth, like his body generally, were unusually sound; on the whole he had very little trouble with them" (II, 486 n. 1).

13. References to Elinor Howells' health problems are from *W. D. Howells: Selected Letters*, I, 146, 149, 218–19; II, 20, 99, 245, 281. Letters in the Howells Papers, Houghton Library, indicate Howells' worries about her being down to 82 pounds shortly after their marriage. In 1875 he notes that she "easily turns the scale at 65." A letter from him to William C. Howells, June 20, 1875, reveals "She has been more than usually feeble this summer, and has had almost constantly a pain in her side"; Arms *et al.*, *W. D. Howells: Selected Letters*, I, 218–19; Arms and Lohmann (eds.), *W. D. Howells: Selected Letters*, I, 20, 92. Howells wrote to William C. Howells, March 7, 1875: "I feel that I need the change, for though my cough is about gone, I have no *tone*, and can't keep up to my work. Elinor commonly has a break-down at this time of year, which we hope to avert by going into different air." Earlier, on January 9, he had written to his father, "We have had a very full week, as to society; I was out four times and Elinor twice, and we had invitations to parties or dinner every night in the week, I believe." The demands made on Elinor to care for three children under twelve amid many social obligations may help explain her breakdowns.

that he will be arriving alone and his stay will be brief from the necessity of getting back home.

In 1880 Elinor's spinal condition is mentioned for the first time. In response to this apparently new condition, Mark Twain wrote directly to her on August 17, 1880: "O dear, I never imagined you were drifting into invalidity as a settled thing. I think we both always looked upon you as a sort of Leyden jar . . . or whatever that thing is which holds lightning & mighty forces captive in a vessel which is apparently much too frail for its office, & yet after all isn't." Howells wrote, "She never *does* quite go to pieces, but it always looks like a thing that might happen." In January, 1881, he writes of her "habitual debility indefinitely intensified," and with the coming of Winny's illness and the extra care it entailed, the times of her being incapacitated or severely fatigued increased. Like Livy, Elinor seems to have enjoyed better health in Europe, and the winter after their return in 1883 was without incident until John's scarlet fever at the end of the year. Howells himself, except for his own collapse in 1881, was seemingly invulnerable to ordinary ills, though he notes in December, 1885, that having been working very hard, he is feeling tired of work, "almost for the first time." Increasingly, invitations to visit the Clemenses are put aside because of Elinor's or Winny's health. After one visit alone, Howells wrote: "You are an awfully good fellow to talk with. I wish you were handier." Three years later, on July 21, 1889, in declining another of Mark Twain's invitations, Howells quietly notes Elinor's growing dependency: "I can see how my wife depends upon me almost momently. I have denied myself a great deal; I would rather see and talk with you than any other man in the world, outside my own blood." [14]

It is a melancholy chronicle when the often vibrant relationship of Howells and Mark Twain is coupled with the sadder facts of their family lives. Although the two men first met in 1869, the first family visit did not come about until March, 1875, in Hartford, and the first visit of Livy to Boston in October. Thereafter, the family visits are relatively infrequent, though greatly enjoyed whether in Hartford or Boston. The last visit before the Clemenses went to Europe in

14. Smith and Gibson (eds.), *Mark Twain–Howells Letters*, I, 323, 328, 347; II, 545, 550, 607.

1891, marking the end of their years in Hartford, was of the Clemenses in Boston in March. In April, Elinor was not well and was staying, as Winny had stayed, in a place of rest in Auburndale.

The personal darknesses of these years are magnified by even as partial a record as this over a period of some twenty years. There were also years of great and satisfying achievements, as personal as John's entering Harvard and Susy's entering Bryn Mawr, and as professional as the completion by both men of some of their best works. The course of their lives, in which illness and aging were inescapable, affected the darkening tone in the works of both as they passed fifty. But in addition, their contemplation of the world around them, particularly its economic and political aspects, led very directly to the darker tones to be found in their later works.

The shift of tone is marked in both writers. The comic of *Innocents Abroad* and *Roughing It* does not disappear from *Connecticut Yankee* or *Pudd'nhead Wilson*, but the underlying seriousness of the latter two sets them clearly apart. Howells' early work was so focused on novels of courting and marriage as to ill prepare his contemporary readers for *Annie Kilburn*, *A Hazard of New Fortunes*, and other social protest novels that dominated his later fiction. The murmurings and misunderstandings of rather dullish young men and somewhat more engaging young women were central to Howells' early fiction, and the Clemens household embraced them as fully as did his other readers. Although he continued to write novels of that sort after 1879, that year and the publication of *The Lady of the Aroostook* brought such novels to the peak of their limited perfectibility. Clemens read installments of it aloud to his family during their European trip of 1878 and 1879. The tale of an up-country Maine girl who finds herself the only woman on board a ship bound for Europe and her subsequent adventures in Venice was well-suited to the interests of American tourists abroad. Clemens' first mention of reading the story places it with the end of the "forlornities" of first arriving in Munich, November 15, 1878. He had brought the tribe from Rome, himself, he claimed, and he found such desolation and inconvenience and grimness on first arrival to make him consider departing immediately for southern France. The next morning, however, the "horribilest . . . most unendurable place" had transformed itself, and within a day or two provided a domestic scene ideally suited to the reading of a Howells novel. "So we gathered around the lamp, after supper, with our beer & my pipe, & in a condition of grateful snugness tackled the new magazines. I read your new story aloud, amid thunders of applause."[15]

Two months later, the reading has progressed about halfway through the novel, and the response of "we three" is that he is "out-Howellsing Howells." What follows is an incisive understanding of and admiration for Howellsian realism. "It is all such truth—truth to the life; everywhere your pen falls it leaves a photograph . . . only *you* see people & their ways & their insides & outsides as they *are*, & make them talk as they *do* talk. I think you are the very greatest artist in these tremendous mysteries that ever lived." The passage ends with an even more elaborate compliment. "You ain't a weed, but an oak; you ain't a summer-house, but a cathedral. In that day *I* shall still be in the Cyclopedias, too—thus: 'Mark Twain; history & occupation unknown—but he was personally acquainted with Howells.'" He next writes, "Confound that February number, I wish it would fetch along The Lady of the Aroostook."[16]

There is no reason to question Mark Twain's praise or the judgment behind it. The novel is still regarded by most critics as the best of its kind Howells wrote. And though Mark Twain did not observe it as the end of a line, his equally enthusiastic response to *A Modern Instance* indicates his acceptance of the deepening seriousness of Howells' novels. Again, it is Howells' ability to convey reality that excites Clemens, though most of his long response is about the difference between Howells' writing and his reading of it. "You *can* read, if you want to, but you *don't* read worth a damn." Howells' delivery as a lecturer was probably not much different from his reading to his friends. A review from a Des Moines paper in 1899 observed that "he has no tricks at all, but reads in a rather doubtful and tentative manner."[17] But in declaring one kind of truth about his friend's art, Mark Twain was provoked to consider the matter fur-

15. *Ibid.*, I, 240.
16. *Ibid.*, I, 245–46, 250.
17. *Ibid.*, 407; Des Moines *Leader*, November 2, 1899, in Howells Papers.

ther. In the end he concluded that Howells' humor and satire are so subtle that a reader needs the kind of pause that reading provides in order "to let the things soak home."

In the midst of lavish praise of *A Woman's Reason*, both a more serious and technically more ambitious novel than the courting ones, Mark Twain catches himself. "We—but *we* ALWAYS think the last one is the best. And why shouldn't it be? Practice helps." When *The Rise of Silas Lapham* appeared, Clemens was beginning a four-month lecture tour with George Washington Cable. Howells attended the reading in Boston, heard portions of *Huckleberry Finn*, and marveled at Mark Twain's artistry. In May Mark Twain shared the program with Howells and others for the American Copyright League in New York. Howells read from *Indian Summer* and *The Minister's Charge*, the one a nostalgic love story set in Europe, the other a novel charged with Howells' growing social concerns. "Heiliger Gott!" Mark Twain wrote later, "but it was good reading . . . Who taught you to read? . . . But you couldn't read worth a damn ⟨when I heard you⟩ a few years ago." Mark Twain's amused delight with Howells' newly-acquired reading ability came at about the same time as his beginning to read *The Rise of Silas Lapham*, "as great & fine & strong & beautiful as Mrs. Clemens had already proclaimed it to be." Livy expressed her belief that the novel "showed more the moral struggles of mortals than any thing Mr. Howells has ever done before." Of *A Hazard of New Fortunes*, the novel that more than any other expresses Howells' criticism of American capitalism, Mark Twain said, "It is a great book; but of course what I prefer in it is the high art by which it is made to preach its great sermon without seeming to take sides or preach at all."[18]

The sermon is not far different from that which is to be found in *A Connecticut Yankee in King Arthur's Court*, almost the last of Mark Twain's books to combine successfully the powers of his fancy, his storytelling genius, and his indignation toward human failings. "Well, my book is written—let it go," he wrote Howells in September, 1889. "But if it were only to write over again there wouldn't

18. Smith and Gibson (eds.), *Mark Twain–Howells Letters*, I, 440; II, 527, 531, 630.

be so many things left out. They burn in me; & they keep multiplying & multiplying; but now they can't ever be said. And besides, they would require a library—& a pen warmed-up in hell." Howells agreed. "It's a mighty great book, and it makes my heart burn and melt."[19]

Most of the things that were burning within both Howells and Mark Twain can be brought together within the categories of economics, politics, justice, religion, and the nature of man. That leaves little out except the natural world, to which both men were extremely sensitive, and which was also being threatened by man and his supposed needs, his actual greed. Much of Mark Twain's offhand indignation surfaced in *The Gilded Age*, the book that had launched him as a novelist in 1874. But it is characteristic of Mark Twain in this earlier period that *The Gilded Age* did not provoke other books similarly satirical of American society, but rather, temporarily focused his attention on capitalizing on the character of Colonel Sellers.

The preoccupation with Colonel Sellers was in part because of his continuing fascination for his brother Orion. A part of Mark Twain admired the innocence and hope that Orion put into his various enterprises, for it was a part of his own character and of the American character. But admiration gave way to vexed amusement and amusement to sympathy and pity and ultimately to despair. Howells had a similarly improvident brother, less engaging in his failure and penury than Orion, but capable of being considered at times as the product of a system that both encouraged and victimized certain kinds of economic failures. His letters to his family are almost as full of references to Sam's unsuccessful life and the assistance he exacted from his successful brother as Mark Twain's correspondence is with references to Orion. He did not choose who was to be his brother, he wrote Aurelia, else he surely would never have chosen Sam. Yet he had been worrying about him before he left Ohio in 1860 and was still doing so as both were becoming old men. At the end of a long recital to Howells of Orion's feckless career

19. *Ibid.*, II, 613, 616.

from political orator to writer to columnist to proofreader to chicken farmer to lawyer to lecturer to reformer to boardinghouse keeper to religionist, Clemens concludes, "Poor old Methuselah, how did he manage to stand it so long?"[20]

Howells was spared the petty vexations that came upon Clemens from Orion's borrowings and various ventures and chronic unsuccess, but he seemed to respond more sensitively than Clemens to Orion's plight. Mark Twain, on the other hand, set aside the realities of American economic life more readily than did Howells, though Howells spoke for both when he acknowledged to Henry James in 1888, "I should hardly like to trust pen and ink with all the audacity of my social ideas." Faced with the economic chance world that he saw all around him, Howells' conscience did not let him rest easy in his own comfort, and his writings of the late eighties and nineties are dominated by his concern for social and economic problems. It may seem odd to read of the Howellses visiting the Andrew Carnegies in New York in 1906 and expressing sympathy for Carnegie: "So long as the competitive conditions endure, sorrowfulness like his must continue."[21] But it is consistent with the impulse fifteen years earlier that established his brief connection with *The Cosmopolitan*, whose masthead bore the slogan "From every man according to his ability; to everyone according to his needs."

The workings of the economic chance world became the central concern of Howells' major fiction from 1885 on. *The Rise of Silas Lapham* depicted the conflict between matter and spirit in one of its simpler forms, the choice of spiritual well-being over material success that constituted Silas' rise. From that novel forward, the subject is rarely absent from Howells' fiction. In the 1880s, Howells' novels became increasingly serious in depicting a basically capitalistic society in which the accumulation of goods depended on chance, exertion of an individual's power, and exploitation of others. The names of the most powerful of these novels have a quaint ring today for even those somewhat acquainted with Howells: *Annie Kilburn*,

20. *Ibid.*, I, 257.
21. Leitz (ed.), *W. D. Howells: Selected Letters*, III, 231; Fischer and Lohmann (eds.), *W. D. Howells: Selected Letters*, V, 197.

named after the rich Bostonian woman who tries to move beyond simplehearted charities as a way of improving the lot of the poor; *The Quality of Mercy*, about an embezzler both responsible for his defalcation and driven to it by the society whose comforts and respect he too much seeks; *The Son of Royal Langbrith*, like the previous novel, one which depicts the hidden corruption behind a facade of business respectability; and *The World of Chance*, in which Howells' own struggles for recognition and financial success as a writer are used to illustrate the workings of the economic chance world within the arts.

The best of these, *A Hazard of New Fortunes*, has as its center a streetcar strike in New York, based directly on a strike occurring at the time, but also standing for the increased number of violent conflicts between capital and labor since the Civil War. The capitalist, Dryfoos, who occupies a central position in the story, provides the money upon which almost everyone else depends: Basil March, the Howells-like figure who has left the insurance business to write for the magazine Dryfoos finances; Fulkerson, the ambitious publisher of the magazine; Dryfoos' son who has rejected his father's business in order to work among the poor; the fashionable artist who lives on commissions from the rich; and a number of characters who depend on the magazine for their livelihood. The story superbly develops the doctrine of complicity, enunciated by the Reverend Peck in an earlier novel, by which each person is bound in trust to every other. It is, Howells pointed out, what the Sermon on the Mount put into practice, and Christian socialism comes as close as any term to defining Howells' belief. Surrounded by the economic facts and human behavior of the American city in the 1890s, Howells' characters all suffer. Father and son are alienated, and the son dies, accidentally shot in the violence of the strike after a quarrel with his father. The old socialist printer is clubbed down by the police. The wealthy woman who has shared young Dryfoos' social convictions joins a religious order. The Dryfoos family retreats to Europe, the elder Dryfoos' grief over the loss of a son somewhat assuaged by the marriage of a daughter into European nobility. The Marches, separately and together, ponder the events and arrive at no conclusions. The secure comforts of religion are denied them, the likelihood of political or social amelioration is questioned, and a stark fatalism hovers at the edge of Basil's marginal belief that somehow the world works toward some undiscovered good.

Ultimately, Mark Twain's faith was even less. Dazzled as he was by man's inventiveness displayed during his lifetime, he came to distrust even that. Formal religion had never offered much to him except an object of satire and a source of as much harm as good. His late stories and essays deny any cosmic purpose. Nothing in Howells' work is as stark as the apocalyptic ending of *A Connecticut Yankee* with its horrifying slaughter made possible by Yankee ingenuity and with its concluding implication that no just and lasting society can be built on corpses. Clemens' reservations about both democracy and aristocracy moved toward scant faith in government's power to control the destructive potential of mankind. Although there are changes and inconsistencies in most of his political views, he seems to have maintained a distinction between a republic and a democracy, the crucial difference lying in his distrust of universal suffrage. The mindless mobocracy was no more to his liking than an oppressive aristocracy. And though he could take up Edward Bellamy's *Looking Backward* as "the latest and best of all the Bibles" in 1888, his more pessimistic view of man's prospects is that that Bible is no better than all the others. In 1897, writing from England in a mood of indifference that he assures Howells will pass, he surveys the difficulties attending the survival of existing republics and adds, "If I were not a hermit I would go the House every day & see those people scuffle over it and blether about the brotherhood of the human race."[22]

In reviewing *A Connecticut Yankee*, Howells seemingly passed over the horror of the book's conclusion. "It all ends," he wrote, "with the Boss's proclamation of the Republic after Arthur's death, and his destruction of the whole chivalry of England by electricity." The review is much taken up with assuring the reader of the "gigantic jollity" of the work, easier to do in his time than any time after World War I. In a later review of *Joan of Arc*, however, he refers to *A*

22. Smith and Gibson (eds.), *Mark Twain–Howells Letters*, II, 579, 665.

Connecticut Yankee with heavy irony. "Faith has ceased to be, but we have some lively hopes of electricity." In the earlier review he had written: "It makes us glad of our republic and our epoch; but it does not flatter us into a fond content with them; there are passages in which we see that the noble of Arthur's day, who fattened on the blood and sweat of his bondmen, is one in essence with the capitalist of Mr. Harrison's day who grows rich on the labor of underpaid wagemen."[23] Howells placed *Connecticut Yankee* at the top of Mark Twain's works, in part because of its forthright identification of capitalist ills.

Beneath Howells' quiet manner is a recognition of a barrenness in modern culture that Matthew Arnold seized upon in lecturing in Boston in November, 1883. Arnold flattered Howells greatly by calling attention to how well he conveyed "a life of hideousness and immense ennui" in his portrayals of New England characters.[24] His reference was to *The Lady of the Aroostook*; how much more pointed it might have been if he had drawn upon Howells' depiction of bogus and impoverished spiritualism in *The Undiscovered Country*, the novel that appeared just after *The Lady of the Aroostook*, or had anticipated the even grimmer depiction of material and spiritual poverty in the rural New England of *The Landlord at Lion's Head* or in the New York street scenes of *A Hazard of New Fortunes*.

Although both Howells and Mark Twain moved toward socialism as a better basis for a just society, neither had the confidence, either in its arrival or its promise, to align with active socialist reformers, though Howells did contribute support for the National Socialist presidential candidate, Eugene Debs. Both were capitalists in fact, and their distress with capitalism was in part the distress of an investor whose stock has fallen. Howells' holdings at his death showed comparatively little in market stocks and bonds; the bulk of investments were in Liberty Bonds, doubtless acquired during the period when everyone was swept into support of World War I. Mark Twain's passion for speculation was extreme, an aspect of his character ac-

23. W. D. Howells, Review of *A Connecticut Yankee in King Arthur's Court*, in *My Mark Twain*, 127, 134, 124–25.

24. Smith and Gibson (eds.), *Mark Twain–Howells Letters*, I, 449–50 n. 2.

knowledged by both hostile critics and ardent admirers, the cause fixed upon the insecurities of his youth, the boom-and-bust character of his times, the need for social respectability necessary to his ambitions. But Mark Twain was seldom attracted to purely financial speculation. He was more stimulated by what such miracles as electric lighting and industrial machinery could do to lift the burden of grinding hard labor and by the way new products and inventions displayed man's power to imagine and fabricate. Anyone who looks at the Paige typesetting machine, now in the basement of Mark Twain's Hartford house, has a better understanding of how it led him to ruin. Whatever its limitations as a practical means of setting type, it is an elegant machine, the model as precisely and intricately turned out as, say, *A Connecticut Yankee*, and with fewer excrescences and unnecessary parts. When it worked it could turn out such a volume of type as to lead Mark Twain to challenge all other typesetting machines in face-to-face competition. It is laborsaving machinery, he tells Howells, that "has made Labor great & powerful," and labor, being human, fails to appreciate it, somewhat as capital fails to acknowledge how labor, despite its ignorance, has educated itself into being a powerful force in the economic system.[25]

Mark Twain's passion for justice was both planted in him earlier and sustained longer than his specific interests in economics and politics. For long periods in his life, except as politicians crossed his path or were useful to his fiction, he was apolitical. His friendship with Howells often had the effect of stirring up his interest in politics, as in their opposed support of Cleveland and Blaine in the campaign of 1884. The only politician that inspired Mark Twain's great ardor was Ulysses S. Grant, and then less as president than as general, and less as either than as a figure to whom great injustice had been done. Grant's tragedy as president is the backdrop for *The Gilded Age*. His impoverished condition as a former president seemed painfully unjust to Mark Twain, and it gave him one of the great opportunities in his life to redress in a substantial way an equally substantial wrong. And having worked the miracle, as he

25. *Ibid.*, II, 597.

might have said, of putting Grant's *Memoirs* before a huge body of readers, there were no miracles left to stave off the cancer that came upon Grant as he was finishing the work. The practical sense of Mark Twain permitted him what satisfaction Providence—or a shrewd analysis of the market—had left available: the vulgar one of launching his own publishing company with the most profitable book to that time in American publishing, and the sentimental one of leaving Grant's widow well provided for. Grant was dead, with only the slender written record to stand for vague but powerful memories of a hero degraded.

For Howells, the climactic event of these years of growing discontent with the comfort he enjoyed was his support of the anarchists executed for the Haymarket Square bombing. His feelings were aroused not by the abstract issue of capital against labor or even by the specific violences breaking out in Homestead, Pennsylvania, and at the C.B.&Q. Railroad (in which he had stock) or at the McCormick Reaper plant in Chicago, which precipitated the Haymarket violence. Rather, he was moved by the obvious injustice that attended the rounding up of men damned by their foreign ancestry, their working-class associations, their courage to protest, and their want of means to defend themselves. The ugliness of police action against striking workers was nothing new, and anarchist writings and actions were a part of the larger struggle between capital and labor. Even though he enjoyed the security that wealth and position gave, Howells strongly sympathized with the laboring classes, too often denied justice in their struggles to better their conditions. The protest against the shooting of strikers in Chicago took place the evening of May 4, 1886, in Haymarket Square. Newspaper reports of the gathering called attention to speeches by several anarchists, but the speeches did not directly precipitate violence. As the crowd began to disperse, a bomb was thrown, and one policeman was killed and a number of others in the crowd fatally wounded. Eight suspects were rounded up and indicted for murder. In the trial that followed, all defendants were found guilty and their convictions upheld by the Illinois Supreme Court in November, six months after the event. One of the accused committed suicide, one was given a prison sentence, two had their sentences commuted to life imprisonment. The other four, Albert Parsons, Adolph Fischer, August Spies, and George Engle, were hanged on November 11, 1887.

During the period of original sentencing and appeal Howells wrote to jurist Roger Pryor who was taking the accused men's appeal to the Supreme Court. When the Court rejected the appeal, Howells, despite the worsening of Winny's condition, wrote a public letter to the New York *Tribune*, stating that he had petitioned the governor of Illinois to commute the death sentences of the men and urging others to join in his plea. "The court," he pointed out, "simply affirmed the legality of the forms under which the Chicago court proceeded . . . it by no means approved the principle of punishing them because of their frantic opinions, for a crime which they were not shown to have committed."[26] There are no extant letters between Howells and Mark Twain from August 22, 1887, to March 31, 1888, so we do not know what may have been Mark Twain's reaction to Howells' act. It was a courageous act, to be sure, but the original letter was buried deep in a column of type, and the angry responses it aroused appeared in small spaces in a scattering of sources. The attention was focused on the anarchists themselves, and the newspaper stories spared little in emphasizing the enormity of anarchistic acts. It was not until 1893 that Governor Altgeld of Illinois pardoned the two who had been sent to prison. Probably the events did not register on Mark Twain as strongly as upon Howells. The year following the original bombing found both of them preoccupied, first with misunderstandings about the Sellers play (a production scheduled for May 24 was apparently postponed), the death of Howells' sister Victoria in December, and Clemens' general involvement in his publishing company and the Paige typesetting machine. The *Library of Humor* was also on their hands, and in addition to his writing fiction, Howells was editing a book, *The Library of Universal Adventures by Sea and Land* with Thomas Sergeant Perry.

Nevertheless, the sparse correspondence we do have strength-

26. William Dean Howells to New York *Tribune*, November 4, 1887, in Kenneth Lynn, *William Dean Howells: An American Life* (New York, 1971), 290–91.

ens a belief that Mark Twain and Howells were in harmony in their radical political and economic beliefs. In his letter of August, 1887, the last to Howells until March of the next year, Mark Twain talks about the changes "age makes in a man while he sleeps." Having just reread Carlyle's *French Revolution*, he recognized himself as "a Sansculotte!—And not a pale, characterless Sansculotte, but a Marat." Noting other changes in himself, he voices approval of Howells' discovery of Tolstoy, the literary passion that came upon Howells in the eighties and that most confirmed his radical social views. Clemens says he has not got him, Tolstoy, in focus yet, though he has Browning. The letter with which the correspondence resumes is entirely concerned with Mark Twain's speech about the Knights of Labor before the Hartford Club in March, 1886, and mentions the anarchist pamphlets that Howells had sent him. How-ells' reply expresses his great satisfaction with Mark Twain's speeches and with a related essay that he had sent. The final crisis of Winny's death, March 3, two days after Howells' birthday, must have curtailed the correspondence of this period as well as the re-sponse Mark Twain might have made to Howells' appeal of the pre-vious fall. What Mark Twain had to say about these matters is in *A Connecticut Yankee*, a product of those same years. He thanked Howells for approving what he had said there about the French Revo-lution, "next to the 4th of July & its results, it was the noblest & the holiest thing & the most precious that ever happened in this earth." [27]

The views Mark Twain expressed in an outpouring of unpub-lished writings in the decade preceding and following the turn of the century find their best-known expression in *The Mysterious Stranger* (begun in 1897) and *The Man That Corrupted Hadleyburg* (1900). Among the unpublished works, two dark strains appear. One is the dream of disaster in which Clemens' struggles with his finances and Susy's death are to be numbered among animating forces. In *Which Was It?* Mark Twain established a Hannibal-like setting in which the central character has achieved not only wealth and fame but an un-blemished record for personal probity. In the course of the narrative, this figure becomes a counterfeiter, a murderer, and a monstrous

27. Smith and Gibson (eds.), *Mark Twain–Howells Letters*, II, 595, 613.

hypocrite concealing from almost everyone but himself the enormity of his sins. The slave, Jasper, finds him out, and a long and effectively written scene shows the Mark Twain central figure forced into becoming Jasper's slave when no one is around and into reverting to the southern slaveowner when company comes. The other dark preoccupation is with man's inconsequence in a vast, uncaring universe. A major vehicle for expressing these views of man as microbe, developed at great length in the spring of 1905, is "Three Thousand Years Among the Microbes," in which a cholera germ is the chief character. One of the other characters, a yellow-fever germ, pronounces, "We live in a strange and unaccountable world; our birth is a mystery, our little life is a mystery and a trouble, we pass and are seen no more; all is mystery, mystery, mystery; we know not whence we came, nor why."[28]

Advancing age helped intensify both Howells' and Mark Twain's darker views, but both had experienced earlier in life the losses and anguish of sicknesses and deaths, the vanity of human endeavors, and the agonizing question of their or any man's purpose in the scheme of things. They were not pessimists by nature, but pessimistic as any human must be who recognizes the truth of Sophoclean tragedy, which counts no mortal happy until he passes the limits of this life free from pain.

28. Tuckey (ed.), *Which Was the Dream?*, 454.

Nine

Honors and Respectabilities

Why should Howells and Clemens not have been friends when they always seemed to be praising each other's work? And by the standards each was so fond of proclaiming—fidelity to truth and reality—isn't there some fudging in the almost uniform praise each gave the other? Howells can scarcely be faulted for recognizing early the genius of Mark Twain and having a part in seeing it realize itself in American writing. Mark Twain's popularity has continued into our time without much diminishing.[1] The reservations academic critics had toward Mark Twain during his lifetime are still to be found among academic critics today, but even so, his works still generate a large body of criticism as well as numerous editions and reprintings.

But what of Clemens' respect for Howells? Every Howells work, Clemens wrote his friend, seemed to be better than the last. And yet, even the best of Howells' many books is scarcely known to readers today. His reputation is kept alive principally by a band of scholars who find his long life and great productivity an obvious subject for research. Even the negative image of Howells has receded into

1. See Louis J. Budd, *Our Mark Twain: The Making of His Public Personality* (Philadelphia, 1983), for a thorough study of Mark Twain's public personality and the hold it continued to have on a large public.

the past. Van Wyck Brooks interviewed him in 1909 and wrote that he had never surprised anybody, thrilled anybody, shocked anybody. Nevertheless he was for Brooks one of the creators of the repressive atmosphere Brooks castigates in *The Ordeal of Mark Twain* in 1920 and against which writers of the twenties could rebel. Forty years later the edge is gone, and Brooks's 1959 book on Howells' life and work endorses Howells with Kipling's praise as "the father of a multitude of heirs who have inherited his treasures but forgotten the paternity."[2]

Still, the fact remains that at the heart of this remarkable friendship is a recognition of each one's claim to more than momentary greatness. That our own public judgment seems to differ from theirs is not so much a measure of Mark Twain's erring vision, clouded by his personal attachment to Howells, but of our collective rejection of much that Howells stood for and a rejection, too, of the life he described in his fiction. To be sure, Mark Twain's judgment was clouded; it is a privilege of being and having friends not to have to judge always by the merciless light of one's clearest intellect. As a headnote to Chapter 11 of *Pudd'nhead Wilson*, Mark Twain wrote: "There are three infallible ways of pleasing an author, and the three form a rising scale of compliment: 1, to tell him you have read one of his books; 2, to tell him you have read all of his books; 3, to ask him to let you read the manuscript of his forthcoming book. No. 1 admits you to his respect; No. 2 admits you to his admiration, No. 3 carries you clear into his heart."[3]

Part of the bond between Howells and Mark Twain was that both were displaying parts of themselves in print that could be responded to with appreciation and affection. And yet that very fact might have been turned quite the other way. The number of writers of fiction that Mark Twain did not like probably exceeded the number for which he had a strong affection. Those he disliked included a good many writers—Jane Austen, George Eliot, Henry James—for whom Howells had great admiration. Distinctive among literary critics,

2. Van Wyck Brooks, *Howells: His Life and World* (New York, 1959), 287.
3. Samuel Clemens [Mark Twain], *Pudd'nhead Wilson* (New York, 1955), 106.

Howells had far more receptiveness to traditional greatness and generosity to writers—foreign authors and young novelists among them. Nevertheless, among the half-dozen American humorists and the larger number of regional writers, none attracted his attention as Mark Twain did. There is some mystery, as there probably should be, in the attraction that brings two people into a good marriage or a close friendship. Some mystery, too, try as literary critics will to dispel it, in what constitutes a good book, or even what constitutes a good book for a particular person. It is possible that Mark Twain and Howells might have become jealous of each other's work, developing into literary snipers rather than friends. One reason they did not was that the times and circumstances allowed each of them ample room in which to operate. They became wealthy and successful authors by following literary lines that are actually quite dissimilar. Their personal friendship made the occasions when these lines crossed sources of interest and opportunity rather than friction. And all along the way, sufficient recognition of the achievements of each made it possible to be generous to the other, even if their temperaments had not been inclined that way.

Within their lifetimes, each received the kind of ultimate recognition that made it possible for Howells, with some amusement, to realize he was "the dean of American letters," and for Mark Twain, with some sadness at the passing of those days when it might really have counted, to know that he was "a prince." We have looked at the course of friendship amid adversity; here it is considered in relation to the honors and respectabilities that accumulated around the two friends.

Recognition as writers stood highest with both Howells and Mark Twain as signs of their worth. They may have prized it more because precise recognition of their worth as authors was mixed with recognition of other abilities and identities: for Howells, editor and critic, for Mark Twain, humorist and lecturer. No doubt Mark Twain responded favorably to Howells' review of *Innocents Abroad* because the *Atlantic Monthly* was seriously interested in literature, and a review there meant recognition of one's standing as an author. Otherwise, *Innocents Abroad* was but another successful subscription book and an affirmation of what Mark Twain already knew: that he could make a successful career as a lecturer and the substance of his lectures would add to his reputation as a literary humorist.

By the seventies, settled in marriage and pursuing writing seriously—Kate Leary mentions the regularity with which he set aside afternoon hours for his writing—being a humorist and lecturer was not enough for Mark Twain, and at times was even the wrong thing. In a long letter to Howells on October 19, 1875, thanking him for the review of his *Sketches*, Mark Twain made a distinction between newspaper notices and a critic's response. "They gratify a body, but they always leave a small pang behind in the shape of a fear that the critic's good words could not safely be depended upon as *authority*." Later in the letter he voices, as Mrs. Clemens' fear, what must have been a fear of his own. "You see, the thing that gravels her is that I am so persistently glorified as a mere buffoon, as if that entirely covered my case—which she denies with venom."[4]

A letter to Orion on March 23, 1878, beginning "Every man must *learn* his trade," acquaints his brother with some of the actualities of being a professional writer. "Nine years ago I mapped out my 'Journey to Heaven.' I discussed it with literary friends whom I could trust to keep it to themselves. I gave it a deal of thought, from time to time. After a year or more I wrote it up. It was not a success. Five years ago I wrote it again, altering the plan. That MS is at my elbow now. It was a considerable improvement on the first attempt, but still it wouldn't do—last year and year before I talked frequently with Howells about the subject, and he kept urging me to do it again."[5] Mark Twain is using his own example to illustrate the foolishness of Orion's trying to "write up hell so it will stand printing." But the general lesson that appears here, and in many of his letters to Howells, is his respect for the hard work and experience that go into being a writer of genuine excellence.

Critical response to Mark Twain's books during most of his lifetime did not give him very clear signs of his literary worth. If we

4. Mary Lawton, *A Lifetime with Mark Twain: The memories of Kate Leary, for thirty years his faithful and devoted servant* (New York, 1925), 11–18; Smith and Gibson (eds.), *Mark Twain–Howells Letters*, I, 107.

5. Paine (ed.), *Mark Twain's Letters*, I, 323.

accord *Huckleberry Finn*, written in the very prime of his life and career, first place among his works, the critical acclaim it received at the time was typically ambiguous.[6] The circumstances of Howells' commitment to *Harpers* probably kept him from reviewing it. Thomas Sergeant Perry, Howells' friend and collaborator on an anthology of adventure stories, reviewed it for the *Century* magazine, and Mark Twain could not have asked for a more learned reviewer nor for a more justly qualified but favorable review. The book's prevailing virtue for Perry was its truthfulness and its restraint from preaching a lesson. Speaking in terms that were to become the watchwords of Howells' own criticism, Perry wrote, "Literature is at its best when it is an imitation of life and not an excuse for instruction." Perry finds it a better book than *Tom Sawyer*, locates its extreme excellence in the characterization of Huck, and makes reference to its humor as a secondary rather than primary quality. Anticipating the most relentlessly pursued strain of modern criticism, Perry finds the ending faulty—"the long account of Tom Sawyer's artificial imitation of escapes from prison is somewhat forced." Brander Matthews, then a thirty-two-year-old critic writing in both American and British periodicals, published an even longer and more favorable review in the British periodical *Saturday Review*. He, too, dwelt upon the superiority of *Huckleberry Finn* over *Tom Sawyer*, telling the reader at the outset that it is a quite different book. Matthews, too, emphasizes the superb characterization of Huck, the realness of all the characters, and the "sober self-restraint" that rules out didactic comments. Like Perry, he leaves his favorable comments about Mark Twain's humor to the last, as if the book could well exist without it but not forgetting to recognize the most established of the author's literary skills. Mark Twain must have been pleased by Matthews' praise, "Mark Twain is a literary artist of a very high order."[7]

6. See Frederick Anderson (ed.), *Mark Twain: The Critical Heritage* (New York, 1971); Richard Lettis, Robert F. McDonnell and William E. Morris (eds.), *Huck Finn and His Critics* (New York, 1962), 275–451; David B. Kesterton (ed.), *Critics on Mark Twain* (Coral Gables, Fla., 1973), 13–36, 62–86; Louis J. Budd (ed.), *Critical Essays on Mark Twain, 1867–1910* (Boston, 1982).

7. T. S. Perry, "Mark Twain," *Century*, XXX (May, 1885), 171–72; review of

Clear as these two reviews were in placing *Huckleberry Finn* with literature of the highest kind and in purposely placing this excellence above that of Mark Twain as humorist, they were but two reviews during the first year of publication to temper the author's anxieties about the book. The troubles of getting it on the market, since it came out under the imprint of the Charles Webster Company, the subscription publishing house Mark Twain had established, were Mark Twain's own. They included the customary ones of delays in printing and distribution, and the more unusual one of some wag engraver drawing in a penis on one of the illustrations for the book. Such troubles helped divert Mark Twain's attention from the unfavorable reviews that appeared in newspapers, most of them triggered by the Concord Public Library's banning of the book in March, 1885, two months before Perry's review appeared. As a publisher, if not as a writer, Mark Twain recognized the value of controversy. It seems entirely possible that if the banning had not occurred, *Huckleberry Finn* would have been received with few reviews in literary periodicals and scant attention given it by libraries. As it was, Mark Twain welcomed the Concord Library's action. It has given us, he wrote to Webster, "a rattling tip-top puff which will go into every paper in the country."[8] He was right in his optimism, for amid the controversy, *Huckleberry Finn* did far better in sales than its initial reception promised. Nevertheless, the side of Mark Twain that aspired to recognition as a writer could not have welcomed, in the middle of his career and in response to a book that had more of his heart in it than any other, his being lumped with dime novelists and being regarded as a vulgar humorist who could not abandon the crudities that had won him success with popular audiences.

Although by the end of his life, *Huckleberry Finn* had received much judicious criticism and was securely placed among Mark Twain's best books, the novel's central character reinforced the ster-

---

The Adventures of Huckleberry Finn, in *Saturday Review,* LIX (January 31, 1885), 153. In Anderson (ed.), *Mark Twain: The Critical Heritage,* 121–25, and J. Sculley Bradley, *et al.* (eds.), *Samuel Langhorne Clemens/Adventures of Huckleberry Finn: An Authoritative Text/Backgrounds and Sources/Criticism* (New York, 1977), 292.

8. Paine (ed.), *Mark Twain's Letters,* II, 452.

eotype of "Mark Twain," the public figure. When *A Connecticut Yankee in King Arthur's Court* appeared in 1889, Mark Twain used it to signal his "retirement from literature," or so he proclaimed to Howells. "I'm not writing for those parties who miscal [*sic*] themselves critics, & I don't care to have them paw the book at all." Nevertheless, he welcomed Howells' review and his earlier responses by letter. "The book is glorious—simply noble. . . . As Stedman says of the whole book, it's Titanic."[9] Although Howells was not alone in recognizing Mark Twain's literary qualities, it is fair to say that most contemporary criticism undervalued Mark Twain as a literary artist.

"Literary fame" in precisely those terms was probably not what Mark Twain set most store by. His most famous aphorism on the subject appears as an imagined retort to an unnamed critic: "Yes, high & fine literature is wine, & mine is only water; but everybody likes water."[10] Without quite realizing it, Mark Twain was establishing a body of writings that helped dislodge "high & fine" as the principal measures of literary greatness. Even twenty years after Mark Twain's death, it was such an unacademic and partisan writer as Bernard DeVoto who championed Mark Twain. And it is probably only after DeVoto's death that academic critics recognized the justice of DeVoto's claim that "American journalism attained its highest reach in the February or Midwinter number of the *Century Magazine* for 1885." For not only did that issue carry a section from *Huckleberry Finn*; it had the ninth and tenth installments of Howells' *The Rise of Silas Lapham* and the beginning chapter of Henry James's *The Bostonians*. But that judgment was DeVoto's, not Mark Twain's. "As for the Bostonians," Mark Twain wrote Howells, "I would rather be damned to John Bunyan's heaven than read that."[11]

Mark Twain, though not wanting to be judged a literary buffoon, saw literary fame of a conventional kind as more appropriate for Howells than for himself. That Mark Twain had not clearly estab-

9. Smith and Gibson (eds.), *Mark Twain–Howells Letters*, II, 610, 617, 619.
10. *Ibid.*, 587.
11. Bernard DeVoto, *Mark Twain's America and Mark Twain at Work* (Boston, 1967), 308; Smith and Gibson (eds.), *Mark Twain–Howells Letters*, II, 534.

lished himself as a great literary figure is clear from the piece
Howells wrote about Mark Twain in a series in the *Century* magazine
in 1882 devoted to new writers. The details of Mark Twain's life and
its relation to his past work take up the first half of Howells' article.
It goes on to identify those characteristics upon which Mark Twain's
literary excellence might be properly based. "I prefer to speak of
Mr. Clemens's artistic qualities," he begins a crucial paragraph,
"because it is to these that his humor will owe its perpetuity." From
that lead, Howells carefully separates Clemens from other western
humorists, as he also separates him from comparison with Dickens
and Thackeray. What he emphasizes most are the universal qualities
of his humor, the strength of his powers as a storyteller, his ability to
create dramatic and convincing characters, and the "indignant sense
of right and wrong, a scorn of all affectation and pretence, an ardent
hate of meanness and injustice" that a reader must recognize if he is
to know Mark Twain at all.[12]

In 1902 Howells again addressed himself to the subject of Mark
Twain's exceptional literary qualities in response to the publication
of Mark Twain's writings in "a uniform edition," which was more
uniform than complete. The conflict between the American Publishing Company and Harpers over publishing a complete, uniform
edition once again illustrates the conflict between Mark Twain the
popular author and Mark Twain the literary one. The American
Publishing Company still held rights to those books brought out
under subscription publishing conditions, and it did not relinquish
them until 1904 when Harpers was able to get exclusive publishing
rights to all of Mark Twain's works. The edition Howells reviewed
included *Huckleberry Finn, Life on the Mississippi, The Prince and
the Pauper, A Connecticut Yankee, Tom Sawyer Abroad* and *Tom
Sawyer Detective and Other Stories.* Howells sidestepped the conflict, but deliberately emphasized the contrast between Mark Twain's
works now having "that dignified presence which most of us have
thought their due," and "the matchlessly ugly subscription volumes
of the earlier issues." The uniform edition, Howells granted, was fit

12. W. D. Howells, *My Mark Twain,* 121, 120.

"to be set on the shelf of a gentleman's library," and yet in those works, moving out of their original contexts, something had been lost, most of all "the accidental and provisional moods of a unique talent finding itself out."[13]

The first part of Howells' piece makes a justified comparison between Mark Twain's wandering and yet intensely engaging path through his books and the essays of Montaigne. "His great charm is his absolute freedom in a region where most of us are fettered and shackled by immemorial convention. He saunters out into the trim world of letters, and lounges across its neatly kept paths, and walks about on the grass at will, in spite of all the signs that have been put up from the beginning of literature, warning people of dangers and penalties for the slightest trespass." More than anything else in this essay, Howells establishes the special province that Mark Twain occupies, referring to Lincoln (as he was to do in *My Mark Twain*) for his closest comparison rather than to any literary figure. In his method of narration, his style, his humor, his American-ness and western American-ness, in his mixture of comic and tragic, Mark Twain is for Howells a unique phenomenon. His work is an addition to the world's literatures by which others are to be measured and, therefore, not to be held up to the measure of those who have preceded him. "A comic force unique in the power of charming us out of our cares and troubles, united with as potent an ethic sense of the duties, public and private, which no man denies in himself without being false to other men" is the summary statement that best catches Howells' assessment of Mark Twain.[14]

The *North American Review* article was written as an expansion of an earlier piece in *Harper's Weekly* in February, 1897, whose crucial points were taken over into the later, more complete essay. The earlier piece came upon Mark Twain at one of the low periods in his life, his struggles to get out of debt, Susy's death, and Livy's confirmed illness all hard upon him. "The words," he wrote Howells, "stir the dead heart of me, & throw a glow of color into a life which

13. *Ibid.*, 143.
14. *Ibid.*, 146, 162.

sometimes seems to have grown wholly wan. I don't mean that I am miserable; no—worse than that, indifferent. Indifferent to nearly everything but work. I like that; I enjoy it, & stick to it. I do it without purpose & without ambition; merely for the love of it." Although, in the next paragraph, he discounts the indifference as a mood that will pass, important parts of what he has avowed remain in his reflections and actions of the succeeding years. They bear importantly on his recognition as a literary artist and his self-recognition of that fact. For, as he reveals to Howells, he is writing as furiously as ever before, but also as discriminatingly. One might interpret his account of the "ill luck of starting a piece of literary work wrong—& again—& again; always aware that there *is* a way" as the floundering of a writer in his decline.[15] But it can be better argued that it is one more assertion of the passion that Mark Twain had very early in his career, both as writer and as lecturer, of getting the thing right. It also attests to the prodigal talent of Mark Twain, capable even in the last decades of his life, of throwing away quantities of work because it did not meet the standard he set for himself.

In April, 1899, Mark Twain writes to Howells: "Jean has been in here examining the poll for the Immortals ("Literature," March 24), in the hope, I think, that at last she would find me at the top & you in second place; & if that is her ambition she has suffered disappointment for the third time—& will never fare any better, I hope, for you are where you belong, by every right."[16] The poll Mark Twain refers to is one taken of the readers of the magazine to give their choices of ten living authors who might best be elected to an American Academy. Howells was first, but Mark Twain was second, followed by John Fiske, Thomas Bailey Aldrich, Henry James, Frank Stockton, and Bret Harte. In 1884, a selection of forty literary immortals in the *Critic* listed Howells in fifth place (Holmes was in first place), and Clemens in fourteenth. Both were elected to the American Academy of Arts and Letters when it was established in 1908, Howells taking slight precedence over Mark Twain in being named its first president.

15. Smith and Gibson (eds.), *Mark Twain–Howells Letters*, II, 664, 675.
16. *Ibid.*, 691.

Howells' own place in history is unmistakably secured, in part, by his association with Mark Twain. It is no small achievement as a critic that he so steadily and convincingly placed Mark Twain's work before the literary world. He knew, long before he ever stated the fact, that Mark Twain was a genius, just as he knew his own work was often estimable but of a more describable and comprehensible sort. During his own rise to recognition, his worth as a writer was in contention with his recognition as an editor and critic. Here, too, Howells valued Mark Twain's responses, for they were invariably to his fiction, which Howells most prized, rather than to his other literary work.

From the first, Howells' acceptance into New England literary circles was only in part because of his artistic literary talents. His first sign of recognition, as he relates in the essay "The Turning Point of My Life," was the acceptance by the *North American Review* of a piece on modern Italian poets. How different this is from the event that Mark Twain picked out as his turning point—not a literary event at all but a series of events beginning with a case of measles and including such good fortune as finding a fifty-dollar bill on the streets of Keokuk in 1856 or 1857. Instead of dwelling, as Howells had, on a crucial event that confirmed his becoming a literary man, Mark Twain saw his life from a wider perspective, that in which circumstances and temperament combined to determine any person's course.

For Howells, literary recognitions were paramount. His career proceeded in a remarkably orderly, step-by-step fashion, from acceptance by James T. Fields as an assistant editor to becoming editor-in-chief of the *Atlantic*, and from the acceptance of his travel sketches, then travel sketches with a mixture of fiction, then fiction with a mixture of travel, and finally to acceptance by himself and others of his full arrival as a novelist. One could carry the progression further and emphasize the stage at which a popular writer of novels about courting and marriage expanded both his range and technique. The image that posterity fastened upon Howells, that of a fussy genteel novelist secure among archly literary and largely feminine readers, is at variance with the public figure speaking out, usually from a liberal point of view, on the public issues of the day. It is at variance, too, with the writer of social protest novels and with his championing of fiction of a socially disturbing kind.

Much as Howells wrote essays confirming Mark Twain's talent, Henry James performed such a service for Howells. The first of these essays appeared in 1886 in *Harper's Weekly*, and the editorial justification for such a piece was probably much like that which provoked the pieces on Mark Twain, Howells, and James in the *Century* in 1882. James had previously reviewed many of Howells' works, beginning with *Italian Journeys* in 1868, and during certain periods of time when James was living in Cambridge, they had discussed literature with an eye to its "art" probably far more intensely than Howells and Mark Twain had. As a consequence, Howells knew James's favorable judgment toward his work, and perhaps might have wished that some immaculately objective judge, one uncompromised in the least by friendship, might set a seal upon his writing. Nevertheless, James's article was the longest and most searching essay written about Howells' work, though an anonymous reviewer writing on American literature in England in *Blackwood's Magazine* in 1883 had devoted most of the space to a close, and not always favorable, examination of Howells' work. At the conclusion of the essay, the reviewer wrote that *A Modern Instance* "is altogether the strongest face which the author has put before us; and if he will forget the foreign reviews, and the stupidity and hostility of the English, and illustrate frankly, without any polemical intention, the society he knows, there is no telling how far he may go."[17]

James's article begins with a brief account of Howells' life with emphasis upon those experiences that have closest relationship to his writing. At the conclusion of the running account of his works to that time, James writes, "Mr. Howells has gone from one success to another, has taken possession of the field, and has become copious without detriment to his freshness." James's reservations are politely phrased, but they raise questions that readers both before and after the date were to raise. His novels "exhibit so constant a study of the

17. Eble, *Howells: A Century of Criticism*, 32–33.

actual and so small a perception of evil," he writes at one point. At another, he calls attention to the "verbal drollery" of some of Howells' characters that does injustice to his "constant sense of the comedy of life." He regrets Howells' reliance on dialogue and openly wishes for more that would be narrative and pictorial. And probably more meaningful to James than any other criticism, he thinks Howells has paid too little respect to style, has appeared "increasingly to hold composition too cheap."[18]

It is an illuminating coincidence that the same year that James wrote his long appreciative essay for *Harper's Weekly*, James Russell Lowell came to Howells personally to ask him to accept the professorship at Harvard that he and Longfellow and George Ticknor had held. Howells declined, saying that he thought it better to pursue his way as a middling novelist than to risk becoming a poor professor. At another point he wrote, "This offer, precious as it was to a man of my self-lettered life, was less precious than his [Lowell's] way of making it." Lowell, still addressing him in correspondence as "My Dear Boy," albeit Howells was approaching fifty, wrote, "Much as I should have liked it, however, I think you are right in your decision."[19]

Offers of academic positions by Harvard and other universities to Howells acknowledge how well he fit conventional ideas of literary respectability. The security they offered tempted him, though only in his earliest years could they match the income he made as editor and writer. As much as the recognition flattered him, there was a part of Howells, as there was a part of Mark Twain, that resisted accepting the status, and the restrictions, that a Harvard or Johns Hopkins position might have conferred. Neither shunned honorary degrees, both collecting a great many, such as Mark Twain's from (appropriately) the University of Missouri in 1902, and both Howells' and Mark Twain's from Yale during its Bicentennial Anniversary in 1901. The culmination of these peculiar honors for both men was the awarding of degrees from Oxford, to Howells in 1904,

18. *Ibid.*, 45, 48, 49.
19. M. Howells (ed.), *Life in Letters*, I, 386, 385.

Mark Twain in 1907. As Mark Twain scholar Lewis Leary once said, Mark Twain was petty enough to seek an Oxford degree and great enough, illustrious enough, to deserve it.

Despite the public recognition that both men received, neither deviated for long from finding his greatest satisfactions in recognition of each other's work. The high aims each held were those of a professional writer, not attached to some abstract pursuit of literary immortality but to the concrete and practical pursuit of characters and situations, and of words that might somehow tell the story at hand. Howells respected Mark Twain's consistent and very often specific praise of his work as a mark of significant recognition. As late as 1899, Mark Twain expresses envy of Howells' ability to look into "the insides of people" and "invent things for them to do & say; & tell *how* they said it." If he could but do that himself, he could write "a fine & readable book now." In 1906 Howells thanked Mark Twain for the only published essay he wrote about Howells and his work. "Your praise," Howells wrote, "has brought back the good great times when the men, Lowell and Longfellow and Holmes, who held the eminence you now hold, spoke well of me. I think round the world, and I find none now living whose praise I could care more for. Perhaps Tolstoy; but I do not love him as I love you, and the honor he could do me would not reach my heart as the honor you have done me does." Friendship alone did not lead Howells to recognize that Mark Twain, as he wrote to his sister Aurelia, was "really a great literary critic."[20]

Since Howells and Mark Twain lived to be old men and their productivity continued on into their late years, they were subject to the customary tributes paid to persons of significant achievement on the occasion of significant birthdays, such as achieving or passing the Bible's allotted three-score-and-ten. Of a number of public celebrations of this sort, the feting of Mark Twain on the occasion of his seventieth birthday and of Howells on his seventy-fifth are most memorable, though Mark Twain did not live to participate in the lat-

20. Smith and Gibson (eds.), *Mark Twain–Howells Letters*, II, 710; Eble, *Howells: A Century of Criticism*, 78–87; Smith and Gibson (eds.), *Mark Twain–Howells Letters*, II, 813–14 n. 1.

ter. Justin Kaplan describes the great banquet for Mark Twain at Delmonico's on December 5, 1905. "After meeting the guest of honor at a reception, they filed into Delmonico's red room to the music of a forty-piece orchestra from the Metropolitan Opera House. Surrounded by potted palms and huge gilt mirrors, they dined on fillet of kingfish, saddle of lamb, Baltimore terrapin, quail, and redhead duck washed down with sauterne, champagne, and brandy. Then they settled back to absorb five hours of toasts, poems, and speeches." Howells was toastmaster and contributed a sonnet for the occasion. It was fully as appreciative but not as engaging as the invention he had worked up for Mark Twain's sixty-fifth birthday. On that occasion, he had done a sketch in which Mark Twain's fictional characters engaged in a dialogue with their creator and with Howells. Howells felt some uneasiness about imitating Mark Twain's voice, and submitted the whole sketch for Mark Twain's approval. Clemens received it apparently as Howells intended, scribbling in response to Howells' invitation to revise it as he might wish, "No, it's lovely." Like the earlier birthday party, a full account of the seventieth celebration was printed by *Harper's Weekly*, this time as a special thirty-two-page supplement with pictures of all the guests.[21] At the head table with Mark Twain were Henry Rogers, Henry Alden, long-time editor of *Harper's Monthly*, Joe Twichell, and three youngish writers, Mary E. Wilkins Freeman, Bliss Carman, and Ruth McEnery Stuart. Andrew Carnegie presided at another table, as did Howells, Henry Van Dyke, Finley Peter Dunne, and Gelett Burgess, and Colonel Harvey, whose rescue of *Harper's* now gave him the privilege of paying the bill. The menu was decorated with sketches of Mark Twain in his various incarnations: printer, pilot, miner, journalist, traveler, lecturer. In the Howells library at Kittery Point is one of the plaster busts of Mark Twain that were given out as souvenirs of the occasion.

Mark Twain's mood at the end of 1905 was such as to make him welcome the splendor of the occasion and to cause him to respond

21. Kaplan, *Mr. Clemens and Mark Twain*, 373; Smith and Gibson (eds.), *Mark Twain–Howells Letters*, II, 726; "Mark Twain's 70th Birthday/Souvenir of its Celebration." Supplement to *Harper's Weekly*, XLIX (1905), 1884–1914.

enthusiastically when it was over. Nevertheless, he had, as Huck said, been there before, and he recognized *Harper's* was doing up the occasion as much for its financial sake as for recognizing the merits of its best and most financially rewarding author. His speech in response to the celebration was not warmed over, but he had had a good deal of practice in responding to such occasions. It ranged back over his years and wished others well in reaching such an age as he had achieved, reminding them only of the maxim that "we can't reach old age by another man's road. My habits protect my life, but they would assassinate you." Howells was as enthusiastic about the event as Mark Twain, writing to Thomas Sergeant Perry that "172 immortals sat down to the best Delmonico could do, and remained glutted and guzzling food for reflection for five hours after the dinner was ended."[22]

The banquet celebrating Howells' seventy-fifth birthday was a similarly splendid affair, though there were more differences in it than just the absence of Mark Twain. Most of Howells' contemporary friends and literary acquaintances had also died before him: John Hay, C. E. Norton, Thomas Bailey Aldrich, E. C. Stedman, R. W. Gilder, and Edward Everett Hale, to name the closest and most prominent. As Livy's death had preceded Mark Twain's seventieth birthday, so Elinor's death preceded Howells seventy-fifth. As a part of his speech, he paid tribute to Mark Twain: "If I had been witness to no other surpassing things of American growth in my fifty years of observation, I should think it glory enough to have lived in the same time and in the same land with the man whose name must always embody American humor to human remembrance."[23]

The birthday dinner, he wrote to his brother Joseph, "was something I could not refuse, but of course I would rather not have been seventy-five years old." Afterwards he reported receiving 150 to 160 letters of congratulations and noted that it was "angelic" of Presi-

22. "Mark Twain's 70th Birthday/Souvenir of its Celebration." Supplement to *Harper's Weekly*, XLIX (1905), 1885; M. Howells (ed.), *Life in Letters*, II, 214.

23. "A Tribute to William Dean Howells/Souvenir of a Dinner Given to the Eminent Author in Celebration of his Seventy-Fifth Birthday," *Harper's Weekly*, LVI (1912), Pt. II, 28–29.

dent Taft to have come up from Washington for the occasion. But looking back upon it a few days after, he wrote Joseph: "I suppose it's what I wanted, but I am able to discount it. . . . Honestly, my real feeling about it is shame. I am no such person, and I oughtn't to be pushed off that way on an unsuspecting world. But if you think I am a good brother, that *is* something I won't deny. You're another."[24] Joseph was to die within the year, on August 10, 1912.

Of all Howells' literary friends from the past, only Henry James was alive to celebrate, from abroad, this occasion. His letter and one from Frank Sanborn were printed in the *North American Review*. The letter is in the late Jamesian style and moves leisurely and movingly through the years in which Howells, in person and in a steady procession of works, placed the younger James so much in his debt. "Stroke by stroke and book by book your work was to become for this exquisite notation of our whole democratic light and shade and give and take in the highest degree *documentary*," he wrote. The essay concludes with the promise of future recognition that is as well known—though, as if in denial of the prophecy still, not very well known—as any summary assessment of Howells' literary worth. "The critical intelligence," James asserts, "has not at all begun to render you its tribute. . . . your really beautiful time will come." Howells' letter of thanks to James curiously mixes a genuine pride he felt in the occasion and the feeling he expressed to Joseph that it was undeserved. He refers to the celebration as being "all wrong and unfit" though it is not clear whether he is describing his own speech of response, the whole affair, or both. Earlier in the letter he had emphasized the magnitude of the affair as he had earlier to Joseph ("I hear it is to be the largest thing of the kind on record"). "Four hundred notables swarmed about a hundred tables on the floor, and we elect sat at a long board on a dais. Mrs. Clifford was among us, two elbows from the President of the United States." His highly formal and effusive letter to President Taft thanking him

24. M. Howells (ed.), *Life in Letters*, II, 313; William D. Howells to Joseph M. Howells, March 26, 1912, in William Dean Howells Papers, Houghton Library, Harvard University.

for his coming is in the same tone of conventional admiration. James took issue with him promptly for the self-disparagement that Howells had expressed. "How can you take any view of your long career of virtue and devotion and self-sacrifice, of labour and courage and admirable and distinguished production, *but* the friendly and understanding and acceptingly 'philosophic' view," he scolded him. "As for the terrible banquet (for I think it must indeed have been terrible,) your account of it confirms [it]. . . . Truly was it an ordeal for you of the 1st water (or I suppose *wine;*) through which, not less clearly, you passed unscathed as to your grace and humour and taste (the only things that were *there* on the table—and quite enough things.)."[25]

Although Howells was as much in the public eye for most of his life as was Mark Twain, he probably genuinely enjoyed it less. As he grew older, his earlier vanities seemed to have been satisfied. If he sought praise at all, it was best coming from those literary men and women he most respected. He is not above, for example, reporting to his grandson William W., then four, that he had heard, indirectly, the great Tolstoy say that Howells was one of four men—others mentioned were Henry George and Henry D. Lloyd—that he would like to bring together. "Pretty good for a little novelist," he wrote to his son John, "what, from the greatest that ever lived? I thought, 'Wull, *Billy* would like it,' and so I report it."[26]

Both Howells and Mark Twain, grown old and famous, reflected often on the vanities of human striving. In Mark Twain's misanthropic moods, the purposelessness of human striving extended to the universe. His vision is basically astronomical, the denial of any purpose posed by man residing in the earth's tiny speck of physical stuff in a universe that brings in and out of being countless larger masses of stuff as a matter of no thought at all. For Howells, human striving had not come much closer to achieving a just society on a large scale than when the Greeks began to organize the polis. And yet, if we

25. In Eble (ed.), *Howells: A Century of Criticism*, 92–93; Gibson and Lohmann (eds.), *W. D. Howells: Selected Letters*, VI, 16; M. Howells (ed.), *Life in Letters*, II, 319.

26. M. Howells (ed.), *Life in Letters*, II, 322.

draw upon Basil March's ponderings as expressions of Howells' own, he stops short of denying meaningfulness to life. He cannot be sure of its meaning, he cannot turn to religion or philosophy for answers, and yet he can justify his own continued writing, his skating around on a surface of impenetrable depths, not so much as cosmic purpose, but as how men and women might conduct their lives to some purpose under the light of common day.

Mark Twain, at least, did not outlive his fame, and for all the gloom that hangs over the last decade of his life, among his moments of satisfaction was the figure he continued to cut in American life. The white suit was adopted in his late years; "a very beautiful costume—and conspicuous," he told his daughters. Howells saw him in December, 1906, testifying in Washington about international copyright. In his white suit and his flowing white hair and still with that walk which set him apart almost as much as his dress and clothes, Mark Twain prompted Howells to write, "Nothing could have been more dramatic."[27] There was pathos mixed with Mark Twain's need for display and admiration, for his moments of loneliness were as stark as those Robert Frost describes in "Desert Places," and arising from familiar human losses, regrets, guilts, illnesses, and death.

Howells realized for the last decade of his life that his works were slipping from literary favor, that he was no longer being read even by readers who were enthusiastically responding to younger writers he had helped create. "I am comparatively a dead cult with my statues cut down and the grass growing over them in the pale moonlight," he wrote Henry James in June, 1915.[28] Still, he continued to write and to publish; two articles on Henry James were the works before him at his death. The Leatherwood God and Years of My Youth, published four years before his death, are both distinguished books. The Home-Towners, an unfinished novel begun during these very last years, is a fragment whose beginning chapters are as strong and powerfully directed as any of his best early novels. He had his

27. Kaplan, Mr. Clemens and Mark Twain, 380; W. D. Howells, "My Mark Twain," 80.
28. M. Howells (ed.), Life in Letters, II, 350.

admirers among living writers—Hamlin Garland, Sarah Orne Jewett, and Booth Tarkington, among others—but the more celebrated young writers were almost unaware of him at his death.

Howells was still alive when H. L. Mencken wrote "The Dean" for *The Smart Set* in January, 1917. He may have read it, for as he was still writing in his late years, so he continued to read. If he did, he could not help but be struck by the resemblance between Mencken and the brash journalist Howells had created almost forty years before, Bartley Hubbard. "The truth about Howells," Mencken wrote, "is that he really has nothing to say, for all the charm he gets into saying it." Few critical pieces have had a higher percentage of harsh truth and an equally high percentage of nonsense, not merely about Howells but about the low state of American letters prior to Mencken. Mark Twain is mentioned at both the beginning and end of the essay. At the beginning, he is set forth as the incomparable artist who could not shake off being the after-dinner comedian, the "flaunter of white dress clothes, the public character, the national wag." In the end, he is described as being descended from the "buccaneers of the literary high seas" whom Howells in his essay "My Mark Twain" completely fails to comprehend. Among the least, and yet the greatest, of Mencken's misperceptions is his finding it incredible that the two men should have enjoyed a friendship lasting forty-four years.[29] The young, both Howells and Mark Twain might have told Mencken, have little sympathy for the old. Friendship, too, may be one of those things the young unthinkingly appropriate as peculiarly their own. Among the honors and respectabilities that rightly belong to Howells and Mark Twain is their friendship itself. And recognizing that friendship is an important part of doing justice to their literary achievements.

29. Eble, *Howells: A Century of Criticism*, 94–98.

Ten

Come—Respect the Capitalist

From Howells' point of view, and almost from the first of their acquaintance, Samuel Clemens had a wealth of which Howells could only dream. The Howellses' first family visit to Hartford provoked him to write his father, "The Clemenses are whole-souled hosts, with inextinguishable money."[1] There is little question that Clemens' wealth attracted Howells. For it was not just a matter of money, though that was the most obvious form it took. It was a wealth of style, of experience, of talent, of the woman he married and her family—and all of it on display. Contrasted with Howells' own possessions of the time, the Clemenses' affluence might have seemed vulgar, just as there was more than a hint of vulgarity in what Howells later called Mark Twain's "Elizabethan breadth of parlance."

Clemens seemed to come into money by quite other means than Howells. It came in great chunks: a house and all its appurtenances as a wedding gift; royalties from a subscription book that went into five figures within months; daily royalties—$150, $200, $350— noted on postcards which, Howells remembered, arrived at Hartford

1. William Dean Howells to William C. Howells, March 14, 1875, in William Dean Howells Papers, Houghton Library, Harvard University.

about dinner time. All of this was quite contrary to Howells' patient acquiring of a yearly salary with annual raises and an income from books more likely to earn $2,000 or $3,000 rather than $20,000 or $30,000. In April, 1874, he wrote to a relative of Elinor's who worked in his publisher's business office: "But, O, you're sure you're not mistaken? My wildest dream was but $200. And $600! Confirm my faltering faith with an early check!"[2] That same year, Clemens was receiving about $900 weekly from the royalties on the stage version of *The Gilded Age*.

Such disparities between two ambitious men early in their careers might have worked against a friendship, might have placed them in such positions as debtor and lender, pensioner and patron, wage earner and capitalist. But though there were frank recognitions of their differences in wealth and style, the differences did not undermine their early friendship. As the years went by, they both acquired the style of living and the associates that wealth brings, making them somewhat equal in financial accomplishments as in literary achievements and recognition. Still, Howells and Mark Twain were closer in their attitudes toward money than the differences in their financial status might indicate. Both were conditioned by experiences and attitudes arising out of their past and by the post–Civil War American culture in which they increasingly prospered.

Too much attention has been given to Howells and Mark Twain as capitalists caught in an inner conflict between their acquisitive desires for and guilty consciences about wealth. Sympathetic literary critics have spawned the persistent criticism that an inordinate need for wealth and respectability somehow crippled or blighted Mark Twain's literary genius. Critics little disposed toward either Mark Twain or Howells have used the writers' wealth and association with men of wealth to cast doubt upon the sincerity and strength of their social satire and economic criticism. At the extreme, Mark Twain becomes a frustrated and baffled genius, bound by his own material needs to be less the artist or the revolutionary than he might have been. Howells, by the same measure, is smug and prudish in his fatal bourgeois condition. Each might better be called

2. Arms and Lohmann (eds.), *W. D. Howells: Selected Letters*, II, 59.

what a recent critic has called Howells: "a humane liberal (some-times a radical)."[3]

Even as knowing a biographer as Justin Kaplan reads much se-rious portent into "a strangely bitter fable" Mark Twain published in 1872 about the upright man who falsifies his income tax return (the income tax, brought into being by the Civil War, expired that same year, not to be revived until 1913). "Clemens believed that the Midas myth had to end tragically," Kaplan comments, "and his own life, culminating in bankruptcy and disasters which he felt were his punishment, was, in part, an acting out of this belief." Kaplan ap-pears to believe that "Mark Twain's disgust with his time," his vic-timization by "the same wild speculative mania he saw all about him," are importantly related to his belief that money is the root of all evil.[4]

Such views disclose as much of Kaplan's American—or hu-man—strain as they do of Mark Twain's. The puritan Christian heri-tage of the nineteenth century clearly preached against the evils of money even as it seemed to make allowances for the accumulation of it, and the Christian tradition, long before America was established, posed an unquestioned superiority of the spiritual over the material. The fascination with speculations that might fulfill one's human dreams probably began about the same time as human dreaming. Mark Twain's being caught up by these two conflicting strains may be viewed simply as a manifestation of the moral and poetic tem-perament essential to his literary genius. Man's acquisitive nature and the conscience that attempts to curb it have been a major source of comedy through the ages. To rail too strongly against their adverse effects on Mark Twain is to deny him the comic genius that is his great literary strength.

Mark Twain's attitude toward money was closer to Aristotle's

3. William Alexander, *William Dean Howells: The Realist as Humanist* (New York, 1981), xi. Alexander's thesis is not new, but he argues well that Howells' "commitment to social reform, and his consciousness of the rationalizations and lies by which he sometimes evaded responsibility give him an honesty, strength and tenacity as man and writer that make it difficult for those who know him and his work to remain unaffected."

4. Kaplan, *Mr. Clemens and Mark Twain*, 116, 158.

than to Christ's; he seldom failed to note the satisfactions money brings even as he was driving, in his public as well as private utterances, the money changers out of the temple. Some of them became his friends; others he excoriated at length. Speculation was attractive to him long before it became ruinous. One can even see a poetic refinement in his speculations as they became attached to inventions. "An inventor," he wrote to his sister in 1870, "is a poet—a true poet—and nothing in any degree less than a high order of poet— . . . littler minds being able to get no higher than a comprehension of a vulgar moneyed success. . . . To invent . . . shows the presence of the patrician blood of intellect." He is faithful to this vision twenty years later when he described James W. Paige, inventor of the typesetting machine that brought him near financial ruin. "He is a poet, a most great and genuine poet, whose sublime creations are written in steel. He is the Shakespeare of mechanical invention."[5] Anyone who looks at the elegant model of the Paige machine, not even having the opportunity to see it operate (and it did operate, magnificently but expensively) might be inclined to accept Mark Twain's judgment.

Samuel Clemens was almost as prolific as his brother Orion in thinking up patentable projects. His idea for a self-pasting scrapbook became an income-producing reality, as ideas for a steam pulley and a cure for chilblains did not. His interest in the Kaolatype process and the Paige typesetter was not idle speculation but an outgrowth of his knowledge of and involvement in printing processes. As to the former's failure, Mark Twain was simply defrauded by an inventor's claim that he had arrived at a new process for molding brass when he had not. "It was exactly as if he had contracted to furnish me a process of making silver out of sawdust for a specific sum," Clemens wrote Charles Webster, "& then claimed the sum on specimens of silver produced in the regular old time-honored way." As to the Paige machine, it was indeed superior to its competition, but expensive to produce and maintain, and it lost out to "a bastard

5. Samuel Charles Webster (ed.), *Mark Twain, Business Man* (Boston, 1946), 114–15; Paine, *Mark Twain: A Biography*, II, 903–904.

cripple like the Mergenthaler." And yet, Mark Twain was right about the impact (and profit) that a successful typesetting machine would have; the Mergenthaler Linotype was indispensable to printing and publishing and has only in recent years begun to be replaced by other methods. It was probably the impact of inventions that dazzled Mark Twain more than the profits. Describing the Kaolatype patent in 1880, he wrote, "Yesterday I thought out a new application of this invention which I think will utterly annihilate & sweep out of existence one of the minor industries of civilization, & take its place."[6]

The minute involvement of Clemens in the business of publishing is most revealing of his divided character. Yet it is a division that few writers cannot sympathize with: the translation into action of those feelings that a publisher is not doing what might be done with an author's book. In a long letter to Charles L. Webster and Company in September, 1887, Clemens outlines a "just and equable" scheme of royalties and runs through a list of books, including his own, Aldrich's *The Story of a Bad Boy*, and Howells' *A Foregone Conclusion*, which might have earned far more income than they did. He ends by saying, more or less accurately, *"The author of The Innocents Abroad tried 2 books in the trade. One of them sold 6,000 copies, the other sold 10,000. Total, 16,000.* He has tried 10 books by subscription. Total sales, 618,000 copies."[7] Although he was sensitive, litigious, quick to blame, he was also thoroughly acquainted with publishing and seldom the fool in his specific involvements in the details of printing, managing, and promotion.

Even his losses from the Paige typesetter—which he set at $300,000 in twenty-seven months—and from his entanglement with the Webster Publishing Company did not end his speculating. Once again, there are reasons (in this instance Livy's chronic ill health) for his being attracted to his last specific costly speculation— Plasmon, a skim-milk food supplement. He first became interested in it in 1898, and it was not until 1909 that he became disentangled

6. Webster (ed.), *Mark Twain, Business Man*, 154; Lewis Leary (ed.), *Mark Twain's Correspondence with Henry Huddleston Rogers 1893–1909* (Berkeley, 1969), 92; Webster (ed.), *Mark Twain, Business Man*, 142.

7. Hill (ed.), *Mark Twain's Letters to His Publishers* (Berkeley, 1967), 234.

from it, incurring, according to one critic, "at least $50,000 in losses and an unpardonable expense of time and energy."[8] One wonders, "unpardonable" by whom? Like the Paige machine, Plasmon was far from being an unpardonable risk. An associated product in the European market, Bovril, flourished, and in America Ovaltine became as well known for a time as Coca Cola.

Clouding the views of those who cannot pardon Mark Twain for expending his energies in money-making schemes is an advocacy of an immaculate conception belief about literature. Samuel Johnson tried to lay to rest such ideas long ago by telling Boswell, "No man but a blockhead ever wrote except for money." The fact is that "the business of literature," in which Howells and Mark Twain were engaged, is not very distant from business of other kinds. The same letter that ends with Mark Twain's informing Howells of $10,000 dropping on him unexpectedly and that leads to "Come—respect the capitalist!" begins with an entire paragraph about his acquiring the wasteful habit (wasteful, that is, of an author's precious time) of putting the full date on his letters. The one is not unlike the other: confining his energy and imagination solely to writing masterpieces would have kept literary critics from accusing him of squandering his talents; dating his letters would have saved literary scholars from guessing about when they were written. Being a speculator never prevented him for long from writing, just as his maintaining friendships did not keep him from writing, and both furnished him a fund of comic observations about his own and other human beings' fortunes and losses of fortunes. "That raven," he wrote of the Kaolatype venture, "flew out of the Ark regularly every thirty days but it never got back with anything and the dove didn't report for duty."[9] *The Gilded Age* and *A Connecticut Yankee* and *The Mysterious Stranger* and *The Man that Corrupted Hadleyburg* would not have been written if he had not been preoccupied with materialism and its good and bad effects. As they emerge, those supposedly fatally flawed unpublished works of his late years are beginning to seem not so fatally

8. Hamlin Hill, *Mark Twain: God's Fool* (New York, 1973), 252.

9. Smith and Gibson (eds.), *Mark Twain–Howells Letters*, II, 683–85; Neider (ed.), *The Autobiography of Mark Twain*, 229.

flawed, making it possible to take quite the opposite view of the baneful effects of Mark Twain's aspiring to wealth. Had he succeeded, he might well have given up the toilsome task of literature altogether, retired in magnificent idleness as he often threatened to do, and left us nothing from his last years.

Howells' financial story is one of careful advancement by virtue of his talents as editor and writer and culminating in expanding markets for his work, higher prices per piece, and generally safe investments of capital. He had some losses, too; his AT&SF stock ($6,000 worth) went from $1.13 per share to $.24 in 1900, and a bank failure in 1907 put him out $8,500. But none of his losses was of the magnitude of Mark Twain's.[10] He resisted such of his father's entrepreneurial notions as selling oars made in Jefferson, Ohio, to Venetian boatmen in 1863.[11] But in 1886 he helped his father produce a better style of grape shears at a cost of $.40 apiece to sell for $1.00.[12] That invention did not make anyone rich, but he had not expected it to. Much of his early correspondence is attended with the difficulties of making ends meet, though his income grew steadily. His lament at thirty-two, "Elinor's sickness and the wet nurse for Johnny have made the past twelve months the most expensive I've ever known," is in the same vein as an outburst sixteen years later. "The expenses! I am on the fire, and I *must boil*. . . . I must give my daughter her chance in this despicable world . . . must get my boy through school and into college." Only much later could he write, "I have worried all my life, and it doesn't pay."[13]

Still, by the time he was fifty Howells was a man of some wealth and troubled by the contrast between his own affluence and the lot of millions of others. A summing up of his financial position to his son John in 1889, when John became twenty-one, showed assets

10. William Dean Howells to William C. Howells, November 16, 1900, William Dean Howells to Joseph A. Howells, November 6, 1907, both in Howells Papers.

11. Arms *et al.* (eds.), *W. D. Howells: Selected Letters*, I, 148.

12. Leitz (ed.), *W. D. Howells: Selected Letters*, III, 96, 101, 105.

13. William Dean Howells to Victoria M. Howells, August 4, 1869, in Howells Papers; Leitz (ed.), *W. D. Howells: Selected Letters*, III, 119–20; William Dean Howells to Joseph A. Howells, June 6, 1907, in Howells Papers.

amounting to $57,450.[14] In 1893 he negotiated eight contracts worth $29,400.[15] In 1915, two years away from eighty, he informed his daughter Mildred that his income was $16,580 that year.[16] At his death, he left an estate of $112,851 plus $59,000 in property.[17] By contrast, in 1900 the average annual earnings of industrial workers, including child laborers, were less than $490. "We left prosperity behind when we left Iowa," he wrote Elinor on his lecture tour of 1899. "Nebraska and Kansas are poor, *poor*. . . . But the thought of taking their money makes me sick, and I shall give it all (except our expenses) back for some public object, unless it pans out richer than I can imagine."[18]

He and Mark Twain shared a distress over the conditions that arose from economic inequality, though he said of Mark Twain that "he never went so far in socialism as I have gone, if he went that way at all."[19] Howells wrote out his reasoned discomfort in a succession of novels and the two Altrurian tracts that posed a Utopia arising from a society that somehow had emerged from man's altruistic rather than acquisitive propensities. Mark Twain let his indignation burst forth intermittently in his longer fiction and in various published and unpublished pieces about plutocrats and plutocracy. Underneath his indignation, and not just in his later years, was a distrust of man as a creature capable of establishing the society that a Howells or a Bellamy set forth. Yet, he became momentarily enthusiastic about Bellamy's *Looking Backward*; he strongly approved of Howells' social views, even as Howells responded with deep feeling to Mark Twain's most pessimistic pronouncements. The romantic and comic dispositions, which are at the center of both men's responses to life, are confirmed here. For the romantic view will per-

14. Leitz (ed.), *W. D. Howells: Selected Letters* III, 254.

15. Edwin H. Cady, *Realist at War: The Mature Years 1885–1920 of William Dean Howells* (Syracuse, N.Y., 1958), 193.

16. Gibson and Lohmann (eds.), *W. D. Howells: Selected Letters*, VI, 86.

17. Copy of Will Probate, June 10, 1920, Howells Papers.

18. Thomas Wortham (ed.), *W. D. Howells: Selected Letters* (6 vols.; Boston, 1981), IV, 222.

19. W. D. Howells, "My Mark Twain," 38.

sist in honoring an ideal even as it may be confuted and abused and defeated by reality. And the comic, in accepting the world as it is, will take the satisfactions that are there to be taken, mundane as they may be, and make us laugh at the endless incongruities between life as it is and as it might be.

In one respect, Mark Twain's behavior as a person—his authorship set aside—does appear to be adversely affected by his pursuit of wealth. The moralist (and Mark Twain's voice would be in the chorus) may confirm the evil effects of gaining wealth by dwelling upon the meanness that comes forth at the prospect of losing it. Out of Mark Twain's failures emerges the Clemens quick to sue, prone to distort the facts, and severe in blame and recrimination. The blame he heaped upon his nephew Charles Webster, whom he put in charge of his publishing company and involved in his other financial affairs, goes beyond what the facts justify. His frequent suits and threats of suits are a mixture of justified legal recourse and splenetic behavior. Webster's son's judgment that "Mark Twain never forgave anyone he had injured" is not so far from Howells'. "He went farther than Heine, who said that he forgave his enemies, but not till they were dead."[20] For it is not always clear, in Mark Twain's rages against individuals who supposedly have injured him, how much of the injury is self-inflicted and how much of the blame and rage is aimed at himself.

Howells lived through the speculations as he did through the outrage and enmities often aroused by them. Often he was a sounding board for a first attack on an enemy, and less obviously a means of tempering Mark Twain's excesses, more by Mark Twain's sense of Howells' fairness and equability than by any direct admonitions on Howells' part. Howells' impact on Mark Twain's writing was more direct, for Howells could and did often perform the necessary questioning and chastening of another's written work that goes with being a skilled editor. In matters of conduct, neither lessoned the other very often except by his presence.

20. Webster (ed.), *Mark Twain, Business Man*, viii; W. D. Howells, "My Mark Twain," 58.

Some critics claim that Mark Twain's association with H. H. Rogers, the Standard Oil millionaire, exemplifies his courting of wealth, his own plutocratic tendencies, his need to be recognized by men of wealth and power. The published correspondence between Mark Twain and Rogers gives a more judicious picture of the relationship, the most important one Mark Twain had with an American capitalist.[21] The bulk of the correspondence—474 letters of which 90 percent are by Mark Twain—is concerned with Mark Twain's business affairs. Curiously, these letters, and the friendship they give witness to, go on at the same time as continuing letters to Howells, but with very few references by one correspondent to the other. In a letter of 1909, however, Mark Twain informed Howells of the use he was making of his three major friends. "I will fire the profanities at Rogers, the indecencies at Howells, the theologies at Twichell." He was referring to his scheme of writing letters to friends and not mailing them. By selecting the right target for each letter, his writings would take on aim and force and, by not sending them, free him to say whatever he wished. "When you are on fire with theology, you'll not write it to Rogers, . . . you'll write it to Twichell, because it would make him writhe & squirm & break the furniture. When you are on fire with a good thing that's indecent, you won't waste it on Twichell, you'll save it for Howells, who will love it. As he will never see it, you can make it really indecenter than he could stand."[22] The letter breaks off at this point, else it might have characterized Rogers in a similarly ironic way. It seems clear that Howells recognized the singular purpose that Rogers served. In the face of Mark Twain's financial plight and their own limited means and experiences, Howells and Twichell as friends need serve other purposes.

Whether Mark Twain first met Rogers in the fall of 1893, or on his yacht a year or two earlier, the meeting, for Mark Twain, had some element of good fortune in it. "All my life," he wrote Rogers in 1896, "I have stumbled upon lucky chances of large size."[23] The meeting was not entirely by chance, at least in one version of it, for

21. Leary (ed.), *Correspondence with Rogers.*
22. Smith and Gibson (eds.), *Mark Twain–Howells Letters,* II, 845.
23. Leary (ed.), *Correspondence with Rogers,* 115.

they were introduced by Dr. Clarence C. Rice, Mark Twain's physician and friend with whom Mark Twain was staying on one of his trips from Europe. The friendship that quickly followed arose both from his need to stave off financial disaster and from his identification with aspects of Rogers' life and character, only one of which was his financial standing. Rogers was only five years younger than Mark Twain, father of four daughters and one son, who, like Langdon Clemens, had died in infancy. His wife was incapacitated with a heart condition and was to die of a tumor in 1894. One of his daughters had died at seventeen in 1890, just before Mark Twain met him, and another daughter nearly died of asphyxiation in 1894, probably bringing to Mark Twain's mind the near disasters that had beset Clara. Much of 1894, while the Clemenses were in Europe, Susy was ill, at times too ill to travel.

Like Mark Twain, Rogers was a poor provincial boy who had gained wealth and power by hard work and application of great talent. In addition, he possessed personal qualities conducive to a friendship with Mark Twain. Lewis Leary, editor of the correspondence, concludes: "The friendship between them was public and often playful, but it was real. . . . If in business Rogers could seem unfeelingly rapacious, in personal relations, in drawing room or club, he could be the most charming of gentlemen, gracious and kindly." Mark Twain described him in a letter to Livy in December, 1893, as one of "two men who make me laugh without difficulty."[24] Allen Nevins writes that Rogers was "adventurous and speculative by instinct . . . kaleidoscopic . . . an unmatchable raconteur and a prince of entertainers. . . . He paid for Helen Keller's education, was a patron of the arts, and loved to be the brilliant center of an

24. *Ibid.*, 5; Howells, as might be expected, is not the other man Mark Twain names. The context of the remark is facetious, for the other is Frank Jenkins, a club member, "when he comments on his opponent's shots in a game of billiards." Leary (ed.), *Correspondence with Rogers*, 27–30. Leary comments earlier: "Joseph Twichell of Hartford was a friend of long standing; William Dean Howells was a literary friend, closer to him than any other, but Rogers, Clemens said, was the 'only man I would give a *damn* for' (SLC to OLC, 15 February, 1894). He could calm the troubled waters of Clemens' spirit; he could laugh, and he could afford expensive play" (6).

intellectual circle." Still, he was called "Hell Hound Rogers" on Wall Street. At his death, a magazine piece titled "The Engaging Personal Side of Henry H. Rogers" surveyed the criticism of his business practices in light of the testimony about his ingratiating personal qualities.[25]

Rogers' financial services to Mark Twain are astounding, and Mark Twain's need and gratitude for them appear to be almost as great. "I am 59 years old," he wrote Rogers in 1894, "yet I never had a friend before who put out a hand and tried to pull me ashore when he found me in deep waters." From the first, Mark Twain was struck with Rogers' decisiveness so much in contrast with his own "indolence, idleness, procrastination, indifference." Within the decade of the 1890s, aided by Mark Twain's own efforts in his celebrated world lecture tour, Rogers was able to disentangle Mark Twain from the Paige typesetting machine venture, salvage what could be salvaged from the Webster Publishing Company, negotiate favorable contracts with publishers, and put Mark Twain back on a solid financial footing. In all this, there is a remarkable geniality between both men. Amid dire prophecies of the poorhouse for himself and his family, Mark Twain was still able to consider the lengthy and complex negotiations over Paige's diabolical invention as a kind of superior game. Something of Rogers' own imagination is conveyed in his remarks about the Paige typesetter. "Certainly it was a marvelous invention. It was the nearest approach to a human being in the wonderful things it could do of any machine I have ever known. But that was just the trouble; it was too much of a human being and not enough of a machine."[26] Clearly, Rogers' availability to Mark Twain was in itself remarkable, and the attraction of each to each was in part that both were most remarkable men.

Although it was an admiration of Mark Twain's books, according to one contemporary source, that led Rogers "to express the desire to help the author financially," there was little that was literary in his

25. Allan Nevins, *Study in Power: John D. Rockefeller, Industrialist and Philanthropist* (2 vols.; New York, 1953), I, 272; "The Engaging Personal Side of Henry Rogers," *Current Literature*, XLVII (1909), 34–37.

26. Leary (ed.), *Twain's Correspondence with Rogers*, 112, 25–26.

relation to Mark Twain. An anecdote attributed to Finley Peter Dunne has Mark Twain asking Dunne about inviting H. H. Rogers to a luncheon with Howells and another literary acquaintance. Since it was to be a literary lunch, Dunne asked Mark Twain: "'Then why ask Rogers?' 'Why ask Rogers?' Mark cried. 'Why ask Rogers? To pay for the lunch, you idiot!'" The story may be apocryphal; Howells' correspondence makes no mention of such a lunch, but it is a story Rogers would have enjoyed. Rogers did come into Mark Twain's life at that point when his optimistic prospects for the Paige machine and for his publishing company promised to give Mark Twain the leisure that would not make writing the wage-earning occupation it had become. Rogers' aid in restoring order to Mark Twain's financial affairs fits in between his telling Howells that the *Connecticut Yankee* is "my swan song, my retirement from literature permanently," in August, 1889, and his "Farewell—a long farewell—to *business!*" that he wrote to Olivia in January, 1894, at the first stage of negotiating an agreement with Paige. "'I will *never* touch it again!' I will live in literature, I will wallow in it, revel in it, I will swim in ink!"[27]

Like other capitalists, Mark Twain was most fervent when he was enjoying the benefits of capitalism to the maximum—not too much different from writers enjoying writing most when it is going well. There are inconsistencies—probably not outright hypocrisies—in Mark Twain's relationships to men of wealth and power. He suppressed some, not all, of his writings that excoriated various capitalists.[28] His dislike of Theodore Roosevelt was intense, not so much personal as directed against his bellicose and imperialistic postures. Although Mark Twain was inconsistent in his own criticism of corporations, he fulminated against Roosevelt's public policies which appeared to betray the very corporations that had brought

27. Finley Peter Dunne, *"Mr. Dooley's Friends," Atlantic Monthly*, CCXII (1963), 95; Smith and Gibson (eds.), *Mark Twain–Howells Letters*, II, 610–611; Charles Neider (ed.), *The Selected Letters of Mark Twain* (New York, 1982), 227.

28. See Maxwell Geismar (ed.), *Mark Twain and the Three R's: Race, Religion, Revolution—and Related Matters* (Indianapolis, 1973), and Frederick Anderson (ed.), *A Pen Warmed-Up in Hell: Mark Twain in Protest*, as well as DeVoto (ed.), *Mark Twain in Eruption*, for collections of materials and commentary on capitalists and other targets.

him into power. Although Roosevelt, then president, did not attend Mark Twain' seventieth birthday dinner, a letter from him was read aloud.[29] Of Andrew Carnegie, and for a multitude of reasons, Mark Twain could say, "I like him; I am ashamed of him." He ridiculed the Bible class of young John D. Rockefeller, Jr., and pointed out that his pious version of the Joseph story was at odds with the real story in which Joseph bought up all the land and cattle and skinned the poor folk of every last penny they had. And yet he could, in Bernard DeVoto's words, "let himself be used" at a propaganda luncheon for the Rockefellers and Standard Oil and stand up with John D. and John D., Jr., and Henry Rogers.[30] Without debating how much Rockefeller's medical philanthropies should atone for Standard Oil's economic savageries, it can be argued that Mark Twain was easily "used" because Rogers was his friend and because Rockefeller money was supporting research in meningitis, the disease that had killed Susy.

Howells was less the friend of plutocrats than was Mark Twain. And yet his fiction recognizes the human dimensions of such a millionaire figure as oil-magnate Dryfoos as much as his personal ac-

29. Theodore Roosevelt provoked more of Mark Twain's harsh words than either Andrew Carnegie or John D. Rockefeller. The most balanced treatment of this relationship is in William M. Gibson, *Theodore Roosevelt Among the Humorists; W. D. Howells, Mark Twain, and Mr. Dooley* (Knoxville, Tenn., 1980). Gibson notes the mixed admiration that caused Mark Twain to write at one time, "For twenty years I have loved Roosevelt the man and hated Roosevelt the statesman and politician," and at another, "'the worst President we have ever had' yet also 'the most admired'" (34, 26).

30. Mark Twain's atttacks on the American plutocracy were linked with reflections about a coming American monarchy. The condition that would create it was "vast power and wealth, which breed commercial and political corruption and incite public favorites to dangerous ambitions." Neither Andrew Carnegie nor the Rockefellers were chiefly associated by him with political corruption or ambitions. Carnegie's "deadliest affliction" was his talking "ever and ever and untiringly of the attentions which have been shown him." In his essay on the Bible class of John D. Rockefeller, Jr., he depicts Rockefeller as an "earnest, uneducated Christian" whose billions cause his Sunday school followers to divide "its worship between him and his Creator—unequally" (Geismar [ed.], *Mark Twain and the Three R's*, 237, 231, 228).

quaintance recognized the human dimensions of Andrew Carnegie. "Somehow I liked him," he wrote his father after having lunch with Carnegie in 1892. "Still, I would rather not be one of his hands." On another occasion, he dined with "a large literary lot at Andrew Carnegie's, in his great new palace on Fifth Avenue. It costs heaps of money, but is very simple and livable, and simplicity is the note of himself and his most amiable wife." On still another occasion, when he and Elinor visited the Carnegies, he found Andrew "rather pathetic . . . like the young man who had great possessions" but who was "always going away exceedingly sorrowful."[31]

Even more than Mark Twain, Howells was the friend of presidents. His campaign biography of Lincoln, though he had little acquaintance with him later, indirectly led to his appointment in Venice. He performed a similar service for Rutherford B. Hayes, to whom he was related through Elinor. And though the Hayes presidency offered him more opportunities than he took (and what favors he took were not for himself), he confined his and Elinor's visiting to six days, late in Hayes's presidency. He had to decline an invitation to visit the Clemenses in order to visit the president, but shortly after he may have evened things up by declining an invitation from Hayes to join him on a transcontinental tour. "Though fat I am not strong," he wrote Hayes in declining. Howells knew Garfield, President Hayes's successor, as an old Ohio friend and political associate of his father. Like Mark Twain, he deplored that side of Theodore Roosevelt that he labeled "a wretched Jingo." Yet he acknowledged to Aurelia, "He is a personal friend, and I like him." In one exchange of letters, Howells praised him for supporting spelling reform, and Roosevelt's reply set aside such praise to point out the much greater importance of his trying to "restrain the accumulation of . . . great fortunes."[32] His support of inheritance and income taxes were measures that gained Howells' strong support.

31. Wortham (ed.), *W. D. Howells: Selected Letters*, IV, 12; Fischer and Lohmann (eds.), *W. D. Howells: Selected Letters*, V, 51 n. 3, 197.

32. Smith and Gibson (eds.), *Mark Twain–Howells Letters*, I, 327, n. 3; William Dean Howells to Aurelia Howells, October 30, 1898, in Howells Papers; M. Howells (ed.), *Life in Letters*, II, 228–29.

The hobnobbing with millionaires by two most often ardent democrats and populists cannot help but raise questions. If they are hypocritical, it is a familiar American hypocrisy, and perhaps nothing is so American about both Howells and Mark Twain as their pursuit of wealth even as they deplored the ills of capitalism. As with the majority of affluent Americans then and now, a guilty conscience is a small price to pay for the comforts that wealth provides. No one was more aware of the naggings of conscience, of the harm it worked upon a person's sense of well-being, and yet its seeming necessity as a check on human greed, than Mark Twain—unless it was William Dean Howells. Howells could admire, but not practice, the disavowal of wealth of a Tolstoy. Mark Twain could recognize what Howells saw in Tolstoy, but admit, "I can't get *him* in focus yet."[33] Neither could disavow friends because they were wealthy. And though neither can be fairly accused of seeking out wealthy individuals for their particular use or companionship, both found it flattering that some men of great wealth and power would seek them out.

Howells' insight into Mark Twain's attitudes toward wealth come closer to the mark than that of most later commentators. "He did not care much for money in itself, but he luxuriated in the lavish use of it, and he was as generous with it as ever a man was." Samuel Webster, whose memory of Mark Twain's treatment of his father gives him no reason to single out Mark Twain's generosity, observed, "Mark Twain always wanted to be on the giving end."[34] In this respect, his own inclinations were strongly enforced by those of Livy, whose characteristic gesture was to give something to others. Mark Twain believed, with Aristotle, that magnanimity resides in having the wherewithal to be magnanimous, though he also responded to the Christian idea of charity enshrined in tales like that of the widow's mite. For the most part, he was a generous man, and with somewhat better returns from his generosity than he got from most of his moneymaking investments.

One example will suffice: the support of the sculptor Karl

33. Smith and Gibson (eds.), *Mark Twain–Howells Letters*, II, 596.
34. W. D. Howells, "My Mark Twain," 66; Webster, *Mark Twain, Business Man*, 180.

Gerhardt and his wife, to which Howells was for a time the only out-side witness. Mark Twain first revealed the matter to him in February, 1881, in a letter marked "Private & Confidential." Gerhardt was a resident of Hartford, an employee of the Pratt & Whitney machine shops, but a sculptor of some obvious but untrained talent. His wife arrived at Mark Twain's door without warning and despite the writer's irritable mood persuaded him to come look at a statue Gerhardt had made and "tell him if there is any promise in it." Both Mark Twain and Charles Dudley Warner went to look at the statue, a life-size female figure nude to the waist for which Gerhardt's young wife had been the model. Having his own favorable assessment of Gerhardt's abilities corroborated by others, Mark Twain supported the couple for three years in Europe while Gerhardt polished his skills. The Howellses visited the Gerhardts on their European trip in 1883 and suggested, as it would not cost much more than their upkeep in Paris, that they be encouraged to visit Italy. "You are those poor little people's god," he wrote Mark Twain, and was as impressed with the young couple as Mark Twain and Warner had been.[35] When Gerhardt returned to the United States in 1884, he had a successful career as a sculptor, among whose works are included busts of Mark Twain and Ulysses S. Grant.

The incident adds two other interesting footnotes. Mark Twain's description of Mrs. Gerhardt posing beside the bare-breasted statue and his coming slowly to realize that she had been the model is a sharp vignette of his (and perhaps of his age's) reaction to feminine beauty, even in its undraped form. "Well, sir," he wrote, "it was perfectly charming, this girl's innocence & purity—exhibiting her naked self, as it were, to a stranger & alone, & never once dreaming that there was the slightest indelicacy about the matter. And so there wasn't; but it will be many a long day before I run across another woman who can do the like & show no trace of self-consciousness." A second footnote is how Howells used the incident as a reinforcement for his beliefs about realism in fiction. Mark Twain had sent

35. Smith and Gibson (eds.), *Mark Twain–Howells Letters*, I, 434. See pages 350–355 for the beginnings of this story as revealed in letters.

him a letter from Mrs. Gerhardt after they had settled in Paris, and he is struck with "that child's artless way of saying the moving thing." Howells replied, "The ideal perfection of some things in life persuades me more and more never to meddle with the ideal in fiction: it is impossible to compete with the facts."[36]

The main point of the incident, however, is the generosity that came to be expected of Mark Twain and the responses he sometimes, but not always, made. The particulars gratified Mark Twain immensely: the unexpected way the story began, the combination of people involved, the struggles of a self-trained artist, the actual opportunity it gave him to support a living and artistic charity. He also must have found some self-gratification in what his money not only enabled him to do, but what it signified to others. As his life went on, he was constantly sought out as a supporter of many charities, and he grumbled about and accepted as many as a basically generous but not mindless person would. Those that went unannounced or as surprises and that had a direct human dimension seemed to please him most, as with his sponsoring of the Saturday Morning Club for young girls in Hartford and his surprise presentation to each of them of engraved pins from Tiffany's.

Among the writings of his late years are those that purport to reveal generosity and other conventional virtues for what they really are. The most of *Which Was It?* is an attempt to prove that selfishness is at the root of all acts. A tale is told of a man's giving a ragged widow his last quarter, forcing him to walk three miles home in a bitter storm. But that quarter, Clemens has his narrator comment, "bought himself free of the tortures of a sharp pain in his heart, he bought himself free of the tortures of a waiting conscience, he bought a whole night's sleep all for twenty-five cents. It should make the sharpest nigger-trader on the river ashamed of himself. On his way home his heart was joyful and it sang—profit on top of profit! usury! Allen, the impulse which moved the man to succor the old woman was wholly selfish, utterly selfish. But there was nothing base about it, nothing ignoble."[37] Lest one jump too quickly to as-

36. *Ibid.*, I, 353, 384, 385.
37. Tuckey (ed.), *Which Was the Dream?*, 308.

suming just where Mark Twain stood in these matters, the spokesman in this passage is Ham-fat Bailey, the Idiot Philosopher, who in
many particulars is drawn from Clemens' brother Orion.

To some extent, Howells contrasted his own less affluent state
with Mark Twain's all his life, refusing most often Mark Twain's generous offers to pay for trips Howells could not easily afford, sym-
pathizing with his friend's financial difficulties, and admiring greatly
the refusal of Mark Twain to take advantage of bankruptcy, choosing
to repay his creditors dollar for dollar. Toward the end of his three
years of paying off his creditors, Mark Twain wrote Howells: "I hope
you will never get the like of the load saddled onto you that was
saddled onto me 3 years ago. And yet there is such a solid pleasure
in *paying* the thing that I reckon maybe it is worth while to get into
that kind of hobble, after all."[38]

Howells' generosity may have been compromised by the lesser
margin of wealth on which he operated and by the constant scraping
for substance that he experienced in his youth. His obligations to
his Ohio family continued on even after his children were grown sufficiently to make him anticipate their financial demands. Often, he
put his own family's needs against and above the support that continued to be needed in Ohio. Aurelia's sacrifice in taking responsibility for Henry is one he tried to both assist and atone for by providing funds. And yet it is hard to judge otherwise than that Aurelia
was one of those family members who was taken advantage of in a
common yet questionable way. Regularly, clothes, gifts, and occasional checks for larger purposes were sent to Ohio. Howells helped
maintain the improvident Sam most of his life, buying the Madison,
Ohio, *Index* for him in 1886, which proved only a temporary solu-
tion to providing him an income. Most often vexed with Sam's pleas
for money in later life—"If he could head a beggar's union, it would
beat the Standard Oil trust"—he informed Aurelia of a week's visit
Sam had made at his house in 1914. "I had reflected with a very bad
conscience that I had never, in all my long housekeeping years, had
him under my roof for a night." He described the two of them as
"two fat old men" who seemed to enjoy the visit. "Morally I think I

38. Smith and Gibson (eds.), *Mark Twain–Howells Letters*, II, 670.

should have been a good deal like him, if some dynamite had not been somehow got into me."[39]

He was generous of his time, influence, and money in easing the lot of his father in his later years. In 1885 he expressed his concern that the elder Howells should work too hard and wrote Aurelia, "I want to pay for the hand and have father stop." He helped Annie in a number of ways in her own career as a writer, and he likewise assisted his elder brother Joseph in his efforts as a writer, though not without some impatience. In 1905 and 1906 a number of letters try to correct Joe (the two brothers were then seventy-three and sixty-eight) in points of grammar. "You are a man of good presence and good manner, and will do yourself credit," William Dean writes, "if you will look out for your syntax."[40]

This is by no means a full accounting of Howells' support of his Ohio family members; even a full accounting leaves questions as to the nature of his domestic acts of thrift and generosity. His helping out back home seems at times to be the customary providing of hand-me-downs and obligatory support. There was a streak of cautious management in his charity that is consistent with his general conduct of life. His son John, writing to Mildred in 1928, noted "that any money I can earn (and I earn more than I want) comes from his patient support of me without comment far beyond the usual age—he never even mentioned or took notice of the fact that he was still supporting me at 30."[41]

Perhaps an anecdote in his relationship with his brother Joseph will disclose some of the ambiguity of Howells' generosity, and of Howells' own questioning of his character in that respect. In 1905 and 1906 Howells was instrumental in securing a consulship for Joseph at Turk's Island in the British West Indies, a post which Joseph recognized as a faraway and minor one and which Howells

39. William Dean Howells to Joseph A. Howells, January 15, 1908, in Howells Papers; Gibson and Lohmann, *W. D. Howells: Selected Letters*, VI, 61.

40. Leitz (ed.), *W. D. Howells: Selected Letters*, III, 124; Fisher and Lohmann (eds.), *W. D. Howells: Selected Letters*, V, 137, 161, 196.

41. John Mead Howells to Mildred Howells, June 5, 1928, in Howells Papers.

urged him to take, largely it seems because it would solve Joseph's financial problems (and relieve some weight of conscience on Howells, too). Joseph did not find life on Turk's Island altogether satisfactory, and again it was William Dean who kept urging him to stick it out, and often at the point of reminding him that with the economy there he could live reasonably well, as he might not be able to do in the United States.

At one point, shortly after he arrived, Joseph wants to spend money to return home, at least temporarily, and Howells speaks against spending such money, reminding him of the money he had provided him for initial passage. "You may think it cheeky of me, who lives wastefully, to preach economy to you," he wrote, "but I have the money to waste, and that is the difference." The bluntness is not characteristic of Howells' letters, but the voiced smugness here must be acknowledged. Just as characteristic is the relenting that followed. In a letter a month later, Howells recognizes his "cheapness" and makes an offer of partial help for passage. Very close upon the first letter was another which, perhaps inadvertently but insensitively nonetheless, reminds Joseph again of the distance between his own condition and that of his wealthy brother. Colonel Harvey, the new publisher of *Harper's*, Howells informs his brother, has offered "to blow Mark Twain and me in for a trip to England on the big Baltic steamer, and a three weeks automobile tour of the island. Wouldn't you like to be one of us?"[42]

There is little question that Howells enjoyed his affluence even as it sometimes afflicted his conscience, that he worked hard for it, and that it placed obligations upon him with respect to his own and his Ohio family. He seldom forgot that his hard and steady work was no harder or steadier than the work of millions for whom it provided little present comfort or future security. "I have had a fair share of luck, taking it 'by and large,'"[43] he wrote Joseph in 1906. Although his Ohio family could not be numbered among the miserably poor

42. William Dean Howells to Joseph A. Howells, July 22 and August 6, 1906, in Howells Papers.
43. Fischer (ed.), *W. D. Howells: Selected Letters*, V, 157.

that he had seen almost everywhere he had lived and traveled, they were still among the millions who had not been particularly favored by the capitalistic economy under which they lived.

Clearly, both Howells and Mark Twain became capitalists, though on a small scale compared with the big capitalists of their time. Both distrusted capitalism as an adequate basis for a just society and that distrust arose from their strong and passionate concern for justice. The voicing of that distrust was a strong and consistent theme in their writing, and it reflected both inner conflicts which arose from their own situations as well as conflicts which seemed to be inescapable in a system that pitted "haves" against "have-nots."

Finally, as they became older and wealthier, they became less optimistic about economic justice and a just society. In those respects, the world had changed little in their lifetimes, and as their reading and writing exposed them to history, they realized what little had changed over the longer span. Materialism was still the basic philosophy of most of those whose struggle for existence gave them little time or inclination to philosophize and for most of those, too, whose economic status gave them leisure to think. Howells and Mark Twain accepted materialism and all its specific savory and unsavory manifestations. The romantic and idealistic and moral in both writers posed various measures and dramatized scenes against which the shortcomings and viciousness, even, of purely materialistic views might be measured. The comic that seldom disappeared completely from their work refused to see a wholly dark world, damned man's worst features, and laughed at and made others laugh at the many infirmities and incongruities of an imperfect world.

Eleven

The Joke Is All out of *That*

One of the mutually admired characteristics of Howells and Mark Twain was their ability to laugh at themselves and at each other. The humor of self-disparagement is as much a part of Mark Twain's comic talent as exaggeration and incongruity, and he often exaggerated his own unfortunate traits in order to heighten the incongruity of so much attention being given to him. In an unpublished sketch of his late years, "Indiantown," the central figures, David and Susan Gridley, are thinly disguised projections of Sam and Olivia Clemens. A long paragraph describes the contrasting traits of "the two Davids."

The real David, the inside David, the hidden David, was of an incurably low tone, and wedded to low ideals; the outside David, Susan Gridley's David, the sham David, was of a lofty tone, with ideals which the angels in heaven might envy. The real David had a native affection for all vulgarities . . . the sham David traded in fine and delicate things only. . . . The real David couldn't keep his word, the sham one couldn't break it. The real David cared but little whether an inconvenient debt was paid or not; the sham one would settle it with his last shirt. The real David was seldom serious; the sham one was a tombstone. . . . The real David was slovenly and preferred it . . . ; the sham David went gloved and clothed like a gentleman. . . . The real David carried a devil's spasmodic temper inside; the sham one was as serene as moonlight. The real David loathed society and its irksome polish and restraints; the sham one was the society model whom the observing and judicious delighted to pattern after.[1]

The passage in its entirety offers as convincing a description of the divided nature of Mark Twain as any set forth by later biographers. And yet, at best, it can be trusted only as a fictional projection, Mark Twain's perception of himself, in part, at a certain point in time.

Howells, too, can be seen as a divided person. Basil March, Howells' chief projection of himself into his novels, is a seriocomic figure. His speech is marked by irony, as one suspects Howells' speech was among his peers. But his manner is never cynical nor merely clever. Rather it consistently reflects a refusal to be overpowered by the seriousness of the world or of himself.

Aging may call forth every ability to view life comically. Both Howells and Mark Twain were very conscious of growing old—at those customary milestones of the decades beyond forty, and at many times in between. Their friendship became important, as all friendships do, not only in assisting them through specific losses and infirmities, but in facing the general sense of loss that accompanies growing old. "Still it would be a good enough world if one didn't have to leave it," Howells wrote Clemens in June, 1899. "This curse of growing old! The joke is all out of *that*." A year and a half earlier Mark Twain had written Howells from Vienna: "If you were here I think we could cry down each other's necks, as in your dream. For we *are* a pair of old derelicts drifting around, now, with some of our passengers gone & the sunniness of the others in ⟨total⟩ eclipse."[2]

Both men were fortunate in living long lives and being relatively free from illnesses and failings that accompany old age. Both, too, were somewhat late starters in their careers. Howells' four years in Venice meant that he was almost thirty before he began as an assistant editor of the *Atlantic*. Mark Twain did not marry until he was

1. Tuckey (ed.), *Which Was the Dream?*, 168.
2. Smith and Gibson (eds.), *Mark Twain–Howells Letters*, II, 701, 670.

almost thirty-five, and *Huckleberry Finn* was written when he was forty-five, about the same age as Howells when he wrote *The Rise of Silas Lapham*. Those seemingly youthful years when Mark Twain was established at Hartford and Howells in Boston and Cambridge took place when both men were in their mid-thirties to mid-forties. Howells' last child was born when he was thirty-five; Jean, Clemens' last-born, did not arrive until he was forty-five. These facts point to a prolonging of youth, even at a time when middle age was regarded as beginning earlier than it does now. The many years still left to them after 1885, when Mark Twain reached fifty, stretched out the period that by any reckoning can be called old age.

It was not fanciful affection that made Livy call her husband "Youth." Howells' description of him at fifty is not, except for the literary touches, far different from Susy's of about the same time. "He had kept, as he did to the end, the slender figure of his youth," Howells wrote, "but the ashes of the burnt-out years were beginning to gray the fires of that splendid shock of red hair which he held to the height of a stature apparently greater than it was, and tilted from side to side in his undulating walk. He glimmered at you from the narrow slits of fine blue-greenish eyes, under branching brows, which with age grew more and more like a sort of plumage, and he was apt to smile into your face with a subtle but amiable perception, and yet with a sort of remote absence; you were all there for him, but he was not all there for you."[3] When Livy reached her fortieth birthday and Clemens neared his fiftieth, he acknowledged to her by letter, and in very conventional prose for Mark Twain, that "our faces are toward the sunset, now," and expressed great satisfaction that their journey had such "gracious company" to "lighten the march." At fifty-six, leaving the family at Lausanne, he drove to a

3. W. D. Howells, "My Mark Twain," 25–26. Susy's description at about same age: "He has beautiful gray hair, not any too thick or any too long, but just right; a Roman nose, which greatly improves the beauty of his features; Kind blue eyes and a small mustache. He has a wonderfully shaped head and profile. He has a very good figure—in short, he is an extraordinarily fine looking man." Edith Colgate Salsbury (ed.), *Susy and Mark Twain: Family Dialogues* (New York, 1965), 195–96.

mountain in Valence in early morning, climbed it and rambled among ruins of a castle.[4] During the nineties, shuttling back and forth from Europe in the early years and traveling around the world in the later ones, he had little time to dwell upon his age. And although some illnesses were upon him, some of which he tried to keep from Livy, he remained vigorous even as he passed sixty-five in 1900.

Howells' severe illness of late 1881 and his convalescing early the next year brought back his earlier morbid fears and recognition of his own aging. "I'm five years older than I was ⟨six⟩ two months ago. I may young up again, but that is the present fact."[5] Like Mark Twain's, his younging up was much a matter of throwing himself into his work. The eighties were a tremendously productive period for Howells, and it was not until the death of Winny in 1889 that his deep melancholy returned, this time to be worked off by those novels and articles most critical of the social and economic system that visited far worse ills upon those in less fortunate circumstances than Howells or Mark Twain.

During the nineties, both families were reminded of their own ages by the deaths of parents and siblings. Howells' father died in 1894 following an illness that had brought Howells back from Europe. He told Norton: "It has aged me as nothing else could have done. I am now of the generation next to death."[6] His father's death was but one of a clustering of reminders of their own mortality for both Howells and Mark Twain. Howells' mother had died within a few years of Howells' return from Venice, but the Howellses were a remarkably long-lived family. Henry and Sam, both of whom were objects of care by the rest of the family, died relatively young in 1906 and 1908, but Joseph, older than Howells by five years, lived to be eighty. Victoria, only a year older than Howells, had died in the mid-eighties, but Aurelia, to whom he stayed very close all his life, lived to be eighty-nine, and Anne, successfully married to Achille Frechette, lived to be ninety-four. Howells' two children carried on the family longevity, John dying in 1959 at ninety-one,

4. Wecter (ed.), *Love Letters*, 246, 260–61.
5. Smith and Gibson (eds.), *Mark Twain–Howells Letters*, I, 385.
6. Wortham (ed.), *W. D. Howells: Selected Letters*, IV, 78.

and Mildred in 1966 at ninety-three. During the decade that Howells lived beyond both Mark Twain and Elinor, he saw most of even his oldest literary acquaintances die, until he seemed a solitary survivor.

Mark Twain lost his father early in his life, and Jane Lampton, a vigorous and articulate woman (Clemens said he would like to see her write something of what she was able to communicate in person), lived well into Mark Twain's middle age. She died in 1890 at eighty-seven, the same age as William Cooper Howells at his death, and during the same year in which Livy's mother died. As painful as were the deaths of Livy's father and of their infant son in the early days of their marriage, by 1890 these had been put aside. But with the death of each of their mothers in 1890, the Clemenses faced a decade of deaths. Theodore Crane, Livy's sister's husband, died in 1889, and during the preceding months, according to Mark Twain, "suffered a good deal of pain of a bodily sort, together with a mental depression & hopelessness that made him yearn for death every day."[7] Susy died in 1896, Orion in 1897, Livy and Mark Twain's sister Pamela in 1904, and finally Jean in 1909, the year before Mark Twain's own death. Of his brothers and sisters and his own children, only Clara, happily married shortly before Mark Twain died and living on until 1965, survived him. Among their close literary friends, Charles Dudley Warner was the first to die, in 1900, followed by Aldrich, Hay, and Norton within the decade.

Howells and Mark Twain had little chance to see each other during much of the 1890s, for with the Clemenses' departure for Europe in 1891, the family was to live outside the United States for much of the next nine years. In the two years between mid-1892 and 1894, Mark Twain went back and forth between Europe and New York eight times, seeing Howells often in 1893 and 1894. In the summer of 1894, they had a chance for leisurely talk in Paris until Howells returned to be with his father before he died. The preparation for their round-the-world trip brought the Clemenses home for about two months, a part of which time Mark Twain was confined to bed in Elmira with carbuncles and gout. Howells only saw them in passing then, and as they departed for Vancouver and thence out onto the

7. Wecter (ed.), *Mark Twain to Mrs. Fairbanks*, 264.

ocean, Mark Twain may have seemed, even to Howells, to be a fictional creation off on another adventure, leaving Howells and much of the rest of the world to mark his progress by items in the newspapers.

As the trip neared its end, bringing Clemens and Livy and Clara to London in late summer of 1896, they planned to have Jean and Susy join them there. Instead, Susy's unexpected death marked the beginning of the losses that plunged Mark Twain into bleak and bitter moods. The exchanges between Howells and Mark Twain are more tender during this period than at any other time of their friendship. In a P.S., Mark Twain responded to the love Howells had expressed for Livy: "I see that I have left out something which I particularly wanted to say. In assuring Mrs. Clemens of your love for her you touched her very deeply, & she has never been more outspokenly grateful for any prized thing which these clouded eighteen months have brought her. She needs all the love she can get, & there is no support that is so good & so welcome as the love of the old, old friends of the days that are gone." Writing from Vienna in January, 1898, Mark Twain observed how he used to write "'Hartford, 1871.' There was no Susy then—there is no Susy now." He mentioned both Susy and Winny, "given us, in miserable sport, & then taken away."[8]

Work, Howells advised Mildred in 1895, is "the only happiness, the only refuge from one's self."[9] Both authors resisted the specific griefs that came upon them as well as the general depressing effects of old age by keeping at their work. Although Mark Twain published no long major work after this time, the amount of writing he did was extraordinary, and much of it as good as any work he had done earlier in his life. Although he may appear to be fumbling at times, he had never found working within established literary forms easy. Even as loose a form as the novel did not accommodate Mark Twain's peculiar genius very well. As readers can find much excellent work among Howells' immense productivity of the last decade, so can they in Mark Twain's. In some ways, Mark Twain's work of the last

8. Smith and Gibson (eds.), *Mark Twain–Howells Letters*, II, 671, 669.
9. Wortham (ed.), *W. D. Howells: Selected Letters*, IV, 116.

decade, were it to be assembled and edited around its major themes, would comprise what he told Howells he was going to do in 1899, now that he had enough security to "put the pot-boiler pen away." "What I have been wanting," he wrote, "was a chance to write a book without reserves—a book which should take account of no one's feelings, no one's prejudices, opinions, beliefs, hopes, illusions, delusions; a book which should say my say, right out of my heart, in the plainest language & without a limitation of any sort. . . . It is under way, now, & it *is* a luxury! an intellectual drunk." [10]

Their personal lives and their literary ones are summed up to a large extent in the correspondence that precedes the Clemenses' coming home from their long exile in 1900. The century's coming to a close complemented their mood. Howells' two-volume novel, done in special binding for the Christmas trade of 1898, was *Their Silver Wedding Journey*, purportedly the European trip of Basil and Isabel March, the couple he had introduced in *Their Wedding Journey* twenty-five years before. The book was a fairly direct account of the Howellses' trip of the year before. The Clemenses read it in Vienna and took as much delight in finding themselves fictionalized there as Howells must have taken in writing them in. With Mark Twain's return to America, his public presence was never more flatteringly celebrated, and his personal life for a time seemed to renew itself with the new century. The Howellses were living at 115 East 16th Street, close to where the Clemenses first rented a place at 14 West 10th. Howells wrote to Thomas Bailey Aldrich, "Clemens is here, settled down for the winter in West 10th Street, and looking younger and jollier than I've seen him for ten years." In February, 1901, he wrote Aurelia: "I see a great deal of Mark Twain nowadays, and we have high good times denouncing everything. We agree perfectly about the Boer War and the Filipino War, and war generally. Then, we are old fellows, and it is pleasant to find the world so much worse than it was when we were young." [11]

10. Smith and Gibson (eds.), *Mark Twain–Howells Letters*, II, 698.
11. Wortham (ed.), *W. D. Howells: Selected Letters*, IV, 254, 258.

Such moods were shoring up the two old friends as the century began. There were enough current events to denounce, and the placing of the present against the past both in and outside their writings was something they could warmly share. Howells' letter to Aldrich on December 8, 1901, gives a sense of Howells' personal joy in having Mark Twain close by and of the public adulation then accorded him.

You ought to have been with Clemens and me yesterday at a Harper lunch. . . . These were gay years, and bless God, we *knew* they were at the time! Well, yesterday it was not so bad either, walking with Clemens to his train under a pink New York sunset sky, that you know the like of. He has no time table, but all the gatemen and train starters are proud to know him, and lay hold of him, and put him aboard of *something* that leaves him at Riverdale. He always has to go to the w.c., me dancing in the corridor, and holding his train for him. But they would not let it go without him, if it was the Chicago limited. What a fame and a force he is![12]

In the public eye, both Howells and Mark Twain became identified as anti-imperialists, with Howells spurring on Mark Twain's unmatched talent for invective. By comparison, his own work, as always, was restrained. The difference in temperament and mood of the two might be measured by comparing Howells' rational Utopia in *A Visitor from Altruria* with Mark Twain's *Mysterious Stranger*. Mark Twain notes the difference in a letter from Vienna in 1898, following some chiding by Howells about his not giving sufficient attention lately to Howells' work. "It's quite true," he wrote, "—I *don't* read you 'as much as I *ought*,' nor anywhere near half as much as I want to; still I read you all I get a chance to." In a subsequent letter, he goes on. "You are old enough to be a weary man, with paling interests, but you do not show it. You do your work in the same old delicate & delicious & forceful & searching & perfect way. I don't know how you can—but I suspect. I suspect that to you there is still dignity in human life, & that Man is not a joke—a poor joke—the poorest joke that was ever contrived. . . . I have lost my pride in him & can't write gaily nor praisefully about him any more."

12. *Ibid.*, 275–76.

Howells does hold out more possibility for man than Mark Twain does. He was also more accepting than Mark Twain of the changes that come over man, both the chance calamities and the inevitable ones, like aging. "Well," he wrote to Joseph, "we must grow old if we live."[13]

Mark Twain's published works of his last decade, such as "To a Person Sitting in Darkness," and "The United States of Lyncherdom," as well as a number of unpublished works, are, like *The Mysterious Stranger*, the product of long-held pessimistic and often obsessive views. His hostility toward God is one subject he felt he could more freely express, and work follows work in which God is depicted as an uncaring Providence that man mistakenly worships or as a superstitious concept on which man has erected even more supersitious beliefs. At times, God is seemingly an angry God ("a malicious Creator" he called him to Howells) whose anger is specifically directed at Mark Twain. "It would be so natural—so remorselessly historical—" he wrote Howells the day after Christmas, 1902, ". . . for Disaster to sneak along in my track for 7 years, disguised as Good Fortune; & then drop his handsome mask & grin at me out of his skinless skull."[14] Although he could claim there was no "subject of a lower grade and less awful than theology," the bulk of his writings manifested theological concerns, however unorthodox his views. One part of them satirized individual religious beliefs, such as that of the Virgin Birth; another focused on the deceptions man indulged in to hide the truth of his meaningless existence in an uncaring and cruel universe.

The subject of religion was one he shared with Howells through the years. Howells never quite abandoned an essentially Christian position, with the life and example of Christ at the center of it. For Mark Twain, Joan of Arc may have embodied something of the same spirit and power of an unsophisticated Christian ethic. The faith that sustained a belief in a personal God and with it a belief in personal

13. Smith and Gibson (eds.), *Mark Twain–Howells Letters*, II, 684, 689; William Dean Howells to Joseph A. Howells, February 19, 1905. Howells Papers, Houghton Library, Harvard.

14. Smith and Gibson (eds.), *Mark Twain–Howells Letters*, II, 757–58.

immortality was almost as weak in Howells as in Mark Twain. In a forgotten short story of 1900, "A Difficult Case," Howells created a central character, suggestive of Mark Twain, who in his deathbed truculence tells his religious comforters: "Why, man, you don't suppose I *want* to live hereafter? Do you think I'm anxious to have it all over again, or *any* of it? . . . I've had enough. I want to be let alone . . . I want to *stop*." Mark Twain read the story, an unusual one for Howells, and reported that he had "got a world of evil joy out of it." [15]

Politics and world affairs were distressing to both of them at the turn of the century. The Civil War that had been at the edge of their lives in their youth was now replaced by the Sino-Japanese War, the Spanish-American War, and the Boer War. The two men denounced all three, and Mark Twain turned out a number of his most powerful pieces on man's tendency to maim and kill each other. Christian Science confirmed for Mark Twain that "in the matter of religions, we progress backward." The existing wars confirmed the same view of man's general progress. In an unpublished sketch, "The Stupendous Procession," written probably in early 1901, the twentieth century, "drunk and disorderly, borne in the arms of Satan," leads a procession that includes most of the objects of Mark Twain's scorn. Christendom comes next, "a majestic matron, in flowing robes drenched with blood." Behind her come her favorite children, England and the mutilated figures of the Transvaal and Orange Free State, Spain and the Inquisition, Russia with a weary column of exiles and floats "piled high with Bloated Corpses—Massacred Manchurian peasants." France, Germany, and America march along with similar horrors in tow. The American eagle appears, "ashamed, bedraggled, moulting; one foot chained," accompanied by a long tabulation of American dead in past and present wars. Tammany Hall, the Philippine Commission, and other targets are introduced, and at the very end, the shade of Lincoln marches, "towering vast and dim toward the sky, brooding with pained aspect over the far-reaching pageant." [16]

15. *Ibid.*, 719. The story is in William Dean Howells, *A Pair of Patient Lovers* (New York, 1901).

16. John S. Tuckey (ed.), *Mark Twain's Fables of Man* (Berkeley, 1972), 405–419.

But for all the parading of cruelty and folly and greed and malice, which history and Providence and man not only condone but foster, Mark Twain's writing has a zest and grim humor that indicated that he had, in some ways, overcome both the financial crises of the nineties and the self-scourging grief that came with the death of Susy. With respect to his old friend Howells, his comic mood reasserted itself in a good number of old-time jokes. One was a letter he sent to Aldrich—which Howells was sure to hear about—in which he enclosed a picture of a dour and menacing sultan of Turkey, Abdul-Hamid II, on which he had inscribed "W. D. H." He explained to Aldrich that this was the newest photo of Howells, one he wished he would use, for it was vastly superior to the picture of the "imposter which he works into book-advertisements." Howells had probably set the joke in motion by sending Mark Twain a recent photograph inscribed to "Old Clemens." When "Old Clemens" replied to "Old Howells," he pointed out that the picture was "a trifle too clerical, too archbishopy; also too intentionally & studiedly holy."[17] There is similar joking about their honorary degrees from Yale in the fall of 1901. For a time, they went around calling each other Doc Clemens and Doc Howells.

Although Mark Twain moved to Riverdale in 1901, making him much less accessible to Howells, they continued to see each other, usually when Mark Twain came down to New York for some occasion, but also at times when Howells made the train trip up the Hudson. Such visiting aroused Howells to set forth as an actual experience a dream about a trip to Riverdale at 3:00 A.M. in which Sam, Mark Twain's man, had turned him away. In an answering letter, Mark Twain reports to Howells the dialogue he had with Sam in trying to set matters straight. Sam described the visitor as "a stumpy little gray man with furtive ways & an evil face," and Clemens tries to pin down just why he was turned away.

"What did he say his name was?"
"He didn't say. He offered his card, but I didn't take it."
"That was stupid. Describe him again—& more in detail."
He did it.

17. Smith and Gibson (eds.), *Mark Twain–Howells Letters*, II, 727, 723, 719.

"I can't seem to locate him—I wish you had taken the card. Why didn't you?"

"I didn't like his manners."

"Why? What did he do?"

"He called me a quadrilateral astronomical incandescent son of a bitch."

"Oh, that was Howells."[18]

The whole dialogue belongs with a supposed copy of a letter to the editor which Mark Twain sent Howells from Tuxedo Park in 1907.

To the Editor:

Sir to you, I would like to know what kind of a goddam govment this is that discriminates between two common carriers & makes a goddam railroad charge everybody equal & lets a goddam man charge any goddam price he wants to for his goddam opera box

W D Howels

Tuxedo Park Oct. 4

(goddam it)

The joke is in part that Howells hated opera and in part in the note that accompanied the letter: "Howells it is an outrage the way the govment is acting so I sent this complaint to N.Y. Times with your name signed because it would have more weight. Mark."[19]

To Howells, the coming of the new century, as reflected in his writings of the next decade, was more of a matter of settling in to new tasks than of indignant opposition to the world around him. He accepted another regular journalistic responsibility in 1900, a column for *Harper's* appropriately named "The Easy Chair." With that commitment came a contract for a novel a year. In 1904 he modified the contract to permit nonfiction travel books as well as novels, and his nonfiction is often better than his fiction. Gathering materials for travel books took him to England in 1904, to Italy and Paris and London in 1907, and to England again in 1909. The best nonfiction book of the period recounts his remarkable trip from Ohio in 1860 to

18. *Ibid.*, 764–65.
19. *Ibid.*, 827.

meet the New England worthies; the sketches of these figures—
Holmes, Lowell, Longfellow, Emerson, and others—in *Literary
Friends and Acquaintance* are some of the best reminiscences we
have of those nineteenth-century literary figures. In 1902 he re-
explored part of the Ohio of his youth by taking a trip down the Ohio
river with his brother Joseph. A children's book the same year, *The
Flight of Pony Baker*, also drew on this Ohio past; Mark Twain, in
reading it, informed Howells that he was in the midst of reviving a
plan to restore Huck Finn in a work of fiction. In his notebook for
February, 1891, he had written: "Huck comes back, 60 years old,
from nobody knows where—& crazy. Thinks he is a boy again, &
scans almost every face for Tom & Becky &c. Tom comes, at last, 60
from wandering the world & tends Huck, & together they talk old
times; both are desolate, life has been a failure, all that was lovable,
all that was beautiful is under the mould. They die together." Like
Howells, he, too, was revisiting in actuality as in his writing, his
western past. The University of Missouri awarded him a Doctor of
Laws degree in 1901, and he revisited Hannibal on the trip back,
spending four days in the town and giving out diplomas and making
a short speech at the high school graduation. The *Hannibal Morning
Journal* commented upon his visit. "There is not a man or woman
in Hannibal who saw him while here but that feels better by his
coming."[20]

Howells' sense of his old age is conveyed in many letters to
many different correspondents. "I do hate to be sixty years old," he
wrote Aurelia, "—it is so near seventy, and so close to the end of my
beloved work." At seventy, to Edmund Clarence Stedman he observed, "What an awfully long day a 70th birthday is!" One of his
longer reflections he addressed to Aldrich, July 3, 1902.

I should not mind being old, so much, if I always had the young, sure grip
of myself. What I hate is this dreamy fumbling about my own identity, in

20. Browning, Frank, and Salamo (eds.), *Mark Twain's Notebooks & Journals*,
III, 606; see Milton Meltzer, *Mark Twain Himself: A Pictorial Biography* (New
York, 1960), for clippings and pictures about this return (pp. 232–35) as well as
of other events in his life.

which I detect myself at odd times. It seems sometimes as if it were some-body else, and I sometimes wish it were. But it will have to go on, and I must get what help I can out of the fact that it always *has* gone on. I think I could deal with the present, bad and bothering as it is, if it were not for visions of the past in which I appear to be mostly running about, full of sound and fury signifying nothing. Once I thought that I meant something by everything I did; but now I don't know.[21]

Confronted with the last ten years of Mark Twain's life, a sensitive reader might well wish Mark Twain had not, as he often wished, survived Livy. Hamlin Hill, who has courageously but narrowly focused on just that period in Mark Twain's life, declares, "The truth is inescapable that, wherever he went after he died, much of the last decade of his life he lived in hell."[22] The hyperbole is one that Mark Twain would appreciate. Certainly, there is much pathos, much strange behavior, much that might be lamented or deplored in the facts Hill chooses to emphasize. But the tone of Mark Twain's *Autobiography*, most of it written during the last five years of his life, belies the claim that these were years of unrelieved gloom and chronic fits of spleen. The accomplishment it represents in itself alters the picture of a great writer whose powers have eroded. Nor does Mark Twain's relation with Howells shift so much in even his very last years to suggest an inescapable misanthropy. The gloomiest year was that which followed the death of Livy in Florence in the spring of 1904. Some of the brighter spots were still those in which he and Howells were able to meet and talk once again.

The years from 1901 to 1904 were the last years in which Howells and Mark Twain met frequently but they were not out of each other's thoughts and writing for very long in the years until Mark Twain's death. "My mainstay for talk, this summer," Howells wrote C. E. Norton in 1902, "has been Mark Twain, only forty trolley minutes away. But how sad old men are! We meet, and strike fire and flicker up, and I come away a heap of cold ashes."[23] Mark Twain was at

21. Wortham (ed.), *W. D. Howells: Selected Letters*, IV, 145; Fischer (ed.), *W. D. Howells: Selected Letters*, V, 210, 32.

22. Hill, *Mark Twain: God's Fool* (New York, 1973), xvii.

23. Fischer (ed.), *W. D. Howells: Selected Letters*, V, 37.

York Harbor, Maine, just up the road from Howells' summer place at Kittery Point. Their visits were frequent in early summer, sadly terminating with the onset of Livy's near-fatal illness in late August to late September, diagnosed as nervous prostration and heart disease. When she returned to Riverdale, Clemens was forbidden to see her, and there began the pathetic daily letter he "sent" to her and the elaborate lies he and Clara engaged in to keep her from being disturbed by such events as Jean's severe illness following epileptic seizures she had experienced on Rogers' yacht, which had taken the family to Maine.

Despite all, Mark Twain did attend social occasions—the dinner honoring his sixty-seventh birthday, for example—and did see and talk with Howells and other friends. Livy improved enough to go to Elmira in the summer of 1903, and Mark Twain began making plans to take her to Florence. From that time on, he and Howells saw little of each other, though Howells saw him off at the dinner *Harper's* publisher gave for him on his departure in October. Howells observed that Mark Twain had changed during these months from "what now seems the almost hopeless case of his wife." Despite the hopelessness, however, the fact of their being able to go to Florence revived Mark Twain's spirits, and his letters to Howells during the early months there are in the old vein. He is full of details about doing his autobiography and is urging upon Howells the great advantages of dictating. For years, Mark Twain had chafed over the physical act of writing; with the crippling of his right hand, some form of dictating became a necessity. As often with Mark Twain, the seemingly mechanical detail of putting words on paper caused him to think about more important aspects of writing. It confirmed the belief that was fundamental to his strength as a writer: that the naturalness of speech was central.

Howells arrived in England with his daughter Mildred on March 25, 1904. Elinor's health had limited her travel as well as increased her periods of invalidism, though this time she was able to join Howells just before the conferring of his Oxford degree. Mildred, who had stayed with the Clemenses at Etretat, France, in the late summer of 1894, was to be Howells' traveling companion often in his late life. They were in London when they received Mark Twain's letter with its blunt opening sentence: "Last night at 9:20 I entered Mrs. Clemens's room to say the usual good-night—& she was dead!" The next to last sentence was just as blunt: "I am tired & old; I wish I were with Livy." Howells wrote two short letters of condolence within two days of each other and another as Mark Twain was about to leave Europe for Livy's burial in Elmira. The Howellses remained in Europe for the summer and following winter. Writing to his sisters, Aurelia and Annie, about the degree ceremony, he observed, "Distinctions all come rather late in life, and if they do not kill, they cure the desire for more."[24] Desired or not, the next year after the Howellses returned to New York, he received a Doctor of Letters from Columbia. Three years later, his "dean of American letters" position firmly established, he was elected first president of the newly founded American Academy of Arts and Letters.

"It seems a poor joke of fate," Howells wrote Mark Twain from San Remo, Italy, January 6, 1905, "that I should be in Italy the year after you, and only twelve hours from Florence."[25] Mark Twain was then in New York wearing out the loss of Livy and facing the facts of Clara's nervous collapse. Resting in a New York sanitarium, she, like Livy, was forbidden to see (or even to correspond with) him and was to be spared all disturbing news. The most disturbing, which Mark Twain did blunderingly inform her of, was Jean's severe injuries when the horse she was riding collided with a trolley car. That autumn was one of the most disturbing times in Mark Twain's life; little correspondence passed between him and Howells during the period, but by the time Howells returned to New York in the spring, Mark Twain was beginning to alleviate if not cure his pains by going back to writing. The world had not changed sufficiently to rob him of immediate objects of outrage. He was working now with Isabel Lyon, who was to be a faithful secretary until her health, her marriage to Ralph Ashcroft, and conflicts with Clara and Jean sundered

24. Smith and Gibson (eds.), *Mark Twain–Howells Letters*, II, 785; Fischer (ed.), *W. D. Howells: Selected Letters*, V, 107.
25. Smith and Gibson (eds.), *Mark Twain–Howells Letters*, II, 795.

that relationship. Mark Twain's personal despair fit the mood of "The War Prayer" and the "Soliloquies" of the Russian czar and King Leopold of Belgium, written early in this period. Howells talked with him at a dinner in April, at about the time he was finishing an essay on Howells, to be published in *Harper's* the next year. The remarks he makes about Howells as a writer are framed between observations about old age. The beginning sentence—"Is it true that the sun of a man's mentality touches noon at forty and then begins to wane toward setting?"—sets up his introduction of Howells as an exception to such a rule. The final paragraph is personal again. "Mr. Howells has done much work, and the spirit of it is as beautiful as the make of it. I have held him in admiration and affection so many years that I know by the number of those years that he is old now; but his heart isn't, nor his pen; and years do not count." Howells responded to the piece when it appeared, "I could not have asked to have anything gentler or kinder said of me." He closed the letter, "Dear friend of forty years, thanks!"[26]

That Mark Twain's spirits had risen and that his affection for Howells was renewed in the old teasing way is implicit in a letter Mark Twain wrote to H. H. Bancroft declining an invitation (also extended to Howells) to visit him in San Francisco. Bancroft pointed out that Henry James had just spent an enjoyable week with him. Comparing himself with Howells, "that shameless old fictitious butterfly" who was flitting around in a way Mark Twain, almost seventy, could not, he adds, "Howells will be 88 in October."[27] Howells' birthday was in March, and at sixty-eight he was a little more than two years younger than Mark Twain. Whatever private reservations he had about reaching seventy, Mark Twain largely put them aside in his enjoyment of his seventieth birthday dinner in November, 1905.

The next three or four years found the two men often in that most familiar of relationships, sharing the literary work they were doing.

26. Samuel L. Clemens, "William Dean Howells," in Eble (ed.), *Howells: A Century of Criticism*, 78, 87; Smith and Gibson (eds.), *Mark Twain–Howells Letters*, II, 813.
27. Smith and Gibson (eds.), *Mark Twain–Howells Letters*, II, 798.

Mark Twain's big project of these years was his *Autobiography*; though a new admirer, Albert Bigelow Paine, was becoming a household attachment, it did not keep Mark Twain wholly confined either to his literary chores or to the crotchets that beset old men with even more placid temperaments than Mark Twain's. Howells, at Mark Twain's request, rounded up "a huge mass of your letters" for Paine's use in doing a biography of Mark Twain. Howells himself repeatedly refused to write such a book. In 1903 he wrote to Thomas Sergeant Perry, with regard to urgings from *Harper's* editors, "He is the most candid, modest and impartial of men, as regards criticism of himself or his work, and I think he would stand almost anything from a man he believed his friend, but all the same it would not do." In a letter dated the day before Mark Twain died, April 20, 1910, to F. A. Duneka, an editor of *Harper's*, Howells wrote: "You know I would *like* to write about Clemens. . . . the most truthful man I *ever* knew. But don't make me—don't *let* me—promise till I get my head out of this cloud in which I have been living with the anxieties of the last two months.—It wrings my heart to think of Clemens dying."[28]

Well before Mark Twain's death, he and Howells were linked together in an unfortunate way in the Maxim Gorky affair in the spring of 1906. Their refusal to support Gorky against general public condemnation of his morals has been most often used as an exemplification of how both men were tied to Victorian morality and how much that compromised the appearance they gave of defending radical views in other respects. Gorky had arrived in New York to raise funds for the Russian revolution, and Mark Twain had responded in a customary way, appearing with Gorky on a number of occasions and letting himself be identified with the revolutionary cause by public statements for the occasion, in case anyone had missed the import of the polemics he had already written. With Howells and other literary New Yorkers, he helped arrange a dinner in Gorky's honor, and he seemed to enter in all these activities with an honest respect for Gorky, his work (though he was not as well acquainted with it as Howells), and his cause.

28. Fischer (ed.), *W. D. Howells: Selected Letters*, V, 68, 317.

In the midst of much newspaper publicity, a reporter dug out the fact that Gorky was not married to the woman with whom he was staying at the hotel. The liaison was not a newly established one, nor could it be regarded, except in newspaper parlance, as "a guilty one." Nevertheless, the couple were expelled from their hotel, and neither Howells nor Mark Twain came to their defense. In recalling the incident in *My Mark Twain*, Howells expressed little sense of personal shame over Gorky's behavior. He acknowledged his own refusal to sign an appeal for funds, prior to Gorky's eviction, out of a feeling that it was "so wholly idle." During at least one period he was with Mark Twain when reporters were laying siege to his apartment seeking out a response to his behavior to Gorky. Despite Howells' advice not to see them, Mark Twain did. "Of course he was right and I wrong," Howells wrote, "and he was right as to the point at issue between Gorky and those who had helplessly treated him with such cruel ignominy. In America it is not the convention for men to live openly in hotels with women who are not their wives."[29] Clearly for their young critics, Mark Twain and Howells' response was another reason for assigning them to the outmoded nineteenth-century past. They were old men who, like Emerson and Lowell and Longfellow before them, had fallen behind the new.

All through these last years, Howells was almost as taken up with the ill health of Elinor as Mark Twain had been with Livy's before her death. There was little new in the situation, and in 1907 and after, they frequently met without their families and talked as they often had. Howells' son was the architect for Mark Twain's last residence, Stormfield, at Redding, Connecticut. It provided a base, as Hartford had done, for entertaining, and New York was close enough that some visiting with Howells went on there as it had before.

But Mark Twain's time there was brief, and much of it beset with paranoia and bad behavior. He complained, at one point, of having fashioned a house for a single visitor, for that had been what he had received for the year. He broke with Isabel Lyon and the man she

29. W. D. Howells, "My Mark Twain," 79.

married, the memory of that relationship, however unfair it may have been to Miss Lyon, furnishing a burst of invective in a letter to Clara in March, 1910: "she was a liar, a forger, a thief, a hypocrite, a drunkard, a sneak, a humbug, a traitor, a conspirator, a filthy-minded & salacious slut pining for seduction & always getting disappointed, poor child." For a few months before her own death, Jean became the manager of her father's affairs. Once again, however, fortune's wheel turned down; this time Kate Leary, the day before Christmas, 1909, discovered Jean's body, dead apparently from an epileptic seizure. Clara, whose marriage Howells had attended in October, was now in Europe, and Mark Twain wrote her of Jean. "I am so glad she is out of it and safe—safe!"[30]

When Howells wrote, November 10, 1909, "All right; I will try to climb your hill some time next week," he was prefacing almost their last meeting. Early in January, Mark Twain left for Bermuda; Howells talked with him for the last time in New York just before he sailed. They did not lose touch entirely; a letter or two passed between them, and Mildred Howells, also in Bermuda for her health, saw him and informed her father of her visits. By now, the effects of heart disease were wearing him down, the chest pains intruding into the tranquility he had found in the absence of telegrams, mobiles, trolleys, trams, tramps, railways, lectures, riots, murders, fires— "no follies but church, & I don't go there." At the onset of Clemens' last illness, Paine was able to bring Mark Twain home to Stormfield on April 14. Howells did not see him during that week and was informed of his death by telegram the night he died. To Clara he wrote: "Shall I dare tell you of the desolation of an old man who has lost a friend, and finds himself alone in the great world which has now wholly perished around?" Howells' essay, *My Mark Twain*, written immediately after, was both an elegy for a friendship and a just estimate of Mark Twain's literary stature. "Emerson, Longfellow, Lowell, Holmes—I knew them all and all the rest of our sages, poets, seers, critics, humorists; they were like one another and like other

30. Mark Twain to Clara Clemens, March 6, 1910, Mark Twain Papers, Bancroft Library, University of California, Berkeley; C. Clemens, *My Father, Mark Twain*, 286.

literary men; but Clemens was sole, incomparable, the Lincoln of our literature." At his own seventy-fifth birthday dinner two years later, he said, "If I had been witness to no other surpassing things of American growth in my fifty years of observation, I should think it glory enough to have lived in the same time and in the same land with the man whose name must always embody American humor to human remembrance."[31]

Three weeks after Mark Twain's death, Elinor Howells died. The stoic in Howells' character comes out in his response to her death. "It is incredible," he wrote to William James, "but it has been happening since the world began." And in a letter to Joseph, close upon that one, the theme is, "I submit, and we must all submit." Whether he and Elinor will meet again, whether life has purpose, are unanswerable questions. "What I am sure of is that it will all be arranged without consulting me, as my birth was, and her death. I feel that we are in the power of an awful force, but whether of fatherly love, I could not honestly say anything." Some four years earlier, Howells had pronounced a gloomy requiem over his own approaching death, then still fifteen years away. "Tomorrow I shall be 69, but I do not seem to care. I did not start the affair, and I have not been consulted about it at any step. I was born to be afraid of dying, but not of getting old. Age has many advantages, and if old men were not so ridiculous, I should not mind being one. But they *are* ridiculous, and they are ugly. The young do not see this so clearly as they do; but some day they will."[32]

Mark Twain had not shared Howells' close friendship with Henry James, the other great American writer of their age. James and Howells' friendship had continued, once their days together in Cambridge were past, at the distance James's residence in Europe had put between them. Mark Twain's references to James and his work are offhanded and equivocal. At one time he could declare he would rather be condemned to John Bunyan's heaven than read James's *The*

Bostonians; at others he seems to recognize James as one of the great literary men of his time. When he was still recovering from Livy's death and staying at Deal Beach, New Jersey, he met James, who had returned to America in 1904 for the first time since 1883. James wrote to William that "delicious poor dear old M T is here and beguiles the sessions on the deep piazza."[33] With Mark Twain's death, preceded as it was by the deaths of Warner and Aldrich and John Hay, James remained Howells' closest literary friend until James's death in 1916. In 1911 Howells worked unsuccessfully with others to try to get the Nobel Prize for James. The prize that year went to Maurice Maeterlinck and to Gerhart Hauptmann in 1912; no American received the prize until Sinclair Lewis in 1930.

Howells returned to New York in the fall of 1910, and with much difficulty—"I am dreading it horribly"—brought himself to preside at the Mark Twain commemoration on November 30. "The Mark Twain business," he wrote after the event, "crowded the Carnegie Hall from floor to roof with 3000 people, and a thousand left on the sidewalk, who couldn't get in." It was a posthumous termination of a friendship that had ended with Mark Twain's death, six months before. In 1912 he read Paine's *Biography* and wrote Paine, "I have lived it all with sorrow as once I lived it all with joy." Appreciative as he was of the book, something of Howells, the scrupulous *Atlantic* editor, as well as Howells, Mark Twain's great friend, surfaces when he chides Paine: "At times it grovels in mere newspaper parlance. *How* can you bear to write 'as does'? What do you mean by an 'ill man'? I suppose, a sick man; but an 'ill man' is a bad man."[34]

Howells turned back to his own past to begin an autobiography during the last decade of his life. His last trip abroad, through Spain in 1911, was linked with his boyhood, as he reveals to Brander Matthews in telling of his plans "to spend September and October in Spain, where most of my boyhood was passed while I was working at case in my father's printing-office in Northern Ohio."[35] The Spain he

33. Smith and Gibson (eds.), *Mark Twain–Howells Letters*, II, 789.

34. Fischer (ed.), *W. D. Howells: Selected Letters*, V, 337; Gibson and Lohmann (eds.), *W. D. Howells: Selected Letters*, VI, 23.

35. Fischer (ed.), *W. D. Howells: Selected Letters*, V, 361.

held in his imagination was that of Cervantes and *Don Quixote*,[36] more than any other book the one which brings together the simplicities and complexities of both William Dean Howells and Mark Twain. *Familiar Spanish Travels*, the book that describes Howells' last foreign journey, ends with an observation that squares more with the indignation of Mark Twain than with the tempered reserve of Howells: "I do not know how to explain the contradictions in the Spanish character. I do not know how the Americans are reputed good and just and law-abiding, although they often shoot one another, and upon mere suspicion rather often burn negroes alive."[37] That part of his autobiography which he finished was published as *Years of My Youth* in 1916, though he projected another volume for the years which followed.

Like Mark Twain, in his very last years, Howells sought a better climate than New England's or New York's during the winter and spent some periods in Bermuda and the South. Hamlin Garland arranged a celebration for his eightieth birthday in 1917, but Howells was in Georgia and declined to attend. Glimpses of him as he passed eighty are mostly benign. He writes to F. M. Duneka from York Harbor in 1917: "The world is still interesting, and there are books that I want to write of"; to Thomas B. Wells: "Yes, Clemens was a good judge of books except when it came to Jane Austen; there he fell down"; to Hamlin Garland: "Never since I came to eighty have I been so well. I work as of old, or of young"; to James Rhodes, who offered him consolation on his eightieth birthday: "I am keeping my health as well as a man of eighty may; but if I could have lived on without becoming eighty I think I should have done it"; to Joseph, on an earthier note than is characteristic of Howells: "All the time, my stomach is a pit of natural gas, which I blow off every morning with a blast that would reduce Henderson Point to a smaller dimension."[38]

36. One of Howells' last literary labors was an introduction and abridgment of *Don Quixote* done for Scribner's. Gibson and Lohmann (eds.), *W. D. Howells: Selected Letters*, VI, 154.
37. William Dean Howells, *Familiar Spanish Travels* (New York, 1913), 327.
38. Gibson and Lohmann (eds.), *W. D. Howells: Selected Letters*, VI, 123,

One of his literary tasks was an essay titled "Eighty Years and After," which appeared in *Harper's Weekly* in December, 1919. It begins with a reflection on his early fears of death and a faith in an afterlife, which gave way to "the prevailing agnosticism of the eighteen-seventies and eighties." He contrasts youth and age in many respects, commenting at one point, "I imagine, in fact, that youth lurks about in holes and corners of us as long as we live." He writes, "Now I wander in a world of lost words," and then turns to examples of the really old—nonagenarians—who have distinguished those years. He regards "old ladies as angelic," and his father as the "most lovable of all octogenarians." In the final paragraph he asks, "Whence is death?" and answers, "All along the line of living, from the moment of birth when we first catch our breath and cry out in terror of life, death has set his signals, beckoning us the way which we must go."[39]

In October, 1919, he spoke of closing the house at York Harbor, a ritual he had performed dozens of times at Kittery Point, which his son John now treasured as much as he had. He was going with Mildred to Boston, New York, and south for the winter. How vital Howells remained to the end is revealed in the unpublished three chapters of a manuscript called both "The Home-Towners" and "An Incident of Convalescence." Mildred's note about this book, written in 1916, characterizes it as being about "the people who sat about in St. Augustine reading their 'home town' papers and talking of them to each other."[40] It is an unfortunate characterization, for it implies similarities with other genteel novels like *The Kentons* and *The Vacation of the Kelwyns*, also completed in his last decade. It is not like them, at all, and is not so much about hometowners in Florida as about the injustices of society and of life, the subject that lay beneath the best of both his and Mark Twain's works. Its opening

---

116–17; M. Howells (ed.), *Life in Letters*, II, 372; William Dean Howells to Joseph A. Howells, September 1, 1906, Howells Papers.

39. W. D. Howells, "Eighty Years and After," in Gibson and Lohmann (eds.), *W. D. Howells: Selected Letters*, VI, 157–67.

40. M. Howells (ed.), *Life in Letters*, II, 363. The manuscript is in Howells Papers.

description of a middle-aged journalist journeying south to recover from some unspecified exhaustion has at its climax the journalist's being awakened into consciousness by the sounds of a lynching.

In January, 1920, from Savannah, he writes of being in bed from a lame back. He passed his eighty-third birthday there, and a little over two months later on May 20, he died in his sleep. In his will, besides other bequests to family members, he gave to his grandson Billy the gold watch he and Elinor had purchased from their joint earnings in Venice almost sixty years before.

Twelve

Friendship

Mark Twain and William Dean Howells, as great in their friendship as in their literary abilities, enjoyed a long and unvarying period of friendship, uncommon among individuals today. Perhaps the condition of our time, as contrasted with theirs, does not provide the circumstances nor the temperaments for such friendships. As often as Howells and Mark Twain moved, ordinary Americans today, according to statistics, move more often still. Maintaining friendships over great distances, even with the help of modern technology, requires effort. Howells documented in both fiction and nonfiction that literary life, as well as most other aspects of American life, became more intensely competitive as he grew older. That competition may underlie a distrust of friendship among twentieth-century intellectuals; H. L. Mencken, in rejecting Howells' *My Mark Twain*, passes over all the undeniable facts and insights that Howells alone could provide because the sentiment offends him. For such skeptics, friendship clouds literary judgment and compromises political wisdom. Since Howells' time, the formal pursuit of literature and the criticism that threatens to replace mere stories and poems and plays have disdained too friendly an interest in the lives of writers. Nonetheless, our age may need the support and security of friendship more than the nineteenth century did. If we have overcome many of the physical ills that plagued Howells and Mark Twain, we have not seen much improvement in our overall mental health. Only the rank sentimentalist would turn to friendship as the cure for twentieth-century anxieties. And yet, it represents one of the few forces any individual can call upon to stave off depression and despair.

Friendship, too, multiplies our joys. What brought and kept Howells and Mark Twain together was, in part, the opportunity friendship gave to expand the joys of the other, joys arising from their professional achievements as well as from their attachments to their families. Much of the satisfaction in achievements of any kind resides in the responses they arouse from others, friends in particular. Critics too easily put Howells into the position of the *Atlantic* editor affixing upon Mark Twain's work the stamp of literary respectability that Mark Twain hungered after. At worst that view, first postulated by Van Wyck Brooks, reduces Mark Twain to a backwoods humorist willing to use and put up with Howells (and Livy) in order to win the favor of polite society and literary men. Howells is placed in a similar position with respect to Lowell and the New England Brahmins (and Elinor). The value of such views lies principally in illustrating the cultural set of the critics themselves, most of them children of the early twentieth century, operating with a self-consciousness toward American culture that both Howells and Mark Twain had outgrown. The professional and personal relation that Mark Twain and Howells enjoyed had at its center the joy in being able to talk to, write to, and experience with someone who also took pleasure in what one said, wrote, and did. Without friends, our own joys become insular, diminished in some relation to the narrowness of the walls we build around us.

A sense of humor is one of the few qualities that no one speaks against. A person may be regarded as too honest or too pious or too courteous or too courageous. But seldom is it said that one has too much of a sense of humor. At most, one can be accused of lacking seriousness (or in literature, "high seriousness," as if to indicate the upper regions in which literature purports to dwell), but that is a different thing. Mark Twain's immense popularity was and is rooted in the human response to the comic. His direct descendants barely exist in literature today, though the passing of S. J. Perelman may bring to mind his and other contemporary writers' great comic gifts that serious criticism tends to undervalue. Feeding the American sense of humor since Mark Twain has been altogether too large a task for writers alone to carry out. Radio, film, and television brought into being a clearer line of his descendants: the Marx brothers, Fred Allen, Jack Benny, Bob Hope, Jonathan Winters, Bill Cosby, and their accompanying set of characters not greatly different from those Mark Twain created on the written pages of *Innocents Abroad* or *Roughing It.*

The success of most of these comedians may remind us that American humor is broad humor. The one-liner, crude as examination reveals it to be, obvious as its corporate manufacture now makes it, is still what makes the largest audience laugh. The quieter understatement and satire that depends on anything but the broadest of experiences and referents finds its audience, but one of smaller dimensions. Howells' humor falls into that category; as compared with Mark Twain's, it was always elusive. It remains so for many readers today, partly because Howells has no way of reaching readers except via the classroom, which usually takes the serious in literature more seriously and the comic less comically than either should be taken. Once past primary school, American students in the classroom laugh by rote; outside, they become human beings again, the manifestations of their sense of humor the most obvious sign of their humanness. Howells' great good time, if it ever comes, will wrest him out of the moral seriousness identified with his life and writings, and place him with those just as morally serious—Chaucer and Cervantes, to choose two examples from greater writers—for whom a sense of humor is the necessary condition for taking the trouble to write.

Mark Twain could appreciate and respond to the comic in Howells far more than most readers then and now because he knew Howells and was not dependent on the written page alone as a source of Howells' comic touch. Their sense of friendship was constantly renewed by the pleasure they took in making fun, in their somewhat different ways, of themselves and the world around them. Each may have imposed on the other something of his own comic perceptions. But again, neither was creator, nor even shaper, of the other in vital ways. So we, in seeking out and finding and holding our friends, may find a sense of humor, however great or deficient our own is, a valuable quality. A sense of humor may be enhanced by a friendship, given opportunities to exercise itself, but it is also one of those vital shared characteristics that bring people together. For in accepting ourselves, which our age seems to prize even more than gold, most of us must have a sense of humor. That longed-for acceptance by others, which we are told will surely follow if we but accept ourselves, may as much depend on the sense of humor in others.

True, we seek friends in adversity, and even the good friend may be excused for avoiding us when our moans become too loud or prolonged. In the very worst of times, we may choose to slink off, like a gravely wounded dog, and lie beneath the porch till we heal. In such times, good friends, like good masters, may hunt us out to save us from wounds that would not heal alone. Howells and Mark Twain's friendship gives us not a model human relationship, but an example of one in which friends both come forward and hold back, grant (without declaring it) the self's priority to be its own comforter.

Among those of us who do not in some way record its presence, friendship often goes as unnoticed as the fact that we do not have anything in particular wrong with us today. We are fortunate, with Mark Twain and Howells as with others who have left a copious written record behind, that we can perceive their friendship more in health than in sickness and consider the happy state a truer measure of its quality. It was a literary friendship, a different and probably less rare thing than had it been between a novelist and a farmer, a banker and a stonemason. There are such friendships, just as there are those between the master and slave, the moralist and rogue. But even such seemingly incongruous pairs as Socrates and Alcibiades, or Mark Twain and Joseph Twichell, have much in common; they are, so to speak, in the same line of work if at opposite ends.

Being in the same line of work is so often a part of friendship that it may be a necessary condition. Work, at any time, defines the birds of a feather who flock together. And why should it not? Most human beings since Eden have occupied the largest part of their waking hours in work. Working together has the same general favorable connotations as being friends together. Friendship may grow out of the shared miseries of toil, just as it may arise from sharing the pleasurable details of that which occupies so much of our time. The friendship of Mark Twain and Howells has a greater appeal to those engaged in the literary line of work than to others. And yet, the talk that dominates their correspondence—what they were writing or about to write, what they were reading, the details of business—is probably less parochial than one might imagine. The correspondence of two literate dentists enjoying a long-term acquaintance would probably be full of what they were doing—the technical details of reaming out and filling in and making stuff stick to teeth, the human details of their patients, and the ends to which their work was directed.

In their separate work, Mark Twain and Howells took on an interest for their peers and for us that is denied even the best of friends of ordinary achievements. Ordinary lives are not without interest. But literature is not life, despite Howells' urge to link the two. Howells' democratic and humanitarian claim that one should write truly about poor commonplace life is a claim that a long-term apathy toward his works brings into question. Howells may have underestimated readers' expectations. His friend Henry James, despite his peculiarities as a novelist, recognized that interesting his readers was the only obligation of a writer of fiction. Starting with that concept, as Mark Twain invariably did, Howells might have introduced ordinary folk both in the light of common day and in the light of the heightened interest that a writer can create by all the resources of his skill. Starting at the other end, Howells risked the reader's disappointment in being asked to interest himself in something that was and was not life, in its commonplace aspects as in its heightened ones. Perhaps, as seems true both before and after Howells' time, the "real" in human lives gains greater acceptance in the case study, the documentary, the transcribed words of working people, for example, that gave Studs Terkel's *Working* such great popularity.

Howells as a person is more interesting than most of the characters and works he created. The claim is less easy to make of Mark Twain, not because Mark Twain is not surpassingly interesting as compared with Howells, but because such creations as Tom Sawyer and Huckleberry Finn, their esteem among literary critics set aside, remain alive as part of the common reader's experience. No Howells' characters achieved this status. Mark Twain was both the significant imaginary and symbolic figure and the real person who comes alive in the re-created details of his life. In *My Mark Twain*, Howells noted that he chose to call him "Clemens" because "Mark Twain . . . seemed always somehow to mask him from my personal sense."

As it may help us conjecture about our friendships, pondering the differences between Howells and Mark Twain is as useful as dwelling upon their similarities. The common reader who certainly knows who Mark Twain was and who never heard of William Dean Howells may find it odd that such a conspicuous figure as Mark Twain would find a personal friend in such an inconspicuous figure as Howells. But Howells and Mark Twain were seen in their time as much more literary equals than they have been since. Their friendship was not dependent on their being exactly on a par in their professional positions, and both recognized in a number of tangible ways—wealth, public recognition, literary reputation—that they were not equals. It is probably also true that their friendship, like most friendships, continued on because they did not move too far apart in these respects. Had one or the other left the literary line altogether, or been cut off in midcareer—had become a Melville, for example—their friendship would likely have waned. If one or the other had shifted the grounds of their relationship, as did Emerson and Thoreau, close friendship might have become strained. But the question is also one of temper and the efforts that persons, brought together by the accident of association and the commonness of views and occupations, make to maintain a friendship. Both Howells and Mark Twain are refreshingly forward in seeking each other out, respectful of each other's separate life and tolerant in looking past their differences. Friendship may not be a thing apart; long friendships may require the fortunate accidents of association and continuing common interests and matching prides and respects, as well as a continuing growth in toleration of another's imperfections. There is even a hint, in a modest investigation of current friendships, that *best* friends are often those who live at some physical distance from each other. The matter rests, as does all human felicity, somewhat on chance. But it also depends upon our own choices and efforts and valuings.

Mark Twain and Howells each had a large capacity for friendship, and probably a higher than average need for friends and acquaintances. Much of each author's discipline of writing, however, was the necessity of cutting himself off from others in order to find time to write. Of living in New York in 1901, Howells wrote Aurelia, "I could go out every night in the week to something curious and interesting, if I could stand it." Mark Twain returned to New York at about the same time and was immediately caught up in a round of banquets, dinners, and other social occasions. "If he had eaten all the dinners proposed," Paine wrote, "he would not have lived to enjoy his public honors a month."[1] As it was, he and Howells, despite their often intense sociability, found ways of getting their work done, both expressing at various times during their lives a wistful intent of getting off in some quiet, remote village where their lives and work could go on without interruption.

Although both were disciplined professional writers, their exercise of self-discipline was greatly aided by conditions that seemed to compromise their writing careers, make them other than "pure" literary men. Howells lamented his ties to journalism, which for most of his life had provided the comfortable existence he seemed to need and yet felt guilty about. The insecurity of his early life may have caused his extraordinary emphasis on security in his later years. But his commitment to journalism, in the acceptable role of editor rather than in the unacceptable one of reporter, was the way he had of

1. Wortham (ed.), *W. D. Howells: Selected Letters*, IV, 263; Paine, *Mark Twain: A Biography*, II, 1115.

being in society, enjoying even as he was lamenting its intrusions into his abstract seclusion and calm. Lecturing occupied a similar position for Mark Twain, and not only from the public platform but as an after-dinner or occasional speaker at hundreds of events. In the aspects of delivery and audience and recognition, speaking was a social deployment of his skills as writing was not. And though he, along with critics thirsting after some idea of supreme literary greatness, lamented how lecturing and speaking took him away from writing, these public activities were an outlet for his inescapable social needs.

Being private and being social are conflicting desires known to all humans, and one's choice of work is often influenced by these contrary needs. Howells wrote, with respect to the typewriter that Mark Twain had wished upon him, "It wastes my time like an old friend." Like our occupations, friendship depends to some extent upon our willingness to give up our private selves, to waste the time necessary to be and have friends. A person's choices lie between having a few extremely close friends or many less intimate ones, being seldom outside the social hum or seeking the social approximation of self-communing in the one great and good friend. Howells and Mark Twain were not unique in combining the two extremes. "I have been a lucky man in my friends," Howells wrote in 1910, specifically referring to Mark Twain. And Mark Twain's life testifies to the Emersonian sentiment he had engraved in brass over the mantel in his Hartford home: "The chief ornament of a house is the guests who frequent it."[2] Clara Clemens records her impression of the two of them in those early days.

One of the most frequent visitors was the novelist, W. D. Howells, who used to come sometime for a few days at a time with his wife. He always brought sunshine and cheer into the house as no one else could. Everyone loved him and wanted him to stay a long time. His sense of humor and capacity to show it refreshed the hearts of all. To see him and Father enjoy

2. Smith and Gibson (eds.), *Mark Twain–Howells Letters*, I, 109; Fischer (ed.), *W. D. Howells: Selected Letters*, V, 331; Smith and Gibson (eds.), *Mark Twain–Howells Letters*, I, 412 n. 3.

a funny story or joke together was a complete show in itself. Both of them red in the face from laughing, with abundant gray hair straggling over their foreheads and restless feet that carried them away from their chairs and back again! I am sure no children ever laughed with more abandon than they did. Anyone hearing them must laugh too.[3]

Much has been written, at times censoriously, about Mark Twain's need for public adulation, as if crowds were always vulgar, the self always morally wrong in responding to their applause. Howells had more modesty, but in the one lecture tour he made he was as receptive to the appreciation and applause as Mark Twain. More to the point is that in the nature of their work they met many people, many whose interests and achievements drew their attention. It was Howells' judgment that "Of all the men I have known he was the farthest from a snob, though he valued recognition, and liked the flattery of the fashionable fair when it came in his way."[4] Their circle of friends was large, including for many years friends from their western days as well as more recently acquired friends among the wealthy and famous. Within that circle are some—Thomas Bailey Aldrich and Charles Dudley Warner for both; Henry James, John Hay, C. E. Norton and Thomas Sergeant Perry for Howells; Joseph Twichell, Mrs. Fairbanks, Henry H. Rogers for Mark Twain—with whom there was a greater degree of intimacy. In addition, both maintained family relationships, some of which were akin to friendships.

For busy people, maintaining active friendships and family relationships often involves temporary and possibly lifelong conflicts. At many times, we are simply too busy, out of tune, inattentive, or worse. For men who made their living by writing, at a time when both telephones and transportation were often more aggravating than convenient, Howells' and Mark Twain's ability and desire to preserve the ties of kinship and friendship must be regarded as extraordinary. If we compare us with them, we can honestly rationalize that they were compulsive writers, and that much of what we perceive of their relationship was through correspondence, the written ex-

3. C. Clemens, *My Father, Mark Twain*, 43.
4. W. D. Howells, "My Mark Twain," 57.

change in which both were facile. In a wry comment about the poor reception given his late novel *Letters Home*, Howells wrote, "In this sophisticated age, people do not want letters nor homes, it seems."[5] Both were as wont as the rest of us to lament the time it took to keep in touch and to feel promptings of conscience over neglects. Unlike us, Mark Twain's lamenting was often the first paragraph of a letter to Howells, and our failing to write was Howells sitting down each Sunday to write to one or another of his family in Ohio.

Their capacity for relationships cannot be held lightly in judging Howells and Mark Twain as eminent literary men. In obvious ways, the ties with friends and families expanded the possibilities for creating and developing characters. That capacity furnished real stories that might be turned to literary use, some extended ones like *Huckleberry Finn*, which explored many deeply felt relationships, others like Mark Twain's mother's long-nursed memories of the man she did not marry, which never found a fictional form. It maintained their sense of audience which meant their work would be read. It kept them tied to the quiet emotions by which human beings live together as well as exposed them to those powerful ones by which our lives are startlingly illuminated or darkened. Above all, the lives they lived, in which ties of friendship and kinship were so strong, embodied the human sympathies with which their writing is so deeply endowed.

Howells, the lesser of the two by most standards, can be called the father of us all. Born within a large family typical of the nineteenth century, his own family shows the restraint of a prudence and planning characteristic of our age. Committed to the family more than fathers of the twentieth century commonly are, he nevertheless discloses our own conflicts between good father, husband, wage earner, professional man, and whatever else our circumstances require of us. In the prevailing pattern of American life, he set store by giving his children a better start in life than he had had. And while he pursued and achieved material success, he did so against the promptings of a conscience that saw in his progress a moving

5. Fischer (ed.), *W. D. Howells: Selected Letters*, V, 69.

away from the many less fortunate than he. Like most fathers, he did not cut a very romantic figure, though he was far more romantic underneath than his life disclosed. He became, through the blessings of fate, a grandfather, as permissive in that role as any grandfather today, and at his death "Fafa," as his grandchildren called him, was loved by them and by those members of his own family who survived him. But his literary fame having vanished, he died almost as unnoticed by the world as all those other fathers who create a world of kin and friends but who have no part in creating fictional worlds that comprise another part of our family heritage.

Mark Twain, to pursue the family metaphor, is an uncle of sorts, as Livy is a charming aunt, always a little indisposed, prettier than most, improbably married to that uncle, and somewhat off to the side as almost everyone must be in the wake of an uncle who comes in from Buffalo or Fredonia, and sometimes, by God, from Zanzibar— an uncle who smokes and swears, as fathers do less of in our presence, who has things in his pockets and stories in his head and a willingness to talk and tell. Like certain of our uncles, we can not claim him for long, though we hear of him often enough, and as we grow into being fathers and uncles ourselves, we wonder what he was really like.

We may even reflect about how our fathers and uncles had friends and what kind of people they were and what their friendships were like. We should know, by then, what a great value they placed on friendship and how that friendship, passed on to us in the words they wrote, enhances the value we place upon it. Few of us are given the friendship of a Howells or a Mark Twain, but we are all given the chances of friendship itself, if we but let it have its person and place and time.

Bibliography

In telling the story of Mark Twain and William Dean Howells' friendship, I drew chiefly on primary materials, letters exchanged, notebook materials, or writings of both men pertinent to their relationship. In the list below, three works clearly stand out for purposes of this book: Henry Nash Smith and William Gibson (eds.), *Mark Twain–Howells Letters* (2 vols., Cambridge, Mass., 1960), Mildred Howells (ed.), *Life in Letters of William Dean Howells* (2 vols.; Garden City, N.Y., 1928), and the six volumes of *W. D. Howells: Selected Letters* (Boston, 1979–83). Since I have mentioned many individual works by the two authors, I have referenced them in the index under each of the author's names. Scholarship about Mark Twain is immense and that about William Dean Howells also large. I am indebted to that scholarship but have listed only those works specifically cited in the text.

Adams, Henry. "*Their Wedding Journey*, by W. D. Howells." *North American Review*, CXIV (1872), 444–45.

Alexander, William. *William Dean Howells: The Realist as Humanist*. New York, 1981.

Anderson, Frederick, ed. *Mark Twain: The Critical Heritage*. New York, 1971.

⸺, ed. *A Pen Warmed-Up in Hell: Mark Twain in Protest*. New York, 1972.

Anderson, Frederick, Michael B. Frank, and Kenneth M. Sanderson, eds. *Mark Twain's Notebooks & Journals*. Vol. I of 3 vols. Berkeley, 1975.

Andrews, Kenneth. *Nook Farm: Mark Twain's Hartford Circle*. Cambridge, Mass., 1950.

Andrews, Wayne. *Architecture in New England: A Photographic History*. Brattleboro, Vt., 1973.

Arms, George, Richard H. Ballinger, Christoph K. Lohmann, and John K. Reeves, eds. *W. D. Howells: Selected Letters*. Vol. I of 6 vols. Boston, 1979.

Arms, George, and Christoph K. Lohmann, eds. *W. D. Howells: Selected Letters*. Vol. II of 6 vols. Boston, 1979.

Bailey, William B. *Modern Social Conditions: A Statistical Study of Birth, Marriage, Divorce, Death, Disease, Suicide, Immigration, Etc., with Special Reference to the United States*. New York, 1906.

Bierce, Ambrose. "W. D. Howells, Artificer, Dispatch from San Francisco, May 22." *Literary Digest*, V (May 28, 1892), 110.

Blair, Walter. *Mark Twain and Huck Finn*. Berkeley, 1960.

Bradley, J. Sculley, *et al.*, eds. *Samuel Langhorne Clemens/Adventures of Huckleberry Finn: An Authoritative Text/Backgrounds and Sources/Criticism*. New York, 1977.

Branch, Edgar, ed. *Clemens of the Call: Mark Twain in San Francisco*. Berkeley, 1969.

Brooks, Van Wyck. *Howells: His Life and World*. New York, 1959.

Brown, George Rothwell, ed. *Reminiscences of Senator William M. Stewart of Nevada*. New York, 1908.

Browning, Robert Pack, Michael B. Frank, and Lin Salamo, eds. *Mark Twain's Notebooks & Journals*. Vol. III of 3 vols. Berkeley, 1979.

Budd, Louis J., ed. *Critical Essays on Mark Twain, 1867–1910*. Boston, 1982.

———. *Our Mark Twain: The Making of His Public Personality*. Philadelphia, 1983.

Buxton, Teresa L. "A Study of the Relationship of William Dean Howells and Samuel L. Clemens." Ph.D. dissertation, Bucknell University, 1930.

Cady. Edwin H. *W. D. Howells as Critic*. London, 1973.

———. "The Neuroticism of William Dean Howells." *Publications of the Modern Language Association*, LXI (March, 1946), 229–38.

———. *The Realist at War: The Mature Years 1885–1920 of William Dean Howells*. Syracuse, N.Y., 1958.

———. *The Road to Realism: The Early Years of William Dean Howells*. Syracuse, N.Y., 1956.

———, ed. *W. D. Howells as Critic*. London, 1973.

Canby, Henry Seidel. *Turn West, Turn East: Mark Twain and Henry James*. Boston, 1951.

Chapman, Helen Post. *My Hartford of the Nineteenth Century*. Hartford, 1928.

Clemens, Clara. *My Father, Mark Twain*. New York, 1931.

Coleman, Terry. *The Liners: A History of the North Atlantic Crossing*. London, 1976.

DeVoto, Bernard, ed. *Mark Twain in Eruption: Hitherto Unpublished Pages about Men and Events*. New York, 1940.

———. *Mark Twain's America and Mark Twain at Work*. Boston, 1967.

Dubos, René, Maya Pines, and the editors of *Life*. *Health and Disease*. New York, 1965.

Duckett, Margaret. *Mark Twain and Bret Harte*. Norman, Okla., 1964.

Dulles, Foster Rhea. *Americans Abroad: Two Centuries of European Travel*. Ann Arbor, 1964.

Dunne, Finley Peter. "Mr. Dooley's Friends." *Atlantic Monthly*, CCXII (1963), 95.

Eble, Kenneth E., ed. *Howells: A Century of Criticism*. Dallas, 1962.

———. *William Dean Howells*. 2nd ed. Boston, 1982.

"The Engaging Personal Side of Henry Rogers." *Current Literature*, XLVII (1909), 34–37.

Fatout, Paul, ed. *Mark Twain Speaking*. Iowa City, 1976.

———, ed. *Mark Twain Speaks for Himself*. West Lafayette, Ind., 1978.

Faude, Wilson H. *The Renaissance of Mark Twain's House: Handbook for Restoration*. Larchmont, N.Y., 1978.

Fischer, William C., and Christoph K. Lohmann, eds. *W. D. Howells: Selected Letters.* Vol. V of 6 vols. Boston, 1983.

French, Bryant Morey. *Mark Twain and the Gilded Age: The Book that Named an Era.* Dallas, 1965.

Geismar, Maxwell, ed. *Mark Twain and the Three R's: Race, Religion, Revolution—and Related Matters.* Indianapolis, 1973.

Gibson, William M. *Theodore Roosevelt Among the Humorists: W. D. Howells, Mark Twain, and Mr. Dooley.* Knoxville, Tenn., 1980.

Gibson, William M., and Christoph K. Lohmann, eds. *W. D. Howells: Selected Letters.* Vol. VI of 6 vols. Boston, 1983.

Gosling, F. G. "American Nervousness: Medicine and Social Values in the Gilded Age, 1870–1900." Ph.D. dissertation, University of Oklahoma, 1976.

Haller, John S., and Robin M. Haller. *The Physician and Sexuality in Victorian America.* Urbana, 1974.

Harnsberger, Caroline Thomas. *Mark Twain, Family Man.* New York, 1960.

Hersey, George L. *High Victorian Gothic: A Study in Associationism.* Baltimore, 1972.

Hill, Hamlin. *Mark Twain: God's Fool.* New York, 1973.

————, ed. *Mark Twain's Letters to His Publishers 1867–1894.* Berkeley, 1967.

Hornberger, Theodore, ed. *Mark Twain's Letters to Will Bowen: "My First, & Oldest & Dearest Friend."* Austin, Texas, 1941.

Howells, Mildred, ed. *Life in Letters of William Dean Howells.* Garden City, N.Y., 1928.

Howells, William Dean. *My Mark Twain: Reminiscences and Criticisms.* Edited by Marilyn Austin Baldwin. Baton Rouge, 1967.

Jerome, Robert D., and Herbert A. Wisbey, Jr. *Mark Twain in Elmira.* Elmira, N.Y., 1977.

Kaplan, Justin. *Mr. Clemens and Mark Twain.* New York, 1966.

Kesterton, David B., ed. *Critics on Mark Twain.* Coral Gables, Fla., 1973.

Krause, Sydney. *Mark Twain as Critic.* Baltimore, 1967.

Lawton, Mary. *A Lifetime with Mark Twain: The memories of Kate Leary, for thirty years his faithful and devoted servant.* New York, 1925.

Leary, Lewis, ed. *Mark Twain's Correspondence with Henry Huddleston Rogers 1893–1909.* Berkeley, 1969.

Leitz, Robert C., III, ed. *W. D. Howells: Selected Letters.* Vol. III of 6 vols. Boston, 1980.

Lettis, Richard, Robert F. McConnell, and William E. Morris, eds. *Huck Finn and His Critics.* New York, 1962.

Lindau, Sarah B. *Edward T. and William A. Potter: American Victorian Architects.* New York, 1979.

Lowenherz, Robert Jack. "Mark Twain and W. D. Howells: A Literary Relationship." Ph.D. dissertation, New York University, 1954.

Lynn, Kenneth S. *William Dean Howells: An American Life.* New York, 1971.

Mark Twain Library and Memorial Commission. *Mark Twain in Hartford.* Hartford, 1958.

"Mark Twain's 70th Birthday/Souvenir of its Celebration." Supplement to *Harper's Weekly*, XLIX (1905), 1884–1914.

Matthiessen, F. O. *The James Family: Including Selections from the Writings of Henry James, Senior, William, Henry, & Alice James.* New York, 1948.

Meltzer, Milton. *Mark Twain Himself: A Pictorial Biography.* New York, 1960.

Meserve, Walter J., ed. *The Complete Plays of W. D. Howells.* New York, 1960.

Neider, Charles, ed. *The Autobiography of Mark Twain Including Chapters Now Published for the First Time.* New York, 1959.

————, ed. *The Selected Letters of Mark Twain.* New York, 1982.

Nevins, Allan. *Study in Power: John D. Rockefeller, Industrialist and Philanthropist.* Vol. I of 2 vols. New York, 1953.

Norton, Charles A. *Writing Tom Sawyer: The Adventures of a Classic.* Jefferson, N.C., 1983.

Oates, Whitney J., and Eugene O'Neill, Jr., eds. *The Complete Greek Drama.* Vol. II of 2 vols. New York, 1938.

Paine, Albert Bigelow. *Mark Twain: A Biography: The Personal and Literary Life of Samuel Langhorne Clemens.* 3 vols. New York, 1912.

————, ed. *Mark Twain's Letters.* 2 vols. New York, 1917.

Perry, T. S. "Mark Twain." *Century*, XXX (May, 1885), 171–72.

Prioleau, Elizabeth Stevens. *The Circle of Eros: Sexuality in the Work of William Dean Howells*. Durham, N.C., 1983.

Rugoff, Milton. *The Beechers: An American Family in the Nineteenth Century*. New York, 1981.

Salsbury, Edith Colgate, ed. *Susy and Mark Twain: Family Dialogues*. New York, 1965.

Shapiro, Sam, Edward R. Schlesinger, and Robert E. L. Nesbitt, Jr. *Infant, Perinatal, Maternal, and Childhood Mortality in the United States*. Cambridge, Mass., 1968.

Smith, Henry Nash. "That Hideous Mistake of Poor Clemens's." *Harvard Library Bulletin*, IX (1953), 145–80.

———. *Mark Twain: The Development of a Writer*. Cambridge, Mass., 1962.

Smith, Henry Nash, and William Gibson, eds., *Mark Twain–Howells Letters: The Correspondence of Samuel L. Clemens and William Dean Howells, 1872–1910*. 2 vols. Cambridge, Mass., 1960.

Strong, Leah A. *Joseph Hopkins Twichell: Mark Twain's Friend and Pastor*. Athens, Ga., 1966.

"A Tribute to William Dean Howells/Souvenir of a Dinner Given to the Eminent Author in Celebration of his Seventy-Fifth Birthday." *Harper's Weekly*, LVI (1912), Part II, 28–29.

Tuckey, John S., ed. *Mark Twain's Fables of Man*. Berkeley, 1972.

———, ed. *Mark Twain's Which Was the Dream? and Other Symbolic Writings of the Later Years*. Berkeley, 1967.

Waller, Franklin, and G. Ezra Dane, eds. *Mark Twain's Travels with Mr. Brown*. New York, 1940.

Warner, Charles Dudley. *Backlog Studies*. Boston, 1872.

Webster, Samuel Charles, ed. *Mark Twain, Business Man*. Boston, 1946.

Wecter, Dixon, ed. *The Love Letters of Mark Twain*. New York, 1949.

———, ed. *Mark Twain to Mrs. Fairbanks*. San Marino, Calif., 1949.

Wortham, Thomas, ed. *W. D. Howells: Selected Letters*. Vol. IV of 6 vols. Boston, 1981.

Index